ROUTLEDGE LIBRARY EDITIONS:
EDUCATION

THE DARK PLACES OF EDUCATION

THE DARK PLACES OF EDUCATION
With a Collection of Seventy-Eight Reports of School Experiences

WILLI SCHOHAUS

Translated by
MARY CHADWICK

Volume 155

LONDON AND NEW YORK

First published in German in 1930
First published in English in 1932

This edition first published in 2012
by Routledge
2 Park Square, Milton Park, Abingdon, Oxfordshire OX14 4RN

Simultaneously published in the USA and Canada
by Routledge
711 Third Avenue, New York, NY 10017

First issued in paperback 2014

Routledge is an imprint of the Taylor and Francis Group, an informa company

© 1932 This translation George Allen & Unwin Ltd

All rights reserved. No part of this book may be reprinted or reproduced or utilised in any form or by any electronic, mechanical, or other means, now known or hereafter invented, including photocopying and recording, or in any information storage or retrieval system, without permission in writing from the publishers.

Trademark notice: Product or corporate names may be trademarks or registered trademarks, and are used only for identification and explanation without intent to infringe.

British Library Cataloguing in Publication Data
A catalogue record for this book is available from the British Library

ISBN 13: 978-0-415-69767-5 (Volume 155)
ISBN 13: 978-0-415-75130-8 (pbk)

Publisher's Note
The publisher has gone to great lengths to ensure the quality of this reprint but points out that some imperfections in the original copies may be apparent.

Disclaimer
The publisher has made every effort to trace copyright holders and would welcome correspondence from those they have been unable to trace.

The Dark Places of Education

by

Dr. Willi Schohaus

*With a Collection of Seventy-Eight
Reports of School Experiences*

TRANSLATED BY MARY CHADWICK

with a Foreword by

P. B. Ballard

M.A., D.LITT.

LONDON
George Allen & Unwin Ltd
MUSEUM STREET

The German original, "Schatten über der Schule," was first published in Zürich in 1930

FIRST PUBLISHED IN ENGLISH 1932

All rights reserved

PRINTED IN GREAT BRITAIN BY
UNWIN BROTHERS LTD., WOKING

FOREWORD

This book is written by a Swiss; but it might have been written by an Englishman, if he had possessed the same psychological insight as Dr. Schohaus, and had hit upon the same plan of procedure. For the medicine here prescribed is not for somebody else: it is for you and me. Make no mistake about it; the dark places here described do not exist merely in a far-off land: they are here in the schools and homes of England—here in the same number, of the same kind, and with the same degrees of darkness.

The plan adopted by the Author was ingenious, and yet so obvious as to leave us wondering why on earth nobody had thought of it before. The editor of an educational paper in the North of Switzerland invited his readers to send him answers to the simple question: "From what did you suffer most at school?" The response, which was generous, led to two notable results. One was that the paper lost 400 of its subscribers, for many of the teachers resented this attempt to peep into the schools and see what happens there. The other result was that Dr. Schohaus selected 78 of the most typical "reports," classified them, prefaced them by a long essay of his own, and published them in book form. Of that book this is an English translation.

Let me earnestly exhort the English teacher to read it—to read it for the good of his soul and for the good of the cause to which he has dedicated his life. And he would do well to read it as I did: to hear the evidence first and to learn the verdict after; in other words to begin with Part II, which contains the reports, and then proceed to Part I, where Dr. Schohaus in a little over a hundred pages discusses the principles at issue. These pages are worth reading over and over again; for they illumine the dark places and set before us an ideal of education which is at once noble, inspiring, and humane. There is here no pettiness: no carping at imaginary ills, no vulgar abuse of any class or section of the community, but a kindly probing of the maladies of our educational systems and a clear pointing of the way to happiness and health. Dr. Schohaus's part is that of the beloved physician.

There is one name that crops up over and over again in these pages; it is that of Pestalozzi. Indeed the beautiful soul of Pestalozzi may almost be felt hovering over the book, touching the sore places with tenderness and healing, and taking the sting out of all the criticisms. For criticisms there are in abundance—bold and trenchant criticisms of all that offends against the spirit of love, liberty, and happiness.

In spite of the title, in spite of the general trend of the reports, the real purport of the book is not negative, but positive and constructive. Dr. Schohaus pins our attention to the things that matter in the school; and the things that matter are not so much physical as spiritual. The only measure of administrative reform to which importance is attached is a reduction in the size of the class, and that only because it enables the teacher to reach the individual child. For the personal relationship between the teacher and the child is everything. "We are obliged," says the Author, "to recognise the fact that each school is as good or as bad as the teachers who work in them."

I cannot refrain from making two more quotations:

"The most elementary, the most obvious condition which the school should achieve, is *that the children will want to go there.*"

"If Pestalozzi could visit our schools to-day as an inspector, he would give more attention to examining the expression in the children's eyes than he would bestow upon the quantity of actual work accomplished and the store of knowledge with which the children's minds had been burdened."

I do not personally know the Author of this book, but I salute him as one of the elect with the seeing eye and the understanding heart, and I urge him to make speed in giving to the world the promised sequel: "The Bright Places of Education."

P. B. BALLARD

CONTENTS

	PAGE
FOREWORD BY P. B. BALLARD, M.A., D.LITT.	9
PREFACE	15

PART I

Diagnosis

WHAT IS WRONG WITH OUR SCHOOLS?

CHAPTER		
I.	DAEMONS	25
II.	SUFFERINGS	31
III.	DISCIPLINE	39
IV.	PLEASURE IN ACHIEVEMENT	46
V.	INTELLECTUALISM	50
VI.	MIS-EDUCATION	59
VII.	EXPENDITURE AND RESULTS	65
VIII.	THE RIGHTS OF PERSONALITY	72
IX.	HUMANITY	78
X.	COMRADESHIP	90
XI.	PROVISIONAL LIFE	97
XII.	MISTAKES	101
	(*a*) Partiality	101
	(*b*) The Fight against Defiance	104
	(*c*) Corporal Punishment	105
	(*d*) Mockery, Contempt and Sarcasm	117

PART II

Reports

	PAGE
INTRODUCTION	123

CHAPTER
- I. DISCIPLINE — 124
  - (*a*) The Most Cheeky Child in the Class — 124
  - (*b*) Blows on the First Day at School — 130

- II. PLEASURE IN ACHIEVEMENT — 134
  - (*a*) I Prefer a Hard Teacher to the School Form — 134
  - (*b*) Sitting Still Hour after Hour — 136
  - (*c*) Compelled to Sit eternally upon the Hard Form with Folded Hands — 142
  - (*d*) The Teacher has Taught from the Same Book for Twenty Years — 144

- III. INTELLECTUALISM — 148
  - (*a*) The Iron Fist was the Order of the Day — 148
  - (*b*) "I can't do Sums" — 153
  - (*c*) Overtaxing the Mind — 157
  - (*d*) I Never Got a Good Report because I Wrote Badly — 161
  - (*e*) It is Shameful to be a Bad Scholar — 164
  - (*f*) Examination Fear — 166
  - (*g*) Those who can't do gymnastics will never be any good! — 168
  - (*h*) Daily Homework until 10 p.m. — 169
  - (*i*) School Ballast — 170
  - (*j*) The More Learning, the Less Knowledge — 172

- IV. MIS-EDUCATION — 175
  - (*a*) Singing as a Torture — 175
  - (*b*) Lack of Understanding — 178
  - (*c*) The Ox is Missing! — 182

- V. EXPENDITURE AND RESULTS — 184
  - (*a*) Strike while the Iron is Hot — 184
  - (*b*) Too Much Homework — 186

CONTENTS

CHAPTER		PAGE
VI.	THE RIGHTS OF PERSONALITY	188
	(a) Fear and Boredom	188
	(b) Youth should be Respected	191
	(c) Ape, Go to Africa!	193
	(d) The Stinking Carcass	197
	(e) Starched, exaggerated Authority	198
	(f) Bad Handwriting	200
VII.	HUMANITY	204
	(a) The Teacher as God	204
	(b) After Sixty-five Years	205
	(c) Individuality and the School	208
	(d) The Rough Country Lad	211
	(e) Only Children	212
	(f) As the Teacher is, so is the Burden	214
	(g) The Blackboard becomes a Pillory	216
	(h) "Ah! S. again, naturally, that Child!"	220
	(i) Judged and Condemned	222
	(j) I Learn the Truth First at the Age of 23	224
	(k) Hands upon the Table	226
	(l) One Froze in Class	228
	(m) Too Many Knowledge-Merchants and not Enough Human Beings	230
	(n) Sexual Enlightenment	232
	(o) The Automatic Official	239
	(p) Lack of Affection	240
VIII.	COMRADESHIP	244
	(a) I want to Sit next to Fritz!	244
	(b) Egoism is encouraged	248
	(c) He would be a Prefect no More	250
	(d) Friendships were Strictly Forbidden	252
	(e) The Battle of All against All	255
	(f) Friends must be Separated	259
	(g) *Divide et Impera*	259
IX.	PROVISIONAL LIFE	262
	(a) With one's Watch in one's Hand	262
	(b) No Greater Aim than to Grow Tall	264

14 THE DARK PLACES OF EDUCATION

CHAPTER		PAGE
	(c) Inactive Day-dreaming	268
	(d) School under a Cloud	271
X.	PARTIALITY	273
	(a) The Hireling	273
	(b) The Final Judgment	275
	(c) A Zeppelin flew past, the Class was doing Arithmetic	277
	(d) The Prejudice against Girls	279
	(e) I Suffered from the Preference shown me	283
	(f) A Rascal and a Good-for-Nothing!	289
	(g) The Scapegoat	292
XI.	THE FIGHT AGAINST DEFIANCE	295
	(a) With a Smiling Face	295
	(b) The Teacher wanted me neither Boiled nor Roasted	298
XII.	CORPORAL PUNISHMENT	301
	(a) The Dummy-sucker	301
	(b) The Consequences of Corporal Punishment	304
	(c) Canes and Hazel-twigs	305
	(d) I will Drive the Midges away!	306
	(e) The Caning Mania	308
	(f) The Monkey-cage	309
	(g) Twenty Hazel-switches	313
	(h) The Disgrace of being Thrashed in the presence of Girls	315
	(i) Thrashing without End	317
	(j) The Dancing Nigger	319
XIII.	MOCKERY, CONTEMPT AND SARCASM	321
	(a) "What! you want to Compel your Teacher?"	321
	(b) A Speech Defect	325
	(c) The Stations of Sorrow	326
	(d) "Not you too, Frederick!"	327
	(e) I was Ridiculed because of my Way of Speaking	328
EPILOGUE		333
INDEX		339

PREFACE

THIS book consists of two main parts.

In the first part we shall attempt to make a systematic statement of the most important inadequacies of our schools in matters of great urgency, and also, if only briefly, to draft out the psychological plan of a school which would seem to us to represent an ideal for the future.

The second part of the book—the collection of reports—has, in point of fact, its own history, and needs some short explanation, in order to make clear the motive which led to their publication.

In October 1927 the Editor of the monthly edition of the *Schweizer-Spiegel* published a questionnaire: "*From what did you suffer most at school?*" A few paragraphs following this question explained its purpose.

"The object of our questionnaire is to persuade as many persons as possible, from the ranks of all classes and professions, to co-operate with us in the investigation of this problem. It is a great pity that, as a rule, only professional teachers concern themselves with this question. Professionals are very often prejudiced, are too much inclined to be biased. They easily lose their sense of proportion when the matter in hand is to subject their own profession to a searching criticism. Then again, we sometimes find writers taking up the problem of the deficiencies of the schools. But then, in the case of our literary critics, we have no real guarantee that they will put their fingers on the deepest wounds, since fundamentally they all write from their own experience, and the experiences of young poets are on the whole different from those of the average person in particular ways.

"For this reason we address the questionnaire to you, honoured readers! We require a great many reports and opinions upon actual experiences of school-life. We want just your impression of it! By means of your answers you will be doing a service in throwing light upon a question of vital importance, and indirectly you will take part in the search for new ways in which schools can be made to bring forth more beautiful and more abundant fruit.

* * *

"This questionnaire does not spring from any hostile feeling against schools nor against teachers. (How could our Editor, representing the opinion of his own profession, take up such an attitude?) We do not ask, because we seek companions to help us abreact old, still undigested school-affects. Nor do we put our question out of idle curiosity. *We ask, rather, because* the matter concerns us all, because it is terribly important, and needs readjustment!

"Why exactly should we make the focus of our enquiry the sorrows and not the joys of our school-days? There are, as a matter of fact, some most excellent teachers, some most sensible educational methods, and consequently happy memories of school-days. Certainly, we are convinced of that. Nevertheless we want to know about the *unhappy* experiences and for two main reasons. First, it is a well-known fact that we are better able to give information about the causes of injuries we have sustained than to trace the sources of our happiness. It is a psychological truth that fundamentally our thoughts are always mobilised through discomfort. Therefore, if this state of affairs be reliable, then with the re-creation of the schools we shall be in as good a position as we were at the beginning. The first necessity for a real reform is nevertheless a critical and thorough recognition of the evils of education. For our sick schools as yet there is no proper diagnosis!

"It is a great pity that practically all people try to shake off all the troubles and memories of this finished epoch when they leave school, that they enter 'life' with a sigh of relief, as though being rid of a burden, and feel that as far as they are concerned schools possess no further interest. Laziness, false good humour and a deficient sense of responsibility hinder practically everyone from taking any steps that the coming generation shall inherit an untroubled childhood.

"Take your share in making the correct diagnosis! Write to us about those things which still echo more or less painfully among the memories of your school-days. Or write about the educational difficulties of your children!"

The result of this questionnaire exceeded our expectation. Several hundred documents came in, which provided startling material, psychologically very interesting, and which was quite unique of its kind. The selection of the reports, which are published here, has been chosen so that each example illustrates an important and typical *dark place of education*. All the occurrences of which we received accounts can be vouched for by several of the documents received. It was not our intention to publish a collection of pathological school curiosities. We have in our selection confined our attention to the most typical, those which appeared most frequently in the reports. And if here and there we selected a strongly marked peculiarity on the part of a school-master, it so happened that it still represented something typical. We wished to show from the common experience of our readers that evils which arise precisely from such abnormal behaviour of a teacher often continue for years and decades, without any responsible person taking a decisive step to terminate it.

As might only be expected, the questionnaire found among the ranks of the teachers themselves not only those in sympathy with it but also violent opponents. (The Editor, who had reckoned upon this attitude, generously took the consequences on his own shoulders. About 400 teachers cancelled their subscriptions to the *Schweizer-Spiegel*. Financially, that meant a loss for the firm of at least 10,000 Swiss francs. Such a sacrifice in the interest of a problem of civilisation is certainly not of daily occurrence.) The anxiety was often expressed that through such a questionnaire as this, instituted by the *Schweizer-Spiegel*, tendencies that were hostile to schools or teachers might derive nourishment by means of the publicity. They feared that unpleasant or senseless complaints might be let loose by those people who were burdened with dammed-up affects against schools, and that in this way a perverted picture of education might be presented by the open forum.

The reports which we received, only a very few, which showed themselves to be mere grievances, prejudiced and unreasonable complaints, were put on one side at once. We publish here only the documents from which we have good reason to believe something of value may be learned. All criticism which does not contain fundamentally the germ of a constructive tendency, which does not conduce to the making of new plans and fresh activity, is negative, sterile and, all told, the work of a sinister mentality.

We are not concerned with persons, but with a problem of civilisation. We are not fighting against a profession, nor with its representatives. In the reports which are included in this book all personal names have been omitted and all clues by which the identity of the writers might be discovered.

From the controversy which arose from our questionnaire it could also be recognised that here and there in educational circles there was an opinion that a wider public should not have been invited to join in the discussion of educational problems. There are certainly some matters which should be left to the members of the professions concerned. We do not wish to promulgate a too democratic lack of respect, but all the same believe that everyone should be entitled to take part in a discussion of this nature. There are indeed some educational problems, amongst which may be classed the special one concerning method, the solution of which is certainly most profitably left to members of the profession.

If, however, the matter in hand is the spirit of education and this aspect of culture as a whole, then, in our opinion, the widest circle is in duty bound to take their part in it and to contribute their views, since there is scarcely any other sphere of culture that gives practically everyone, because of their intimate and rich experience, such a great personal right to take up a position of offering criticism.

In spite of all the explanation we published in the text accompanying the questionnaire, which we have quoted above, the question was put to us: Why had we asked for information about the troubles of school-days, and not simply about experiences in general which had left a deep impression? Another argument may be brought forward here concerning the origin of our *partiality*. If one wishes to persuade people to offer their advice for a work of improvement, one most profitably enquires about their objections and grievances. In this way one reaches one's goal in the shortest possible time. The obvious and existing good parts can be left to take care of themselves for the time being. Then they will, precisely because of the sharp contrast, appear in their most significant light, showing up against the dark side.

We should like to mention to our readers here that before long we intend to launch another school questionnaire in the *Schweizer-Spiegel*, to enquire into the happy experiences of school-life. In this, primarily, we shall ask parents what favourable evidence they can find if they compare the experiences of their own school-days with those of their children who are still at school. We hope in this way to collect material from which the tendency to contemporary revival of the spirit of education and the changing attitude of the school may be clearly recognised.

Nevertheless, among the answers to our first questionnaire there were a large number from both men and women teachers in different types of schools. These writers provided a considerable amount of evidence for the fact that the sorrows of the children were all fundamentally the troubles of the teachers.

* * *

It may be that someone may object to a lack of reality in our collection of material, upon the grounds that the conditions described in the examples are now obsolete and that the majority of the teachers mentioned in them are no longer living. In order to be able to refute this argument, we have asked a statistician to compute what percentage of these same teachers is probably still alive and carrying on their work, based upon the ages of the writers of these reports. The results worked out at 50 per cent. And if we take into consideration the extreme difficulty with which a person breaks away precisely from his professional habits that arise from weak points in his character, we can hardly doubt that by far the larger number of the evils described in these depositions go merrily on.

* * *

This book will be a criticism of the *old* type of school, which has still not yet been abolished at the present day. It is written for the following people:

I. *For the lay public*, to awaken their interest in the conditions of our school organisation. It will serve to give those outside educational circles some idea of the inadequacy of this most important institution of our culture, and will help them to form a more definite ideal for a school of the future. The efforts of our educationists who are in favour of reform have no more powerful enemy in Switzerland than this very significant opposition to publicity.

II. *To teachers of all grades*. It will be of assistance to them in recognising the difficulties which have always complicated their profession, and always will do so, because although the school came into existence in response to a cultural necessity, yet it can never be brought fully into accord with human nature. It will help to comfort them and to show that certain educational defects are as obvious and inevitable as the imperfections in their own characters, so that they will not squander their strength in a struggle against the unalterable conditions of destiny.

On the other hand, this book will nevertheless give the teachers some information about school evils which, with good luck, we may hope will be abolished in course of time. It will strengthen their self-criticism and point out things to them which they constantly overlook because of their proximity to the matters under discussion. It will also assist them to overcome the dangers of professional aloofness, precisely because it will bring before their notice in what ways the weaknesses and inadequacies of their professional work are reflected in the public mind.

"The essentials of a good school are the same as those that are necessary for all human happiness, and nothing else than the true wisdom of life." (Pestalozzi, *Lienhard und Gertrud*.)

PART I

DIAGNOSIS

What is Wrong With Our Schools?

CHAPTER I

DAEMONS

IF anyone should build a house thinking he will be able to live in it in comfort, he will have to beware that the house really belongs to him and not he to the house. There are so many people who are simply the managers and caretakers of their own property, and thus subordinate themselves to their possessions without actually being aware of doing so.

Even the man who wants to be a tram-conductor has to face a similar predicament in connection with his calling. He must be careful that in the innermost recesses of his being he does not allow his relation to his profession to get topsy-turvy; that he does not eventually come to think that the purpose of traffic control lies in the maintenance of the tramways and their employees, and that the public should be grateful for being allowed to ride on the trams.

A similar confusion of ideas is to be found in the police force, among customs officials and many other public functionaries. From misapprehensions of this kind springs everything to which we refer as *bureaucracy*. And it is always the public themselves who sanction and aggravate this state of affairs, because of a mentality which needs gratification for the instinct of veneration, and through an incapacity to believe that the life of an individual and his happiness are important in themselves.

A nation creates an army to protect the country. The army, however, gains power in that country until it mounts from being its servant and becomes its master. This modern Moloch devours possessions and people, which are offered up to it readily enough. The military authorities establish a government which takes steps to increase the birth-rate. The army must increase and flourish; therefore they believe that the population of the country exists for no other purpose.

Men make machines which in relation to civilisation, taken as a whole, should have but the one purpose of diminishing the individual burden of necessary work and providing a greater amount of freedom and happiness. But finally machines threaten mankind. They increase but the unrest of his life. They co-operate in the destruction of his capacity for contemplation. They demand an enormous amount of attention; they facilitate only economic projects which tyrannise over men's lives. To-day one of the most important duties of human beings is to maintain their intellectual mastery over their own mechanical inventions.

It would seem to be a law of life that our organisations may become *daemons*, evil spirits, against which we must exert ourselves in order to protect our liberty. Otherwise the *means* will be magnified until it becomes an *end* in itself; the instrument will exist for itself alone, and the creature will at last threaten to overpower its creator.

The schools, likewise, are in the grip of these daemons. From their very nature they should be both a multiplicity and yet a unity of methods for training youthful ability. They should make the coming generation as efficient as possible for the requirements of life. Life, however, is in a constant state of flux. Its aspects and demands are subject to perpetual changes, and for this reason the school should possess the greatest possible internal flexibility and adaptability that are contrary to its usual devotion to good tradition, and indeed become the pioneer of a richly flowing life.

Instead of this, it often degenerates into autocratic rigidity. This is one of the tragedies of education, that it finds it so difficult to make contacts with the tendencies that are characteristic and distinctive for the psychological trend of any given period of time. Somehow the school always remains aloof from real life, and is generally in direct antithesis to it. It is easy to say that on the average it is modelled upon the requirements and conditions of life and society that obtained some fifteen or twenty years ago. And according to this same standard it will arrange its habits, values and ideals. It is this spirit of estrangement and self-sufficiency to which an impartial person who stands in the midst of the stream of life refers when he speaks of *school-masterishness*. According to this attitude the pedagogic attainment of the child will be regarded as more important than his general development. School learning will have a higher currency value than efficiency for life; school goodness will be estimated more highly than the possession of an independent character and a charming ingenuousness. The school claims the sphere of protecting human immaturity and thus assumes a dangerous importance.

From this spirit also arises the deficient sense of humour to be found in exaggerated discipline. Veneration for tradition is greater than a reverence for human life which is displayed in the children.

This kind of mentality is to be seen most clearly in schools which specialise in certain subjects. It is a familiar fact that one constantly finds that more interest is bestowed upon special studies than upon the general work of the school. Each teacher considers his subject to be of particular importance, as the corner-stone of a solid education, and the worried school-boy must see to it that he fulfils all the demands which are made upon him.

We have a striking example of this tendency in the following educational controversy. Large numbers of educated people have now grasped the fact that the study of the classics is a useless burden, and merely provides an opportunity of wasting endless time and energy. It is obvious that it is sheer quixotism to devote time to the classics in regard to the future interests and life work of many intelligent young people. Yet in spite of this it has taken decades before the reality of this has been grasped. There are, in fact, so many teachers of Greek and Latin who are not capable of earning their living in any other way, and there are so many large editions of Greek and Latin grammars and text-books! Therefore there must also be young people available, so that this wisdom and these books may be used up. This connection of cause and effect is familiar enough, but many people seem to be without a sense-organ through which they can realise the horror of such a situation.

The tendency of the school is so much inclined to autocracy, and is influenced so much by common human weaknesses, that the danger exists for each individual teacher to represent this spurious importance, this claim to reverence in his own person. The danger overtakes many of them. In every profession there are typical *professional diseases*. The most prevalent professional disease of the educational world is this lack of ability to estimate one's personal value in relation to one's professional capacity. It is indeed tremendously difficult to remain humble in a position where one is the most mature and possessed of the greatest knowledge instead of being of an average ability. It is hard always to be an authority and at the same time to remain conscious of the fact that one is a servant. It is difficult to gain a correct perspective of the position, that as teacher in the class-room one is burdened with the most responsibility and in spite of that is the least important person present.

The children feel the autocratic demands of the system and the teaching staff. Everyone is familiar with the well-meant remark, which teachers repeat constantly for the encouragement of the children, "You do not learn for the sake of the school nor for your teachers, but for your own benefit, and for life." The children receive these assurances characteristically, with the greatest scepticism; not because they are not able to grasp such an idea, but because they constantly gain the opposite impression from the school itself. But to the same extent that in any school school-masterishness competes with and exceeds an appropriate training for life, thus far the children are right in their belief that they *do* learn for the benefit of the school and their teachers.

The most difficult problem of the teaching profession lies in its own organisation. The representatives of all other professions have on the one hand finished with their school education and also have acquired a certain amount of knowledge and training connected with their profession, on account of which they are enabled to take up some position in the social organisation. They have a share in the functions of the community which belong upon the other side of the preparatory stages, in the definite position of maturity. Those who become teachers, however, remain for ever stuck in the preparatory phase. In actual fact, they never leave school. For this reason they only know that life which lies beyond school, for which they are educating the young folks, from *below*, we might say. The teacher as a professional type is therefore a product of educational in-breeding.

It is because of these reasons that the school gains such a fatal attitude of self-sufficiency through the behaviour of the teachers. The school-master so frequently knows nothing but the school world from his own experience: only there does he feel sure of himself and at home. How then can he make it correspond with that world beyond his class-room and make it of practical use?

An elementary school without professional teachers is quite conceivable. One might liberate sensible people who have pedagogic ability from their various professions for, let us say, three to five years, and make use of them for our teaching staff. In this way the most natural and many-sided relationships with life, in the forms it takes in maturity, could be established for the children. And the school-masterish professional disease would never come into existence. What these lay-teachers lacked in educational method would find compensation through their sense of real values and their impartiality.

But we do not wish to elaborate these ideas any further. Nothing remains for us to do than to remark, by way of summary, that the education of children does not necessarily require a professional teaching staff.

We certainly appreciate fully the positive side of the trained teaching profession. There are a great number of true leaders whose work for children signifies a vocation of great and real value. A teacher who in his heart feels a proud humility and pious thankfulness that he is permitted to share in the work of helping the young soul to unfold will rise victorious over the most fundamental difficulties of this most complicated problem of his profession.

CHAPTER II

SUFFERINGS

THE most obvious evidence of the arrogance of the school which we have described is that it is regarded by so many children as a compulsion, as a worry and a torture.

We must investigate this unpleasant fact at the beginning of this book.

Which of us wants to pour blessings upon his school-days? Who can look back without aversion to the time when his own existence was compelled to subjection by that merciless organisation? Which of us can quite honestly wish his school-days back again?

There are a great many grown-up people whose anxiety dreams always have the same content. These were mentioned in many of the depositions received. One is faced with terror in one's heart with some terrible situation which had been caused by the hated and unreasonable demands of the educational system. In these school dreams is concentrated everything which our soul avoids as humiliating, repellent and fear-provoking. How deeply, therefore, must the sorrows of our school-days penetrate into the depths of the unconscious mind.

We watch the small child trot to school for the first time. What will he gain from this encounter between his own individuality and the organisation? Would it not be better to bestow our condolence upon the child than congratulations?

We all know that the majority of our children go unwillingly to school. We know more than this, that the percentage of school-boys and girls to whom each new day at school is a source of fresh, bitter affliction is appallingly great. A heavy shadow and a painful repression lie upon eight years at least of our youth; *the burdensome necessity of education.* Eight years that are thirsting for life and hungry for happiness are passed by large numbers of children even to-day under daily, hourly compulsion, against which they revolt from the depths of their heart.

One may say without exaggeration that it is frequently precisely the normal, healthy children who can find no real positive attitude to the school. *The model children,* however, only too often lack any great degree of strength and are frequently deficient in vitality.

Such a statement of facts is a heavy indictment. We should entertain suspicions of all prophets who advocate the blessing of a childhood passed in hardship! You may try to comfort yourself for the oppression of your own unhappy childhood with such theories. But it is on the whole a dangerous old superstition to believe that hard times make the character more able to bear future burdens. Where such an effect is to be found, it is probably, at most, only a case of a not very beneficial dulling of mental sensitiveness. Usually, however, the following is the true state of affairs. We can be sure that a person who learned to know the deepest joys of life in happy days of childhood will meet a sorrow-laden destiny with courage, confidence and true deliberation, and "hold all Powers at defiance." Therefore let us do away with this gloomy wisdom and wish and bequeath to our children a happy and pleasant existence. It may be perhaps that *for adults* trouble has the effect of deepening their characters, adding penetration to their minds and strengthening their wills, but the period of growth needs happiness and a zest for life.

Development is only possible in growing persons where there is a free unfolding of their powers. When the natural rhythm of youthful expansion is interrupted for years together through unnatural compulsion, development must suffer and serious distortions will take place. We have grown up so entirely under the influence of these bad conditions that frequently we are not able to recognise them clearly as such.

When developing abilities are trained in reasonable ways through exercise this experience will naturally be accompanied with feelings of pleasure. When we allow our talents to unfold strongly and according to their own natural tendencies, we feel happy, yet not entirely: the necessity of overcoming difficulties always provides us with discomfort; but not usually as a predominating feeling over stretches of time. A permanent condition of clouded happiness for years on end gives us a sure criterion that it prevents young people from taking the opportunity for healthy and natural activities in life through personal or environmental causes. If, however, the school does not provide that atmosphere of cheerfulness which is just as important an element in the children's lives as suitable food and fresh air, it is then depriving them of an essential factor. The most elementary, the most obvious condition which the school should achieve, is *that the children will want to go there*. Then only has it some sort of purpose, an object, a claim to be considered part of life's development. A school, however, which continues to be a place of compulsion against the sympathies of the children is a highly questionable institution which actually defeats its own object.

Nevertheless, we do not subscribe to the opinion that no real effort should ever be required of the child and no serious work ever imposed upon him. The modern theory of "play instruction" and the like arises chiefly from weak sentimentality or from a silly longing on the part of the adult for the absence of responsibility and romance of his own childhood. Those who make no demands for self-denial from the children weaken them and injure the development of their will-power. Moreover, hard work in reasonable amounts and carried out in good company gives those who take part in it a feeling of pleasure.

Many years ago now Pestalozzi was never weary of reiterating that the whole business of education was worth nothing if courage and joy had no part in it. "A person, if he is to become what he should be, must as a child be and do what provides happiness for him in his childhood." He always expressed this opinion. And if Pestalozzi could visit our schools to-day as an inspector, he would give more attention to examining the expression in the children's eyes than he would bestow upon the quantity of actual work accomplished and the store of knowledge with which the children's minds had been burdened. He would, however, even to-day, observe a shocking amount of boredom, disgust, dullness and weariness of the school, defiance, resignation and shame in these eyes which, on the contrary, should be bright with the joy of discovery and pleasure gained from achievement. This is the criterion of a report upon a school.

And for such reasons we should not rest until, let us say, 90 per cent of our children go to school willingly, until 90 per cent of the adult population have a preponderance of happy school memories. *Then* would such school happiness be possible. This has been proved by a large number of ideal schools in our country, which provide us with evidence enough that healthy children bring a strong urge to acquire knowledge to school and an intense love of achievement. But this is only to be had as the result of the right training during the preschool years.

* * *

The school misses a great many opportunities precisely where this function is concerned of filling the pupils with happiness in their work and life. This may easily be proved.

We may reveal the whole difficulty of the problem with the questions: What are the particular conditions which make school-days such a time of affliction? Wherein lie the causes of the unhappiness? Here is a whirlpool of uncertainty. At this point we stand at the beginning of our quest. Because individual persons suffer from such different factors at school it appears very difficult, or almost impossible, to bring the needs, hardships and complaints under a few common headings. The variety of school troubles is so extensive because they arise from the characteristic peculiarities of the different pupils. The same conditions of school management constantly produce quite different, sometimes entirely opposite, reactions in the children. For example:

Here is a child who is always seeking attention and cannot find in the school the reassurance for his self-confidence which he needs. There is another who learns well and has gained an over-estimation of his abilities upon the score of small successes and a rich harvest of praise, which must become fatal for his future development.

The system of good and bad marks keeps one child in a constant state of nervous tension, destroys ease of mind and threatens his psychological balance. Another derives from these marks untold pleasure, through the gratification of ambition, vanity and self-complacency, and it will only be noticed later, or perhaps never, how much this injurious dependence upon external success in school has damaged his character.

There are still nowadays quite enough children who tremble beneath the blows of a bad-tempered or sadistically inclined school tyrant. But there are others who would never be influenced, who perhaps would never be taught by a very *gentle* teacher, and yet suffer just as much perhaps from the effect of an unconscious compulsion, which is difficult to realise, which under certain circumstances is more brutal than the thrashing discipline.

Again, one particularly gifted scholar may suffer exceedingly because the teaching is based upon such a very low average intelligence, and that for this reason he can advance so slowly with his own learning. In the same class there will be others who can only keep up with the greatest difficulty and are under the impression that the teacher pays too little attention to their comfort and their rate of learning.

We constantly hear complaints about *overburdening the memory*, about *one-sided culture*, about education which lays too much stress upon the teaching of too many subjects, and about the present-day repudiation of the old ideal of *general education*. Other people, on the contrary, are anxious about the lightness of the modern school satchel. They suffer from a certain remoteness from the world and reproach the school with supplying too little knowledge.

One friend assures me that he would have gone to school willingly enough if only comradeship, good fellowship and co-operation had been more encouraged and better provided for. The school, on the whole, usually offers more or less opposition to these requirements. Yet in contradiction to this view one may quote the opinion of another of my school-fellows. His chief cause of suffering was that the school had the effect of making the minds of all the scholars too much alike, and that for this reason the individuality of each had too little opportunity to develop.

These suggestions will be enough to show how deep the sources of the troubles often lie and what difficulties lie in the way of discovering the evils. And the hundred great and small reforms, which in our days try to patch up the whole school system without much deliberation, show in themselves how little clarity exists about the question of the most fundamental needs or where the school of to-day fails.

In the last chapter we have given some information about the deepest root of the evils—that of the fetishism of the schools, their autocracy and rigidity (want of flexibility).

In the following section we shall try to explain a number of other inadequacies which are especially prejudicial to successful educational work. These arise entirely from the injurious after-effects of that mental confusion through which the child in the school is pushed away from being the centre of interest to a position more or less at its periphery.

* * *

All school difficulties can be traced back to three main causes. They lie primarily in the system of our schools, in the power of a frequently dilapidated tradition, against which the individual teacher is helpless.

Another cause is principally that in the teaching profession a large number of persons are employed in whom there is not sufficient pedagogic qualification.

The source of the difficulty may also lie essentially in the child itself, in his over-sensitiveness, in his dreamy ways, in his lack of self-discipline, in his exaggerated need of affection, in his tenacious clinging to romantic expectations which cannot be fulfilled.

Lastly, it may often have been the home training of the child before he reached school-age which has been responsible for the state of affairs. We must always be prepared for this fact, that necessarily most of the mistakes of parental training work themselves out in school-life, otherwise we should be unjust to the teachers and the schools. The child's predisposition to find causes for suffering is extraordinarily active in many ways. To deal with them thoroughly would be a matter for investigation which should be carried out in co-operation with research concerning problems of domestic training. In this book, therefore, we will confine our attention to the first two causes of trouble—that means, with the inadequacies of the educational system and with the most prevalent failings of the teachers.

CHAPTER III

DISCIPLINE

THERE must be order in every school. That is evident. But order, discipline, is a complicated conception. We must therefore give our careful consideration to the problem as to what form we can most reasonably introduce to the class-room.

I. To follow the teaching of Pestalozzi, we can say that the child should develop from the stage of *wild animal* to that of *domesticated human being*. He must learn to impose limits upon his egotism and the cravings of his instincts in order to obtain the privilege of being included in the cultural system of social organisations. Everything that the school demands of the child in the way of reasonable discipline, serves the purpose of the development of his moral will. When he is given no opportunity for the exercise of such self-control the most important help will be withheld from the child for the development of his ethical personality.

II. In particular the school has to provide for the child the realisation that the needs, opinions and efforts of his fellow-men should be respected. The maintenance of silence and order during instruction is nothing else than an expression of respect for the work of the teacher and for the wishes of the pupils who share it with him.

III. Discipline, therefore, in school management is to a certain extent a technical necessity. The correct carrying out of a specific programme would be impossible without it.

These requirements are so natural that school discipline arranged upon these lines might occasionally be rather inconvenient to a child, but never a source of suffering. Children as a rule respond to reasonable demands for discipline instinctively and without further trouble. They allow themselves to be guided within these limitations with perseverance, reasonableness, good faith and good humour.

Why then should customary school discipline cause children so frequently real suffering? Troubles of this kind in childhood are usually the personal expression of inhibited development.

The cause of this is on the whole because the school compels the children to a discipline which is foreign to their nature, to a life controlled by rules that not only are in direct opposition to their requirements for uninhibited instinctual development, but also the entirely justified need for free bodily movement which is favourable to their general development.

In most of our schools the children are still kept for hours together sitting still as in the stocks, in unchildlike immobility, unnatural passivity and compulsory *goodness*. Thus unreasonable demands are made of the children. Such discipline destroys so much of the strong, efficient, healthy ego-instinct of the child. It is actually injurious to development in a purely biological sense as well, because it hampers the development of their physical strength and stifles their vitality.

The demand for discipline is exaggerated. It is often exalted to the position of being an end in itself. One constantly forgets that even discipline, as far as it is necessary, exists for the sake of the children and not the children for the sake of the discipline. Frequently the school in this way resembles a temple in which the teacher, as a sinister high priest, forces the children to worship in the service of a merciless false god, *Discipline*. All discipline which does not further development and does not increase the benefits and happiness of life is finally nothing but the service of a false god.

DISCIPLINE

Fortunately at the present time an understanding for the human free behaviour of the children has increased considerably. The children are allowed a freer existence. One allows them more time out of doors and here and there permits them to have an outlet for childish naughtiness and high spirits. The radicals among us would like to see the school-form and the sitting-still done away with altogether. Still we cannot discuss now the rights and wrongs of these requirements.

One should not forget in any case that the solution of such problems is extraordinarily difficult, especially for schools with large numbers of children, and particularly for those which have to do with many different classes, which is the rule in the country cantons of Switzerland. But primarily it is essential that we should bear in mind that here is an unsolved problem of very great weight—and we should pay attention to these questions.

Nevertheless there are a large number of pedagogues who believe the former compulsory methods of education to be an indispensable necessity, who put their faith in the old traditional school discipline as serving its purpose, as in an indisputable dogma. Again, there are teachers who do not stand in any particular odour of pedantry who still maintain the conviction that the rule of strict silence which they call discipline is the most important and absolutely the most indispensable fundamental principle of systematised education.

This fatal superstition seems impossible to root out. What an unnatural thing to do with children to compel them hour after hour to petrify their spontaneous love of movement into the attitude of the wooden doll! What sort of education is this, the success of which could be jeopardised by occasional cheery interruptions and all the other manifestations of harmless *naughtiness*, which are so entirely without malice. Are we justified in our anxiety that natural freedom in the class-room would inevitably degenerate into lawlessness?

One trains the children to persevere in cramped goodness. Is it not a more noble aim for education to train them in such a way that they can be liberated to audacity without ugliness?

There are numerous reasons for losing one's sense of proportion over such soulless discipline. Love of power often plays its part. Teachers who find it necessary to feel their supremacy and power fairly often to prove its extent in a practical way are usually inclined to cling to this discipline fetishism without noticing its deficient sense of humour. Human laziness, or perhaps an intense weariness, a deeply rooted tiredness in the teachers, plays a great part in this widely spread exaggerated discipline to which old school-masters are especially prone. Authoritative severity is not always a sign of an abundance of energy but frequently of its lack. Military discipline, once established, provides the teacher with the possibility of giving a lesson with the minimum of expenditure of energy. Everything goes as though by clockwork—on oiled wheels; there will be no occasion to deal with unforeseen happenings. Greater freedom for the children provides quite other conditions for the teacher. Automatonism disappears from his system, he will have to treat each individual pupil as such to a great extent; he will be obliged with greater personal flexibility to seek to justify the spontaneous, vivacious requirements of his pupils anew. He will have to be more the experienced artist than a mere automaton.

Again, behind this discipline that is wanting in all sense of humour will often be a quite genuine fear on the part of the teacher that without it he will never be able to reach the goal of the curriculum. He too also suffers from the rigidity and the schematisation of the demands which the system makes upon his labours which, perhaps, are only to be actually achieved by putting constant pressure upon the children. The system will, however, be supported by school authorities and *public* opinion who are obsessed with the overestimation of intellectual aims of education. But we will discuss this question again in another connection.

Then further, the fear of the teacher plays an important part in another way; by securing them greater freedom one might one day be no longer able to control the children, largely dependent of course upon a strong suspicion of the impulses of youth. It will be easily recognised that the particularly severe teachers with their overstrict rules behave fundamentally as strong men because they have so much personal uncertainty and weakness to disguise. Those who have not come to terms with themselves, who suffer from a strong feeling of inferiority, are easily inclined to see in the young the beginnings of a hostile power which must be controlled so that they do not get out of hand in case they are finally overcome by them. For those who are not sure of themselves, the problem of authority easily becomes a highly personal matter. Their wavering self-confidence makes it necessary for them to fight for their personal position, when all that is needful is to establish in the children a happy respect for all those high aims which all of us as human beings are bound to honour. It requires a good deal of personal assurance to be able to endure children being children in all their unbroken strength and natural delight in criticism.

The inclination to establish an unnatural discipline will often be strengthened in the case of those who are personally deficient in liberty and inhibited because of the circumstance that they are rigorous and moralistic in their requirements of themselves. They make ascetic demands of themselves, and therefore require a similar attitude of atonement towards life from the children. This is often the most frequent as well as the most important cause of what we call pedantry. A pedant is a person who has made no satisfactory adjustment to life where its central problem is concerned, and who tries to compensate this failure by a compulsion to overconscientiousness in a hundred trifles of everyday life. What the pedant has established as the norm for his own existence he is obliged for the same reasons to demand from others as their attitude to life. In this way only is he able to maintain the fiction of the actual value of his substitutive ideal for himself. That such a teacher carries on his work with a strong dose of chronic irritability and *nervousness* one can understand without further explanation because of the general cramping of his ideals. And because of this conviction, which keeps his suspicion tormentingly alive, and through this moralistic displacement, their ethical severity will be extensively condemned to be of no effect.

For this reason external discipline will constantly be rated so high in the currency that one can obtain no deep personal discipline for reasonable behaviour. A better ideal would be that the urge for achievement, real interests and a community feeling should be brought before the children as living realities, and that by means of these elements alone a natural and a voluntary school discipline should be established. Everyone should be made to contribute to this end. When people are in mutual agreement, and respect a common work of which they are all fond, reasonable discipline will be its fruit which ripens without any further trouble on our part.

But as yet people are usually far from being able to understand these obvious facts. Even the young teachers who are first put in charge of a class-room are often dominated by the superstition that the first necessity is to control the children entrusted to them, to suppress by stern regulations their inclinations to disobedience, which at the same time will be regarded as though through a magnifying glass. Then the struggle begins, and it is fought out with the weapon of external authority in worried anxiety concerning their own worthiness. If they meet with success, the event is considered a victory somehow in the sense of the subjecting of the children —a crippling discipline this and devoid of all sense of humour.

But it should be possible to establish a discipline with the co-operation of the children and not against their will. One may win children, not so much for oneself as for the common good of the class and in the interests of comradeship.

Experience shows us constantly that a personality endowed with pedagogic talent succeeds easily enough, even when its possessor is still quite young. A gifted teacher knows, if he is not led astray by the influence of tradition, no difficulties in connection with the maintenance of discipline.

This talent is of course exceptional. Unfortunately the inability rooted in some characters of being able to mix as a human being with others in a human and simple way is widely spread. This impossibility consequently compels the pupils to fall upon their knees before the idol of external discipline. Because naturally discipline of some kind must be maintained.

CHAPTER IV

PLEASURE IN ACHIEVEMENT

The school does not realise sufficiently how to construct its work upon the child's natural love of achievement and therefore allows this to become stunted.

If we watch children of pre-school age playing on a sand-heap, we are always delighted with their wealth of imagination, inventive phantasy and determination, their endless good nature and the touching creativeness of the little builders. Similar impressions are gained by every father who occasionally allows his boys to have the use of his tools in his workshop; and every mother can bear witness to the same pleasure derived from simple activity and the zeal with which her girls work with her in the kitchen without compulsion or affectation.

The school, nevertheless, is generally far from being able seriously to grasp or make use of these enormous possibilities, which lie in this play-development of the children's abilities and which are being considered at the present time. It is difficult to realise what torments a child may suffer in school, who is highly-strung and longing for achievement without being aware of the source of these feelings of discomfort through being condemned to such extreme passivity and to the compulsory acceptance of well-rationed, pre-digested material, so little adapted to his own natural interests.

In old-fashioned schools in which the child is more or less nothing but a vessel to be filled, the daemon of boredom creeps in inevitably and weakens the mental energy which has a dangerous tendency to become chronic. Boredom is a spectre which slowly but surely sucks the living marrow from any school. Boredom may only be abolished permanently through providing gratification for the children's love of achievement.

Nowadays, energetic educationists, but still relatively only a small number of them, are in favour of practical work, whereby learning may be connected not merely with development obtained from experiment, but extensively with practical manual work. Unfortunately, however, in Switzerland, this movement remains as yet only in its early stages.

The idea is by no means new. Indeed first Pestalozzi, and after him many other pedagogues, drew attention to the importance of practical experiment as essential to all kinds of instruction so that the child works out his knowledge through his own observation, discovery and thought, in opposition to the customary method of the schools, where all the teaching material is given to the pupils already chewed, formulated in prepared opinions, ready to be stored away in their memory.

The modern practical schools work upon a different plan; the co-operation of the brain is required to be balanced by the practical work of the body. In the timetables of the old schools we also found classes for repairs, carpentry and gardening for the boys, and for the girls needlework and cooking. But as a matter of fact these activities occupied a far too modest place in the old curriculum. According to more recent theories, hand work and opportunities for practical work connected with it should find a place daily to accompany theoretical work, and should be related with it as intimately as possible. Drawing, cutting-out, modelling, building, are of the greatest importance, especially in the first schoolyear. In this way the school would then be making use of the natural creative ability of the child and giving it food for development, thus encouraging love and respect for manual talents, and helping hidden gifts to come to the light as soon as possible and not only when the time has come to choose the subsequent life-work at the end of school-days.

However, one meets with a good deal of misunderstanding upon this question, as though the idea of practical work were only to serve the purpose of increasing the manual dexterity of the children. Also as though it were simply a matter of obtaining a better balance for the traditional head-work by the increased activity of the hands. Nevertheless, according to the principles of self-experiment, the theoretical gain of knowledge should be transferable.

The modern theories point out that it is not so essential merely to amass knowledge. The chief thing is that the child should observe correctly and learn to make his own deductions whenever possible. Children should not be kept away from life, but be brought into nearer contact with it. They should, for example, learn less history and geography of the countries far away and long ago, and be educated to have a lively understanding of the present and the future, and a real knowledge of their own country. They should be worried less with abstract grammar when learning languages and be brought to a better knowledge of the complexities and acquire fluency in the use of a spoken language through constant practice. By means of composition the child shall gain the ability to describe its own experiences, and to learn how to acquire a correct, individual use of language full of directness and originality. The pattern essay with its conventional, meaningless phrases upon such subjects as the *First Snow, Spring, The Love of Brothers and Sisters*, leads to nothing but a formal use of words, and a cramped style, and at the same time to the habit of simulating feelings and ideas when there is no personal experience of them.

The wide sphere of practical work can also be supplemented by the nature-study subjects in which the children can often be taken out into the country for excursions for the purpose of observation and personal discovery, instead of being bored in the class-room with pictures, or at best with preserved, dried or stuffed portions of natural objects.

These schools which shall be nearer to nature will first have to be established. For the time being the first attempts at them are already in existence and are to be found represented by a few courageous experimental schools. Frequently, nevertheless, the enthusiasm of the teachers, especially in relation to a pioneer movement in reforms of this nature, is crippled by paltry opposition and the chicanery which is provided by a lack of understanding and suspicion on the part of the parents and school authorities.

It is caused by this transformed ideal; formerly the children were considered to be a sort of receiving apparatus, their behaviour must be *receptive* before anything else. The new school wishes to make the personal achievement of the children the corner-stone of the modern educational methods. The child shall not in the first place accept, he shall develop what he has within himself. He shall not be exclusively receptive but also productive. The children shall grow up in an atmosphere of happy development of all their active powers which may obtain achievement quite naturally in our ideal state of civilisation.

CHAPTER V

INTELLECTUALISM

An infinite number of the hardships of children arise from the fact that the school with its generalised demands makes them upon individual children who are not yet capable of fulfilling them. Everything is still even to-day based upon the ability of the *average child* who is relatively fairly highly gifted, upon a *normal child*, that is to say upon a being who does not really exist. The actual child, with his typical one-sidedness, that is generally to be found is dominated then by the preference given to this illusionary *normal* type.

It frequently happens that the whole of the school-days of the ordinarily intelligent *normal* child is embittered because it is weak in one subject, such as composition, history or arithmetic. In this way one sphere of learning may become an unending source of worry and fear. The spectre of arithmetic, for example, persecutes many a school-child from his first waking in the morning through every hour of the day until his troubled falling asleep at night, or may even follow him in anxiety dreams in his sleep. A distorted intellectual viewpoint where this matter is concerned prevents us from taking the only reasonable attitude to the problem. "Now, good heavens, their arithmetic is awful, but everything else goes well enough. Let us give up trying to get an average achievement from this painful subject. Let us be thankful with what they can do, and see to it that the children retain their happiness, courage and self-confidence in the sacred interest of their general development."

But instead of this these children will usually be remorselessly harried because of the superstitious reverence for the importance of each subject as a thing in itself, and the rigid, ridiculous notion about the necessity of our so-called *general education.*

To-day we hear many complaints about the intellectualism of our times. We do not want to join in this chorus unconditionally. The energy and conscientiousness which are being devoted at the present day to scientific investigation of natural and cultural problems call for our respect and love. A civilisation based upon thought freed from countless inhibitions and all that contributes to the furtherance of the love of truth, would in course of time also make men personally stronger, less concentrated upon their own gain and more good-natured.

But still there is a variety of intellectualism which is characteristic of our times against which we are right in contesting. Our age suffers from a dangerous overestimation of school learning, which is as current in the home as in the school and in the whole of society in general. People are obsessed with this idea of the exaggerated importance of a knowledge of facts, and accordingly treat the young people as though their memories were their most valuable mental possession. The schools fill the heads of the children with a ballast of the most heterogeneous knowledge which, in the most favourable cases, leads to a "know-all" tendency which is far from *education.* Often, however, it leads to an entirely wrong conception of the true values of education, and hence simply to magnified self-deception. This memory-stuffing, such as we have described, consists for the most part of ready-made opinions, which the scholars have but to swallow whole. The exercise of their own faculty of thinking receives but little attention as a rule.

The teaching obtained in the school should provide the children with a general theoretical knowledge which, however, should also comprise the capacity of teaching them to orient themselves with regard to the truth and to enable them to use their own judgment. The develop ment of this ability to recognise reality is the foundation of everything else. People should be able as much as possible to adjust themselves in their own sphere of work—that is to their environment.

The acquisition of knowledge, therefore, is not *the end* but *the means*, a means to the education of understanding and to enable them to form judgments. For this reason all that is carried out in the school should be accomplished by the children themselves with the guidance of their teachers. And so we return from a wider viewpoint to the requirements of practical work which was the subject of the last chapter.

Similarly the basis of instruction should reasonably be always only the means and not the end or aim. It is to be achieved not from remembering but from understanding. To be able to remember well is important only to this extent—that it facilitates the work of comparison between what has been learned in the past and what may be learned in the future.

The child should be given a general education certainly. That should only mean, however, that his capacity to form judgments upon the many varied problems of our universe should be put into practice, which will enable him to acquire a theoretical orientation useful for his general development.

The demand for a general education in this sense that each young person should acquire as much knowledge as possible in all the most important scientific subjects is a cultural impossibility. It arises from the idea that education is an aim in itself, whereas it ought to be nothing more than a means for correctly directing one's life. Intellectualism may be seen in its worst form in this superstitious overestimation of the value of acquiring a great deal of knowledge upon many different subjects. To a certain extent it arises from a materialistic evaluation of the worth of education. A person wishes to possess as much learning as he can and neglects his more practical interests through which he might arrive at the goal of mastering this knowledge and yet remaining unsubjugated by it.

Most of the oppression and threatening of youth comes then from the overestimation of the subjects of school-learning and from the overloaded curriculum. This is indeed the most obvious expression of our distorted ideal, through which education will be regarded as being more complete the wider its extent, to be gained at the inevitable cost of its depth in certain special directions, for which the most advanced of all our grades of schools constantly long in vain.

Because of this view of the acquisition of learning the general comfortless special lessons are the order of the day, which are doled out even to the pupils of the elementary schools, who are thus daily under the necessity of accepting the finely chopped-up food of various sorts of knowledge in rapid succession. Someone has already named this aspect of the usual experience of education the faulty metabolism disease of the school. And how *many* of these educational treasures which the school offers for the acceptance of the children remain for the actual needs of life are highly questionable! We do not want to establish a sterile standard of preciousness by which only the subsequent usefulness for the struggle for existence decides the relative value or worthlessness of the subjects of instruction. Yet one thing is evident —that everything that is learned should be connected in some practical way with life. But the school often offers the children stones instead of bread. They lay before the child a paper world, and allow his mind to starve. They create for the young people a theoretical picture of life, which is really nothing but a shadowy stereotype, a ridiculous, school-masterish caricature of reality.

Wherever we find the use of this subject cult in vogue

we see the easy domination of fatal indifference, aridness, a lack of elasticity and impoverished phantasy. All these evils limit the development of the child's emotional nature and his will and therefore become a danger for the maturing of an harmonious personality.

Intellectualism in the bad sense stimulates the attempt which to some extent is found even in the infants' department, to deal with subjects taught in a too scientific way, as though the object were to make all the children into miniature professors. Through this scientific systematisation and dissection which at this stage can be nothing but superficial, much happy enjoyment will be destroyed. For example, let us give a moment's consideration to the extent of happy experience that can be provided for a child who is unspoiled by education by watching a wasp out of doors. He will be fascinated by the gleaming golden body, by the flexibility of the movements and through the charm and wonder of trying to realise how this creature is connected with the rest of the kingdom of nature. But in school he would only be taught that the wasp is an insect that sometimes steals honey from the useful bees, that it is in the first place an insect divided into different parts, head, thorax, abdomen and legs (three pairs). The child at the same time has something divided in his own mind as well, namely the experience and finally the capacity for any intense observation of natural objects.

Even in his time Pestalozzi fought against intellectual one-sidedness, but probably never realised that hundreds of years after his death a people would exist who always attempted to establish a soulless culture with such materialistic educational aims.

We find much in his writings against the "beasts of reason," as he in his irritation called the people who tried to further culture through the acquisition of much knowledge, and attempted to make mankind happier by this means; who estimated the worth of an individual mainly through the development of his reason. In one passage he writes as follows:

"I tell you that the mere training of the mind (reason) isolated from the development of the other physical and moral powers of men, is nothing but a mistake, which must eventually lead on to the ruin of the unity of human ability."

In Pestalozzi's time the spirit of *reasoning* was dominant. The most extensive expectations were connected with the possibility of achieving world-reform and release from the power of *reason*. The years which followed have corrected this delusion. To-day, nevertheless, we have only again every cause to strive against the dangers of intellectual one-sidedness for an harmonious education and general ability in the sense of Pestalozzi's writings.

Let us now summarise a few more of the consequences of the former intellectualised ideals.

The need of satisfying an extensive time-table in all its subjects leads to a thousand compulsions in school-life which readily create in the child a sense of general embarrassment and fear. The school threatens the sunny carefree attitude of the child, its primitive liberty, its ingenuous mind, through spreading a net of a thousand troubles around it, by means of the general and particular demands, without giving him sufficient opportunity for happy and healthy recreational development by way of compensation.

Furthermore, the system of marks, certificates and examinations constantly provides a humiliating experience of failure for so many individual children, through which will be established a fatal consciousness of their own intellectual inferiority and often also that of their moral inferiority.

Thus it follows that many teachers, prejudiced upon this point, are only too eager to show the scholars that they can do and know very little, whereas it is much more essential to bring to their consciousness their ability and progress, which will lead to the awakening of their courage and joy in further work. In this way the schools carry on a fight as against windmills, against the imaginary danger of youthful self-overestimation; that is, against an evil which actually would never exist in a fairly human and sensible educational system. If we find one child with an exaggerated sense of self-esteem, we certainly see ten with deficient self-confidence. Practically all children would be able to do relatively more at school if they possessed a greater belief in their capacity for achievement. A teacher who has once grasped this fact can set free an astonishing amount of energy.

In the previous statements made in this chapter we have always had the normal, good and averagely gifted children in mind. We must now give some attention to the intellectually weak pupils. We will, however, leave the actually mentally-defective children out of our consideration because the ordinary schools are not at all suitable for these as a means of education.

For the child who is weak in some subjects, or in all, school-life is, as a rule, a veritable torture. Confused, tormenting efforts alternate with humiliating failure and a dull resignation. In the case of these children that are so unsuited for school-learning, it is particularly tragic that the school believes so implicitly in intellectual attainment because in this way the individual as a whole comes in for too little attention. Under this prejudiced estimation of mental achievement, capacities which do not come directly within the sphere of intellectual attainment are little valued or overlooked altogether. One can hardly imagine how much hardship is brought into the lives of all those children whom fate has endowed with a greater capacity for work with their hands than with their brains by a system whose valuation depends exclusively upon standards of intellectual attainment. The majority of these intellectually weak children are actually not altogether ungifted, but are *differently gifted*. In the ordinary school organisation, however, they are as a rule as much out of place as an armless man in a rowing club.

The elementary school, reconstructed upon lines of greater humanity and with a less prejudiced outlook, would nevertheless be a true place of education for these children. This new school would reckon the practical talents side by side with intellectual ability and would accept among its functions not only the fostering of mental capacity in the usual sense but also the ability for phantasy and sense of beauty far more than is usual to-day.

It would mean in order to fulfil this requirement that each child in the school should be judged according to the standard of its own individual attainment and possibilities rather than according to an abstract picture of the attainment of a *normal pupil*. Life does not want standardised adults only; it requires locksmiths, gardeners, solicitors and poets. There are so many varied and pleasure-giving personal values outside the category of recognised school-virtues about which a school-masterish brain scarcely even dreams.

We have reason to rejoice to-day that intellectual prejudice is recognised to a great extent and contested by the teachers themselves. The dawn is breaking. How much nearer to real life, how much more interested in the entire personality of the young human being are the new methods of teaching, for instance, which attempt to satisfy the childish hunger for life and pleasure more extensively than the colourless and humourless products of past decades. Moreover, the progress of that project method, which we have already mentioned, stands as a witness of increased interest in the whole of human nature and an understanding for the fulness and riches of life.

It means, to state the truth clearly, that school education exists not so much for the attainment of knowledge as for the all-round development of the psychological powers. The subjects of instruction are fundamentally only of indirect importance. *What* one achieves in the way of knowledge is insignificant in comparison with the importance of *how* one attains it. The great essential is that one understands how to stimulate the young mind to material of some kind and to bring about happy vibrations. All growth takes place through stimulation of this kind. Teaching is improved the more intensively and happily it is carried out.

Anyone who has once experienced this for himself in its entirety will be set free personally from the tyranny of time-tables and the curriculum, and will work to the limit of his powers that school regulations shall allow an increasingly greater expression of such freedom for development.

CHAPTER VI

MIS-EDUCATION

The school provides for the young not only fluency and knowledge but also ideals, an infinite number of ready-made opinions by which they may estimate their environment.

That is without question an important function of the school. It should develop in the children a sense of discrimination between good and bad, right and wrong, beautiful and ugly, important and unimportant. But it should do so only in so far as to enable them to use this power of discrimination when necessary. Instead of this, however, it is a general weakness of members of the teaching profession to want to provide the young people with their own values through the power of suggestion. The older generation cannot refrain from trying to create the new generation in their own image by forcing them along their own pathways in life. In order to provide a constant renewal of culture, however, we might wish for an entirely opposite state of affairs; that one might be able to educate the young folks so far in the spirit of intellectual independence, by renouncing all conscious suggestion where they were concerned, that they might evolve from the needs of their own minds and emotions an attitude untainted by tradition upon all problems of history, religion and art, as well as upon social, economic and other matters of communal life.

At the end of their education the school releases the boys and girls with a more or less concrete attitude to life and a general philosophy. If the teachers were less arrogant in this respect, and more inclined to increase the capacity of the children to discover their own attitude instead of trying to inoculate them with their own, then we should find less condemnation, less rigidity, and consequently a greater freedom in mental flexibility, true originality and a faculty for far more independent criticism and receptivity where new ideas were concerned. The school, however, always tends to furnish its protégés, up to a certain age, with a most complete and permanent intellectual and emotional attitude to the world, so that a correct view of life should be established in their minds, as they believe. In this way education readily creates an arid precosity which hinders the development of a true, deep and far-reaching knowledge of life.

Naturally it is very difficult for an enthusiastic teacher to practise really tactful self-control in this respect. It is so easy to transfer one's own preferences and antipathies to things, to ethics and the various problems of culture, to the children. Yet, after all, the suggestions which emanate from a truly earnest, vital personality, and carry the stamp of a real individuality, need not finally be considered too much in the light of a tragedy. There is also much that is of true educational value for the young in influence of this kind.

The mental impressions which are derived from an emaciated, anaemic school ethic, behind which no single teacher actually stands as its representative, is far more injurious. Side by side with the ideal of the general education stands this equally questionable superficial general morality, with its outworn theories of goodness, industry, endurance, thrift, obedience, etc.

The school teaches the children that bees are useful; that cockchafer grubs are injurious; the old Confederates were brave and devoted to their country; the Austrians were avaricious and boastful; the good child loves his sisters and brothers and tells his mother everything!

One may recognise plainly enough how prejudicially

this school spirit has influenced the moral opinions and attitude of the children when one investigates the actual reactions of the pupils which the school is always trying to suppress and those which it overlooks. Let us enquire into these in relation to the notes upon their behaviour which are placed in the beginning of the usual little mark books. According to this rubric one was supposed to give the children good marks at first to encourage them. They were to get a *very good*; this, if one wished to take it that way, provided a standard. But what kind of conduct does "very good" represent in a moral sense? Let us, however, go into the question of the standard of this highest mark.

It will be a critical moment for the child when the teacher bestows one of a lower grade. What sort of conduct will have deserved it? It will in fact imply a certain amount of naughtiness by this means, one that has a particularly disturbing effect upon the life or peace of the school and one which is particularly obvious, such as chattering, the tendency to interrupt, disobedience, lack of modesty, individual acts of untruthfulness, etc. These are considered most regrettable faults, which must be eradicated at all costs. But how many other psychological uglinesses are there, which cannot be recognised in the schools, or that are habitually condoned, moral faults which are never accorded a bad mark, egoistic eccentricity, lack of the spirit of comradeship, envy of the success of another, moral superiority, vanity, pharisaical behaviour, hypocrisy, indirect untruthfulness, smutty phantasies. Many of the children are prone to faults of this kind who in the schools are regarded as particularly exemplary and gain the highest marks.

The unreasonableness of such a practice may be clearly understood if we consider the subject of truthfulness, for example. The child who is mentally or indirectly untruthful in his behaviour, who deceives himself as well as others, who wishes to appear in his own sight and to the rest of the school as something which he is not, will, in spite of the scrupulosity of the school, be hardly ever objected to. In point of fact, the school authorities are scarcely ever in a position of registering the matter of this form of untruthfulness. The teaching-staff also has usually neither the knowledge nor the interest to observe the working of any deeper psychological mechanisms. Another child, however, who now and then tells a direct lie to the teacher, will have the enormity of his transgression pointed out on every occasion. He will be scolded with intense moral indignation, and punished with the utmost rigour of judicial pathos. And yet mentally this child may be more truthful and frank essentially than the other, who hardly ever lies openly and yet inwardly is much more unscrupulous in regard to the truth.

In this way it happens that the school quite unintentionally sanctions a great deal of hypocrisy, boring goodness and lack of enthusiasm through the partiality of its moral opinions and standards of correction which, however, constantly bring to light behaviour which may lack virtue but which is relatively unimportant.

The greatest danger of this result is that these values will be established for life in the case of a large number of persons. The authority of the school has enslaved their conscience once and for all, has put its stamp upon it, and never allows it to develop to full stature nor to freedom.

There are indeed many more persons than one imagines who remain mentally fixated to the authority of their teacher for the remainder of their lives. There are countless persons who carry through life the narrow and cramped general conscience of the school instead of an individual conscience. They keep the gloomy moral spectacles of the school upon their noses, and through them they view life according to school standards. All that is connected with silence and quietness is good, as well as industry, love of order and subjection. Everything which disturbs the peace of the citizen and annoys authorities is bad. All strong will is open to suspicion; all revolutionary impulses, everything different from the ordinary daily life which can provide an unforeseen stimulus. A man is good if he is able to withdraw the depths of his personality respectably from our gaze; he is *bad* if he reveals the inadequacies of his uncovered nakedness.

That is a specious ethic. And in this philosophy may be found the most tragic form of mis-education for life —that people find it is difficult to outgrow a conviction or a fundamental viewpoint which has been fed from a thousand channels during the most impressionable years of life from the inexhaustible and venerated spirit of the school.

In a reading-book, which is still used to-day in the lower classes, we find the following poem. And many people who are now grey-haired own a sensitive conscience because they realise how far the path of their life's virtue has strayed from the ideal represented in the verses.

DER FLEISSIGE SCHÜLER

Der Knabe lernt daheim mit Fleiss,
Bis ganz genau er alles weiss.
Und dann er gern zur Schule geht
Und betet fromm das Schulgebet.

Und in der Schule gibt er Acht,
Das er dem Lehrer Freude macht,
Schreibt sein Aufgab' mäuschenstill,
Wie es die Ordnung haben will.

Auf alles, was der Lehrer fragt,
Er stets die rechte Antwort sagt.
So lernt er froh, was er vermag
Und wird geschickter jeden Tag.

THE INDUSTRIOUS PUPIL

The boy learns at home with diligence, until he knows everything by heart.
Then he goes to school gladly and prays the pious school prayer.

And in school he is careful to please his teacher.
He writes his exercise sitting as still as a mouse, as discipline requires.

To all the questions of his teacher, he gives the correct reply,
Therefore he cheerfully learns what he can and becomes more clever every day.

CHAPTER VII

EXPENDITURE AND RESULTS

THE school makes an extraordinary high demand upon the time of the child to obtain its objective. What is the actual relationship between this expenditure of time and the success that is gained?

During the eight obligatory years of education the children spend some 9,000 to 10,000 hours in school. Nine to ten thousand! And in addition to these we must also reckon those which the child spends over homework to satisfy the demands of the school.

In relation to this we must also take into our consideration *the benefits* which the school has conferred upon the pupils who leave from the highest class. We will give a short review of the results gained in the separate school subjects.

Arithmetic.—Theory of number and practical use of numbers are usually satisfactorily developed in all children. The young folks acquire the simple methods of so-called general arithmetic, and by this means have at their disposal an extraordinarily valuable equipment for holding their own in the practical struggle for existence.

Writing.—Handwriting is usually clumsy and untidy. There is commonly a fairly widespread uncertainty regarding orthography. The feeling for language is very slightly developed. Few are in a position to write a correct letter and are incapable of recording an experience with even a semi-adequate description. Writing, too, as a vehicle of expression is to most of the pupils such an unnatural function that one might call it a writing-phobia in a great many cases.

Reading.—Good results as a rule. One can record on the whole a thorough mastery of the technique of reading. The gateway to the kingdom of the written and printed word is therefore definitely open.

German Literature.—The condition of knowledge gained in this subject is very arid and the result of chance. The young people mostly have not the least idea of the significance and deeper cultural meaning of literary productions.

History.—Knowledge is highly fragmentary. Generally one finds a recollection of a mass of single, disconnected facts. The realisation of the relation between them is hardly ever developed. One cannot mention the possibility of historical sense or the capacity for historical conception.

Geography.—The children of to-day have a special interest in geography. One often finds that the pupils in the highest class have a very good and comprehensive idea of geographical facts.

Nature Study.—This is a very scanty sphere of learning. The capacity for observation and a mental grasp of natural laws are scarcely developed. There is also a handicap in this direction, because it is not possible to awaken enough enthusiasm in the children for direct and intensive study of nature.

Drawing.—The results show wide deviation. Recently these have been most encouraging here and there. Many children find in this subject an opportunity to develop their sense of beauty and in drawing also they obtain a free individual means of giving expression to their feelings and ideas.

Singing.—This often establishes a satisfactory foundation for a certain amount of understanding of music and makes it possible for some scholars to find pleasure later in part-singing. Most of those who are capable of learning music achieve this standard of proficiency.

Handicrafts.—Recently results in this subject have been most gratifying. Frequently a respectable and versatile dexterity will be acquired. The possibility of discovering talent in many different kinds of work and recording their proficiency, provides very useful material for the subsequent choosing of a profession or trade.

Gymnastics.—So little time is generally given to this subject in proportion to the amount required from the children in the class-room that it is in urgent need of more attention. Results are handicapped because of the long hours spent in sitting still, through which physical growth is hampered and malformations take place. Pleasure in bodily movements of all kinds gains its gratification outside school hours.

These are the apparently slender results which are to be had from the fairly high educational requirement of so many thousand hours of school-work. The chief lack of this system of education lies in the fact that when everything is taken into consideration the work is un-organised, that the results are patchy and fall asunder for want of any internal cohesion. The results, nevertheless, considered on their own merits, are not to be estimated too poorly. Upon the foundation of this educational system rests the relatively high average standard of the cultural attainment of our population.

Still, in comparison with the enormous expenditure of time, the results attained must be considered as extremely modest. What the school achieves from the young people in all these many years in the way of ability to form a judgment and of actual knowledge and fluency is on the whole very meagre indeed, so that we have every reason to be astonished over the disproportion, should we not have long ago forgotten how to be surprised or shocked at our reflections over such a state of affairs.

Those who are even occasionally in contact with children know their natural ability, their great average fund of mental activity and capacity for receiving instruction. How then is it possible that the schools in all those many thousand hours, at work upon this human material in their workshops, do not achieve relatively better results upon individual scholars as a rule, according to their own standards of education?

One may find many examples to illustrate this fact; the normal, not unusually gifted child, who on account of illness or because of other reasons, only starts to receive instruction at the age of nine, ten, eleven or even twelve years old, with fairly favourable guidance from the teaching-staff will easily overtake his contemporaries in a period of time extending from one to two years.

In order to get the whole problem of school results into a right perspective, we must now put our question into this form. What more do the children learn up to the end of the eighth school-year than if one were to let them run wild and occupy themselves from time to time at home, in the workshop, the stable or the fields? What the children would observe, learn and experience in these environments would certainly be very valuable to them. Should we regard the matter in this light the results attained by the school seem perhaps to be all the more scanty. We now come to the next question. What do the schools accomplish over and above the results of development gained by the children without attending school?

One cannot deny the disproportion between the expenditure of time and the success gained in work. What then is the cause of this discrepancy?

To start with, one may suggest that there are many teaching methods that are not entirely satisfactory, or indeed are quite contrary to the purpose they wish to achieve. A further investigation shows us that in this connection many of them are not so ineffectual as one might suppose. During the last ten years great progress has been made in the technique of teaching, and it now stands to-day relatively high. It has reached a level of considerable refinement and has extensive psychological grounding. These advances are to be noticed in other directions besides those of reading and writing, which, for example, have now been brought to such a state of perfection that we may expect a certain success which was not to be had some fifteen years ago. And yet other educational subjects show a pitifully small improvement throughout the whole experience of education.

Next we may ask whether there are in point of fact a large number of teachers who do not put enough enthusiasm into their school work. But this must also be denied. The majority of our elementary school teachers work conscientiously and give a high degree of concentrated attention to their work. Many of them indeed suffer also from the slowness of the progress and from the impossibility of reaching a higher level.

The cause of this discrepancy between the outlay of time and the results gained lies principally not in the methods used nor in the teachers, but elsewhere. Primarily it is to be attributed to the size of the classes, which, in the country districts especially, makes the work in the class-rooms extremely difficult and handicaps it. There are in Switzerland plenty of class-rooms where one might find sixty or seventy children at one time. In the country cantons a class of over fifty children per teacher is the rule at the present time. In many cases, also, the system provides that a teacher may have to work with several classes simultaneously, up to eight classes. It is obvious that the most conscientious school-master under these circumstances cannot have any serious contact with the individual children. He can no longer be an educator, but merely a teaching official, the shepherd of a flock. His highest hopes and attempts to carry out the excellent ideals of reform break to pieces before the mass-production with which he is faced.

A teacher in a school of this type can only pay attention to one class or one group of pupils at a time. The others must then be employed with silent work. Everyone only half initiated into educational secrets knows what that means. In these overpopulated schools it is by no means possible to see that classes occupied in this way use their time in working in a serious or concentrated way. In point of fact the few who do so are in daily danger of being sacrificed to the many idlers who do not. The school itself teaches them, therefore, to waste their time, and trains them to artistic day-dreaming.

But apart from the possibility of such injuries to character, it is a serious wrong done to the children to shorten their youth in this fashion, to demand such an enormous sacrifice of time from them, without providing them with an adequate return in the way of educational gain. We should also treat the child's personality with as much respect as we do his time. He knows well enough what to do with it, and uses it in a hundred sensible and recreative ways when we grown-ups only allow him to do so.

In the interest of economy of work in the schools, to make them as free as possible of pedagogic reproach, regulations should be made that no teacher in any elementary school should be allowed to have more than thirty-five children at a time in a class-room. In a secondary school there should be a still smaller maximum. It is important that this need should be recognised as soon as possible for the common good of all those involved. Another essential factor for the realisation of the public is that as large a proportion of taxes as possible should be laid out in necessary improvements of the free education of our children.

But there are still some other reasons for the want of proportion between the expenditure of time and the results gained. Some of these lie in the gloomy atmosphere of the schools. By this we mean all that remains in our schools of grumbling, lack of a sense of humour, pedantry, severity and boredom; everything in fact that leads to the widely spread weariness of school-life from which the child suffers. This spirit alone is enough to cancel the child's pleasure in his work, and will cripple his best powers. It is so foreign to the natural and vital life-rhythm of youth. And for this reason it fails to produce any stimulating effect or to stir any enthusiasm.

It seems to us that something should be done to deal with this problem of the discrepancy between the hours spent in school and the achievement in the form of knowledge gained. It might be possible to accomplish a satisfactory result by increasing the intensity of the work and shortening the hours of daily instruction. In the elementary schools it would be quite sufficient for all classes if the teaching of school subjects took place in the mornings only. The afternoons could then be devoted to handicraft, games, expeditions and excursions. Naturally in order that these should have some educational value for the children, their own teachers should act as the leaders of these expeditions, so that they should be organised as profitably as possible. Reforms of this kind would increase the interest of school-life for the children and make it much more tolerable.

The most necessary reform of all is to decrease the size of the classes. Next in importance is to change the atmosphere to be found in many schools. We need the stimulation for more zeal, greater love of achievement, an increased happiness as well as a more healthy freedom from inhibitions for the pupils. Again there is still room for further progress in reform in educational method in order that the time given to instruction can be shortened. But the most decisive factor of all which is essential for all changes is the introduction of the dynamic force of a new spirit in our schools.

CHAPTER VIII

THE RIGHTS OF PERSONALITY

ONE great danger of all school education lies in the tendency to turn all the children out upon the same mental pattern, by which we shall find that not only are unwelcome social tendencies eliminated, but also some valuable individual characteristics of the children are threatened. Thus the school turns them into a flock. It has the effect of making them feel as though they belonged to a group at the cost of allowing them freedom to develop a consciousness of their own personality. This will frequently lead to a stunting of their feeling of responsibility. Modern crowd psychology has discovered that the individual as one of a crowd behaves as a conscienceless, dull and undifferentiated unit in ethical matters.

In this same fashion the individual in the school finds it easy to compound with the daily demands by suppressing his own judgment and personal discrimination. The general behaviour of the crowd, that is of the class, will be a supreme authority to him, against which his own conscience never comes into conflict. The standard of correct behaviour will be that each does what the others do; and what the others reject will be regarded as worthy of rejection. Weak reactions of this type will be increased in some by their natural cowardice and laziness, and will be shown principally in the unpleasing side of what in schools we call the *class spirit*. This usually produces a stupid, barren and inelastic average type of behaviour throughout the class. Sometimes it may break through into a romantic, comradely solidarity, but then almost without exception it will show a hostile tendency, being directed against authority represented by the person of the teacher. We will mention the beneficial aspect of the class spirit later. The evil of group behaviour such as we described above is naturally greater in proportion to the numbers that are crowded into a class-room.

One constantly finds that the unsatisfactory effect of this crowd spirit upon the individual and his subordination to the rest of the herd, has the most demoralising effect upon sensitive pupils without the cause being apparent to themselves. The hall-mark of mass-production is by no means the most unimportant of these factors which cause the school to be a destroying agent where the self-confidence of the children is concerned.

In the interest of its schemes for organisation the school constantly strives to suppress the individuality of the pupil. Each teacher carries this work out unconsciously. He requires the subordination of the individual to the group as a matter of course, and takes for granted that even those who cannot be forced entirely into the common mould, shall at least follow upon the same lines. Therefore the stronger characters, those with greater originality and gifted with a certain amount of dynamic energy, whose guidance requires a high level of understanding and broadminded handling, if they are to retain their individuality, suffer most from the school and the experiences they meet with there. This is especially noticeable in the Middle Schools. It is, however, a fact which to-day wins general recognition, that the people who in later life show themselves as exceptionally gifted and useful members of society, became involved in their youth in the most vigorous conflicts with their personal teachers, or with school authorities in general. Many outstanding personalities in all spheres of work give us, in a description of their youthful troubles, a record that they were regarded as the outcasts of their school, that they were considered there as mentally defective, naughty, peculiar or rebels, and there they found no means of escape from this bad character they had won. "There is nothing to be done with you!" was only too often the prognosis, and it was only the actual subsequent success of the individual which contradicted this arrogant prophecy of the school-master.

The school, in a great many instances, although naturally not always, is unable to endure the presence of a genius of any kind. It seems that it feels its fundamental principles and methods threatened by any form of unusual talent, and cannot assimilate it. It therefore (I speak here chiefly of the Middle Schools) regards all outstanding characteristics as irregular and for this reason takes up a position of hostility and opposition to all those children who show signs of talent as well as those of a difficult, surly or reserved nature.

It is obvious also that the school continually finds it difficult to condone youthful emotional difficulties, especially in those cases when the teachers have failed to recognise the manifest symptoms which appear from time to time as in any way similar to the more familiar signs of pubertal disturbance—that is to say if they are not able to interpret the unfamiliar in terms of the familiar.

The school also shows a constant habit to prune the self-confidence and self-assurance of the average pupil by reminding him perpetually of the painful limitations of his position as a school-boy, whenever his youthful desire for power may occasionally lead him to assert himself intellectually. It has such a firm belief in the necessity of preserving the external show of authority that frequently boring goodness and pliancy of will are cultivated in the scholars of the highest class, at the expense of any healthy originality, which will thus be eliminated for the rest of the school period, being considered ideal behaviour for a senior pupil.

In this way the school not only inculcates the production of an inferiority complex but fosters the retention of a sense of inferiority, although generally quite unintentionally. Usually the children who will be most affected by this attitude will be those who are especially sensitive and highly strung, who at certain periods of their development easily acquire conflicts of conscience that are difficult to resolve later, and feelings of guilt.

It should, however, be considered one of the most important functions of the school to establish or to strengthen a healthy and happy self-confidence in children of this type upon sound lines. But, contrarily, the school often works in the opposite direction and actually strengthens and increases the feelings of inferiority and incapacity.

In order to arrive at a proper readjustment of this evil, there is but one thing to be done. The teachers must carry out their work as though the children were of more importance to them than the educational system, and that the development of one personality were of greater value than the maintenance of the plans of the school organisation. Finally, moreover, everything must be based upon a deep love of humanity, in a faith in human nature, which will affirm all the manifold phenomena of youthful development, even when these seem to us as most strange or are exceedingly difficult for us, who look on, to understand.

The chief requirement for the correct pedagogic treatment of individual pupils is the acquisition of a thorough understanding of the individual characters of the children themselves. This will comprise not only the theoretical psychological knowledge of all the different stages of development, but an extensive understanding of character-construction. To understand really means to possess a discriminating sense of the hidden values of the personalities of these young people, for their longings which are so often kept a profound secret, for personal truthfulness, goodness and strength. Educational understanding means an active faith and a sharp-sighted love for all the good possibilities which as yet lie dormant within the character of the children. If these ideas were to be put into practice, we should find that understanding which would penetrate the surface would be eminently educational, because it would be a source of liberating and uplifting strength.

Boys and girls, especially the older ones, who are approaching puberty, long for understanding of this description. The age is one which presents many problems, and those who are going through the stage are often at a loss to understand their own reactions and their tormenting doubts concerning their own worth or worthlessness. For this reason the understanding of an adult will give them comfort, consolation and encouragement.

It is particularly necessary for girls to have some contact with an older, understanding person at this age. For them it will be a most significant factor for their development. If the relationship of the girls with their teachers is favourable, if they respect and love them, and find a ready understanding of their personal difficulties, their school-days will generally be found to pass by peacefully and happily. This was made particularly clear in the documents received in connection with our questionnaire. The girls will usually be glad enough to go to school if and when this condition is fulfilled—that where love-requirements are satisfied respecting some man or woman teacher.

The boys are more exacting in their demands. They have a larger number of different interests which seek gratification from the instruction offered them by the school. Therefore we find that their happiness at school depends fundamentally upon other factors besides that of the contact with their school-master. Among these we must reckon the amount of freedom they are allowed, possibilities for individual achievement, and opportunities for comradeship. But we must also not forget the essential condition of being understood, which is a fundamental of their educability through the school.

This individual understanding being an established principle in the school, it will also be inevitable that the teachers shall treat the pupils with respect or politeness. If one should regard children as individuals of a certain worth, and allow this belief to be reflected in one's behaviour towards them, the assumption will be that one expects equally good manners from them in return. This will put them on their honour to conduct themselves as well-bred and cultured persons. They will feel in duty bound to justify these expectations and exert themselves to comply with them. But if one should treat them as people of second-class quality they will behave as such and appear lazy, careless and churlish.

This is such a simple axiom. We may see it borne out by our daily experience. And yet many teachers find it terribly difficult to treat children with courtesy or in a cultured way. But our attitude to the children reflects our educational aims, which often makes us blind to the truth, that the children's happy respect for themselves provides a greater stimulus for their psychological growth than all our more or less successful educational methods.

If only every teacher would, body and soul, remember this fundamental truth that pedagogically there is not the smallest reason why children should not be treated every bit as politely as grown-up people!

CHAPTER IX

HUMANITY

THERE can be no leadership unless those who are to be led regard the leader with a certain amount of esteem. The teacher's claim to a position of authority is therefore necessary in the interest of his function. Yet it is unfortunate if he is obliged to strive to attain it with special efforts, and does not gain it naturally by reason of the difference in age between himself and his pupils, as well as the instinct for reverence which is to be found generally present in most children.

There is a something about the school-master which marks him out in our childhood as different from the other people we know. He does not resemble the baker, the postman, the milkman, even the family doctor, or Uncle Fred and Uncle Henry, and so many others who come to the house to visit our parents. They behave naturally and treat us in a free-and-easy way, because they do not always feel bound to make an impression on us.

There are various methods which are used for acquiring this respect and superstitious reverence. There is one teacher who poses as the strong person, always very dignified. Here is another who adopts an attitude of judicial knowledge and infallibility. A third coquets with the claim to be thought a connoisseur in music, languages, sport or some other accomplishment, and yet another will adopt the rather silly attitude of being a friend of children. This means that he believes he comes down to their level in the pose of a demagogue which provokes all kinds of unpleasant familiarities.

We often find that behaviour of this description is a mask which makes an honourable human relationship between teacher and pupil quite impossible.

HUMANITY

The children take these poses for the genuine article, and thus gain a perverted idea of human dignity and significance. The playing of a part by the grown-ups easily deceives children. In this way it will be nourished by the childish tendency to be imposed upon by unreal gestures. They will have to keep up their position through all forms of pretending and exaggeration of assumed perfections.

Chief among these poses we find the unctuous, ceremonious, pathetic attitude, through which the teacher takes unto himself the appearance of immense moral superiority which, in the way we have just been describing, has such a demoralising effect. A further danger lies in the fact that the weak, dependent natures among the children, who take this apparent dignity for reality, and believe in the infallibility of their teacher, will magnify the disparity between their own shortcomings and his perfection, in which they believe so implicitly so that they have no courage left for their own moral strivings.

The more robust children, who are more certain of their own instincts, usually soon see through this lazy magic and revenge themselves upon its perpetrator in their own fashion, by the cultivation of endless prejudiced and most unloving criticism, and often express quite astonishingly appropriate satire. In this way they will escape from the teacher's suggestions in one direction but fall into the opposite danger that they will now react in a negative way to all the usual or unusual demands which are put before them by authorities. Their urge to freedom has broken all bounds and has led on to a new form of slavery and to a fatal distortion.

Another especially widespread pose causes the teacher to play the part of the severe person, whereby he tends easily enough to establish a relationship of overlord and subjects. The children will now be burdened by a tyrannical oppression, through which will be developed in the children themselves often a personal desire to acquire power, to an unpleasant degree. Oppression creates counter-oppression, but their courage often fails them to make open rebellion against their teacher. Their awakened desire for self-assertion will then be directed against weaker objects, such as brothers and sisters and class-mates. Constantly do we find that tyranny of this kind awakens a desire for power in the oppressed, and strengthens the impulse for selfish assertion of the ego which is lacking in all sense of humour. In this way the school itself will often establish an unhappy exaggerated striving for self-advancement and inflated self-feeling. Other results of the despotism of teachers have already been discussed in the chapter upon Discipline.

One must as a teacher constantly keep one's eyes open to the fact that the respect which one requires from the pupils should fundamentally be related not to the person but to the idea, an impersonal conception of authority, to which all are bound to do homage.

"Es gilt, in der Erziehung all persönliche Eitelkeit, all Geltungssucht, allen Machtwillen und Verehrungshunger beiseite zu stellen. Es gilt, die Anbetung der Kinder vom Realen und auch von uns selber weg allmählich auf das hinzulenken, was allein wahrhaft anbetungswürdig ist, auf das Ewige, das in der Wirklichkeit nie ganz aufgeht."[1] (Paul Häberlin in *Eltern und Kinder*.)

Some of these forms of artificial behaviour have of late years almost forfeited their currency value, especially the two poses of dignity and severity. A recognition has happily gained ground that the most favourable relationship for education is that of a quite natural, respectful friendship. The full realisation is now in progress of

---

[1] "In education we must abolish all personal vanity, all seeking after esteem for ourselves, all our love of power, our hunger for honour. It means diverting the adoration of the children from material things and from ourselves entirely to that which is only worthy of adoration, to the eternal which in reality can never be accomplished completely."

development that one has the most satisfactory influence upon the young folks, if one remains true to one's own character, keeping an honest and impartial estimation of the fact that we are human beings, each with his own imperfections.

Fundamentally the possibility of such a free natural attitude is a matter of temperament. The profession of education demands unusual psychological qualities. Let us give a brief summary of what the backbone of the teacher's character should comprise. It seems to us that it should be composed of the three cardinal virtues of *wisdom*, *goodness* and *happiness*.

Wisdom does not mean an inexhaustible fund of school learning, not being replete with general education, but possessing a free capacity to form judgments and a sure intuition respecting the essentials and worth of things.

Goodness in the educational sense has nothing to do with boring piety, weakness and sentimentality. Goodness is a characteristic which arises from forgetting oneself out of sympathy with the psychological development of another. Goodness of this kind arises from a fundamental reality of character, and very strong cultural externalisation of personal interests. It is based upon maturity which means well-developed mental freedom. It is to be found in persons whose development is constantly active and who, moreover, are as free as possible from their own complexes (fixated subjective inhibitions).

In this requirement, indeed, lies the characteristic of the teaching profession, which it shares with very few others. It means work carried out exclusively for love of humanity. For this reason it demands an unusual amount of interest in the future and in the growth of human beings, a highly developed gift of appreciation of social life, and a peculiar blend of an ideal ability for enthusiasm with a serious grasp of real values. It requires also a specific predominance of the idea of the importance of the function of the teacher as opposed to any material gain which may accrue to his position. In many professions, the clearly defined idea of gain leads to the exercise of greater zeal. The teacher, however, must to a great extent be able to forget that he has rented his working energy to the school authorities for the purpose of earning his daily bread. Otherwise he will easily become a time-worker who is niggardly about the expenditure of his energy. The teacher from vocation is glad to give his services without computing the reward.

Neither has *happiness* anything in common with the trivial habit of joviality or an infantile love of making jokes. Happiness is a condition of mature stability in relation to the oppressing forces of life. It means not taking one's personality too seriously, nor the hardships which come upon us either from without or within. Happiness is compatible with the deepest ethical seriousness and indeed cannot be imagined without it. The right kind of goodness provides the warmth of a flourishing educational climate, and happiness its light.

Beyond these three essential virtues, or side by side with them, we must add another specific pedagogic characteristic. An inexhaustible interest for the most minute details and a capacity to be able to renounce rapid, visible success in our work. A teacher should distinguish himself especially through a particular interest in practical matters and have a real ability to explain and pass on knowledge and skill. A great deal is required to make a good teacher!

One always comes back again to this point in all discussions upon the inadequacies of our schools and about reforms which might ensure fruitful and happy school-days for our children. It is the question of the pedagogic personality and the best method of bestowing educational talents upon the teaching profession. After a period during which we laid too much stress upon external reforms, financial subsidies and skilful organisation which after all are comparatively easy enough to accomplish, one realises to-day more than ever before that the central problem is the education talent of the teaching staff. The realisation is brought before us with greater vividness than ever, that the spirit of schoolmasterishness in the bad sense, working in a new schoolbuilding that resembled a palace, run upon a model rational time-table, and equipped with the most perfect educational material, would provide nothing but a daily oppression for the children, an occasion for stultifying boredom, and be a provider of abortive productiveness and sterile ambition. One realises also, however, the contrary state of affairs, that a teacher only half-blessed with these urgent necessities, and working with all the cramped conditions of obsolete school regulations, contrives, in spite of these drawbacks to influence their development favourably, because the chief need has been his personal contact with the young folks. He allows every school-day to be an interesting experience and to be filled with the joy of growth. Therefore we are obliged to recognise the fact that each school is as good or bad as the teachers who work in them.

Realisations of this description draw into prominence an important problem for all those who are striving for the rebirth of the school; how is it possible to gain the people who have the best qualifications from a pedagogic standpoint, according to their ability from the whole population, for the teaching profession?

We cannot discuss this question fully here, and must limit ourselves consequently to an explanation of the two steps which seem to us to be of particular importance.

I. We must give teachers, and especially those in our elementary schools, higher average salaries. It would be an advantage if they could be paid sufficiently well for their school-work to free them from all anxiety about the acquisition of a certain amount of comfort in the externals of daily life, which would make it unnecessary for them to seek for additional sources of income which waste their energy outside their real work.

As long as the calling of teacher cannot offer better advantages in the economic field, it cannot be expected that it will attract a very large number of young people from the ranks of the most talented. The estimation of a profession to-day depends to a great extent upon the financial gain to be derived from it. The higher the emolument, the greater the satisfactoriness of the profession. We have indeed stated above that the teaching profession particularly requires men who would carry out their work faithfully without the incentive of material gain, and for whom this was relatively a matter of small importance. Yet, in spite of this, those who are possessed of educational talent are after all men and women of the present-day world, and therefore are only relatively free from the hall-mark of general estimation of values. Adequate payment would also raise the professional status of the teacher, improve the quality of his work and would have a beneficial effect upon the choice of this calling, through which the training colleges for teachers would have greater facilities for selecting those who seemed the most suited for the work, from a larger number of candidates.

II. According to the present regulations of educational authorities obtaining in Switzerland in most of the cantons, aspirants for the teaching profession are recruited at the age of fifteen or sixteen years. They are then usually so immature that their choice of a profession is then only to the smallest extent objective, that is, can follow logically from an impartial consideration of general characteristics and the more or less correctly estimated cultural requirements of the teaching profession.

For this reason we have made the following suggestion

to a Swiss training college—that they should allow their students to write essays upon this subject: "Why I came to the Training College." As preparation it was made quite clear that no one expected to hear about a "spiritual call," "an urge to help with the development of the child mind," if no such thing really existed, and that everyone might quite frankly state without any diffidence what the factors were besides the considerations placed before them by their relations and others who had advised the taking of this step which had led them to enter the College.

The results were highly satisfactory. They showed that the principal and decisive motives had throughout been unconnected with material gain. That is, that the deciding factors arose predominantly from subjective wishes and desires.

The most dynamic factors may be obtained from a summary of the essays themselves:

(*a*) A consideration of the good social position of the teacher. The wish to move in a certain social circle, generally supported by the motive of definite ambitions of the relations in this respect.

(*b*) Consideration of the financial certainty of an official position, especially relative to the receipt of the pension. Usually behind this motive could be seen a definite anxiety connected with the exigencies of life, neurotic sense of inferiority and lack of sufficient strength for the struggle for existence.

(*c*) Dependence upon comfort; the reflection that the teacher carried out his job dry-shod, that he had long, free evenings, and enjoyed excellent holidays several times in the year. Such considerations were to be found mainly among the sons and daughters of the small peasant class, who had been brought up surrounded by a hard struggle for existence and who came but little in contact with quiet conditions or with refinement.

(*d*) Defective physical strength, a delicate constitution and a consciousness of lack of capacity for agriculture, or manual work, together with a relatively good school record. ("He will have to be a teacher; he is not strong enough for any other work!" is the idea that sums up this attitude.)

(e) Want of information respecting the training requisite for the profession on the part of the children, who always found learning easy. One would like to be able to give children extended facilities for education after they leave school. If any of these should happen to want to live in a town in order to attend a public school or a trade school, the boy or girl is advised to go to a training college instead. Because otherwise the cost of providing them with board and lodging would be prohibitive in many cases. The training school for teachers is a simple expedient, as it is relatively inexpensive. Therefore the training for the teaching profession will be adopted because among all the other learned professions it is relatively the least costly and most accessible.

(f) Identification with the admired teaching staff in the past. This is closely connected with the frequent devotion to be found on the part of boys and girls for a school-master or mistress, which constructs a professional ideal, through the adopting of which it becomes possible to follow the footsteps of a loved and honoured person.

The wish to adopt a certain profession that arises from such reasons may be the result of a quickly passing impulse, but it can nevertheless become a permanent desire in the mind of the young person, especially when it has taken shape in comparatively early childhood. Because the child's intention springs from the stimulus of an ideal of this kind, it is very difficult to bring to his conscious mind, the instinctual (erotic) tendencies which determine the choice of his profession, that are not actual objective reasons. The fact that the sons and daughters of school-masters choose the profession of education in large numbers, comes from a positive identification with the father.

(g) A strongly developed love of power drives a great many young people to the idea of becoming a teacher. The factor which always calls forth the greatest admiration in the inexperienced eyes of the children is his almost unlimited power in every aspect of his function. The teacher in his own kingdom, which is the class-room, is the greatest, the strongest, the most clever and the best-dressed person there and so becomes the highest possible standard. The teacher is also in the social life of the community a significant figure that is regarded by the children as through a magnifying glass. This power of domination is the great essential in the rôle of the teacher from the pupils' point of view. We can gain a great deal of information in this respect by observing children playing at schools, which is always a favourite game with them. The greatest charm for those who take part will be on the one hand to play at being the teacher, and thereby tasting all the delights of dictatorship which lie in the rôle, and upon the other, to take the part of pupil and negate this power through exaggerating every form of insubordination. This power is always the central point, and for this reason we often find that the game comprises punishment in the form of beating extraordinarily frequently.

It therefore happens that the boys and girls who have an especially strong inclination to be the top dog readily acquire a wish to be a teacher. There is no question that one finds among the students at the Training College a more decided desire to be esteemed than among the pupils, let us say, who are still at school training for other professions or those in workshops as apprentices.

(*b*) The emotional fixation to the school atmosphere. Many children were so happy at school that they want to become teachers in order never to be obliged to leave it. They are naturally those who have a relatively small urge to experience life in its full extent. They are the good children, the recluses, those who can do feats in memory acrobatics, etc. They are the scholars who are completely satisfied with the school as it is and from whom one may expect in the future to find little genius for reform.

These are the most important subjective motives to be found in the essays which have led to the choice of the profession of teacher. As we have already said they can be regarded as the decisive factors, or those which have been one of the most determining causes of the choice. This may sound serious. As a matter of fact it may not be as grave as we think because the existence of these reasons by no means precludes the presence of real pedagogic qualifications. Because such subjective reasons have been the deciding factor for entry to a training college, it does not mean that they will continue to preponderate in the choice of the profession for all time. These facts only serve to show us that at this early age, before the person is sixteen, an ability for true, objective consideration relative to the choice of a profession is not highly developed.

Still it requires our attention that a great deal rests upon chance, whether, in the case of these young folk who come to the training colleges, a real wish to be a member of the profession and a true gift of teaching is to be found in any way. Also it is well established that the number of unsuitable aspirants is by no means small.

Unfortunately, however, in the choice of reliable adults, we have also no means of knowing with any degree of certainty whether we shall find in them the lack or the presence of those qualities which are important in this respect.

Indeed, our common experience of human beings, supported by various methods of examination, occasionally guide us in a trustworthy way, where the candidates for the college are concerned. Here and there will be some who show clearly enough that they are unsuited for the teaching profession, their intellectual flexibility is not sufficient, nor their ethical balance, etc. We may only postulate this certainty, however, that where obvious partiality or an outstanding lack of predisposition for the vocation shows itself, the person is unsuited for the profession.

Positive judgment, however, "Here we have educational talent," can only very seldom be made, because at this problematic age such a wide field of possibilities for development lie before the normal adolescent that we ought not to try to take their measure, nor to make prognostications even with the aid of our psychological insight.

In the case of boys and girls between the age of fifteen and sixteen, their mental development is normally in a state of considerable upheaval. At this age particularly they have all the ethical tendencies which incline them towards the profession of a teacher which will not be founded entirely upon an actual preference. The definite mental-spiritual habits of a person can only be conjectured at this age, and not determined with any degree of certainty because for many years yet they will be subjected to extensive changes through the operation of partly if not entirely unexpected factors of development.

Therefore the requirements for the accurate selection of students can only be obtained by carrying out extensive reforms in the training of our teachers. The course of instruction for the candidates at the colleges must be reconstituted so that the final decision to adopt the profession is put off for several years. The decision would then take place normally at the comparatively favourable age of perhaps nineteen or twenty on an average, when greater experience of life's opportunities, freer self-knowledge and a more educated realisation of the responsibility of a teacher will lead the students to accomplish it automatically.

In the interest of a more substantial and extensive theoretical and practical education for future teachers, reform of educational training is required in respect of an increase in the time that is required for the various sections of the training. It is much to be desired that through these reforms new paths may be blazed by which this central problem may also find its solution. The accuracy in forming a decision regarding a profession is in itself more important than the amount of knowledge and proficiency which can be provided in the training of a teacher.

CHAPTER X

COMRADESHIP

If one should ask grown-up people what are the joys of their school-days they like best to remember one usually hears first about experiences in the forefront of which the happiness gained from youthful friendships stands as the focus point. Here we find the most intense aspects of life which gripped the whole of the personality. Emotions were experienced in which heart and mind played a significant part and stand out as a more vital factor than instruction gained at school.

This is perhaps a no less important function of the school than that of bringing children together. The school constitutes a natural community in which the social tendencies of the children may unfold and develop. It offers to every child a choice of contemporary companions, among whom it can establish to its heart's content friendships or hostilities. It will provide numerous opportunities for the construction of social groups, in which the several talents for leadership or co-operation may be developed. School-life is an unsurpassed source for all the romantic rapture of collective experience in which the child may find a happy possibility of breaking through the barriers of his individual isolation.

Anyone who does not learn to feel a member of a wider community as a child, or fails to achieve incorporation into a circle of contemporaries in childhood in a positive spirit, remains a self-satisfied and asocial person for the rest of his life.

Healthy childhood has a natural inclination and talent for comradeship which needs no help of ours. Still it sometimes fails to develop without some assistance. For this reason it should be regarded as an important function of the school to construct a bridge leading over to friendships, for those children, who, because of some unfavourable influences in the pre-school period, suffer from inhibitions in the development of their impulse for social contacts.

Primarily it is a matter of the greatest importance for all children that their need for contacts should be connected up from the start upon lines which serve a cultural purpose. The hunger for comradeship is originally in fact nothing but an impulsive erotic manifestation. But it is possible when this instinct is sublimated, which means developed among the young people in a sense of brotherly and sisterly affection, it will lead on to a solidarity in which will be included a realisation of responsibility, readiness to help one another and self-sacrifice.

School-teachers, however, are frequently so very much occupied with their time-tables that they neglect entirely or extensively the practical side of the education of the young folks among each other and for one another's good.

And yet this function is so pertinent that these strong and most useful strivings for affection on the part of the children can be made use of for the cultivation of social service. The class-room is a place where the children of widely different social circles meet. Here they have almost unlimited opportunities at their disposal for bridging over socially hostile and opposite tendencies which will be supported by the far-reaching natural community interests of childhood.

The psychological structure of the family rests extensively upon the tendency of the self-assertion of its several members. Within this group therefore will always be found predominantly the egoistic instinctual components. The school, on the contrary, should be the promoter of the social educational habit.

Wherever the school accepts this most noble obligation it will in the first place take care to avoid those mistakes in its handling of the children through which their community life will be destroyed. Many of the reports which follow in the second section of this book show clearly enough how the irony of the teachers, the preference shown to one child, the neglect of another, the teasing or injustice shown to some of those who contributed them, cut off individual children from the class-spirit and destroyed the comradely unity of the whole class.

Factors which disturb the community feeling arise, however, not only from mistakes of this kind, but chiefly from the system of present-day educational organisation. It is particularly necessary to accomplish a realisation of this fact, that our whole educational system in many respects is far more likely to estrange children from one another than to bring them together. We strive, without recognising that we are doing it, to make the individual interests of the school-life more prominent than the general interests of the school as a whole.

This phenomenon is indisputably connected with the worship of the idol of external, visible success. When we allow the pupils to write essays or other written exercises, then it becomes so terribly important for us to point out the isolated achievement of each child and to stamp it with a good or bad mark. (With what grotesque solemnity therefore do we condemn *copying* as a criminal offence!) The evaluation of work through a system of marks must of necessity always remain relative, which means that one pupil receives a better or worse mark according to the standard of the work of the others. The success of the one is conditioned by the failure of the others and vice versa.

We find a similar state of affairs in oral repetition and

COMRADESHIP 93

in the hearing of lessons. The upraised hand of each one who knows is of more or less importance in relation to the number of raised hands that are visible. The whispered hints of the uncovetous, however, are frequently counted as weighty school offences, regarded pathetically as *deceit*, because they interrupt the inventory-keeping of the teacher of the memory capacity of single individuals, and will consequently undermine the pupils' hope of any possibility of release from the power of the schoolmaster.

And the system of school reports and the giving of marks which is regarded to-day as being so indispensable, is nothing but this manifestation of the spirit of rivalry. It becomes a ruling which leads to the necessity of every child seeking his own personal advancement, his personal success before anything else. The marks in themselves neither please nor depress the child, but the knowledge that his greater or less success in marks will be counted in comparison with those of his schoolfellows.

As a symbol of this spirit we may take the astounding school form through the use of which every pupil enjoys nothing but a view of his comrades' backs because they sit one behind the other. Such furniture is constructed upon the most asocial pattern possible. If one were to carry the idea a step further quite consistently in making the isolation as complete as possible, why should we not have partitions made between all the pupils sitting in the same row, so that each would sit in a similarly constructed box with only one possible focus of orientation—that of the desk of the teacher?

If one had wished intentionally to work out a system through which the children could be most surely brought up to self-seeking, to envy, and by which their happiness might be most effectually destroyed, we could not have devised anything more to the purpose than this prevailing method of oral inquisition, seclusion, marks and reports because these regulations constantly allow the children no other opportunity but to work in competition against one another.

As long as school authorities base education upon personal success it encourages individual ambition to be the chief incentive of school achievement and necessarily becomes an education of the asocial instincts. In this way it will create in the children a cessation of the operation of the emotions and judgment which can hardly ever be entirely eradicated afterwards, giving them the impression that life is primarily a battle-field where each is obliged to seek his own advancement naturally in opposition to the interests of the other combatants. The natural need for contacts which is never quite destroyed in the pupils is hardly sufficient to hold the balance even.

Among the Middle Schools we may frequently see in how many ways the teaching staff takes steps to hinder the construction of a firmer community feeling among the young folks. It was entirely symbolic of this mental attitude that it was prohibited to wear class colours for many years in a large Swiss boys' school. Teachers are suspicious of alliances among the children because they are afraid of loss of their own prestige thereby. Whenever we find a person troubled about the preservation of his position of authority it proves the maintenance of the old Roman maxim of *divide et impera*. Through that method of education the spirit of Bernard Shaw's definition of education is carried out. "Education is the organised defence of adults against children." In this way the fear of the solidarity of the pupils becomes especially easy to understand. The teaching staff feel that they have not got complete mastery over the children somehow, because they have failed in the conception of the educational spirit which grips them from within.

All true happiness and culture depend upon the necessity of co-ordinating all our more purposeful schemes increasingly in the community. The schools which in fact are the natural organisations for carrying out the work of social education, ought to contribute their help. It could be accomplished if only they could be reorganised in respect of this essential factor that they should make the principle of communal work, of mutual help, the corner-stone of school-life. They must allow the children to work for and with one another instead of against one another.

Here and there in Germany and other countries successful experiments upon these lines have been carried out, principally in connection with the institution of *work-projects*. All school work, essay-writing, arithmetic, nature study, research, drawing, handicraft, have been as far as possible dominated by the school-groups. Naturally among these groups, details of work have to be carried out by individuals when of necessity they could only be done as the work of a single person. The feeling and realisation of co-operation for a special purpose provide a happy incentive for all to work together and bestow upon it a consecrating benediction. Mutual help thus becomes a virtue without dross and provides no further opposition to the wishes of the leaders. Each becomes dominated by the community spirit that true work means service to the group and that selfishness is the source of most of our misfortunes. Such ideas make culture of the mind possible. Ambition, however, is an intellectual energy which isolates the individual and makes all true heroism impossible, and is based usually upon the renunciation of all personal interests.

Moreover, in community education, the stimulus of competition should have no place. But here we must make some provision for the natural impulse of youth that desires to measure its growing strength against that of another. This spirit of rivalry can be directed into channels, where it can have no more dangerous significance than that of happy, comradely sportsmanship, where the various contestants have a full respect for one another, which as a rule is to be found among the most celebrated representatives of modern sport. By such means the good teacher will have a hundred better opportunities of keeping before his eyes the progress of the development of the individual than by means of the former incentives of exaggerated personal efforts.

Should the teacher in the school of to-morrow consciously place the creation of the community spirit in the central position of his work, and devote only one quarter of the mental energy which he gives to-day to educational technique, to daily cultivation of the spirit of comradeship, more will be accomplished for the training of moral strength, efficiency and happiness than by the institution of the most clever reforms in methods of education.

CHAPTER XI

PROVISIONAL LIFE

> Und er weiss von allen Schätzen
> Sich nicht in Besitz zu setzen.
> Glück und Unglück wird zur Grille,
> Er verhungert in der Fülle;
> Sei es Wonne, sei es Plage,
> Schiebt er's zu dem andern Tage,
> Ist der Zukunft nur gewärtig
> Und so wird er niemals fertig.

THESE lines come from the second part of Goethe's poem of Faust. They describe a mental attitude which many people carry about with them like a chronic illness throughout their entire life. They always live provisionally and never definitely. They are perpetually expecting and hoping for a time to come in the future when they may achieve something, but it never actually arrives. They put off making all important decisions. They will definitely take themselves in hand later on. They will prove their worth presently. Always some time in the *future*. They live every day for a constantly receding, unachievable to-morrow. They can never make up their minds to be really sad or happy to-day. The present gives them only a lukewarm feeling in comparison with what is to come. The future only can bring them the fullness of life. But the future fails to work this miracle. It continues to recede before the unalterably sterile present.

In neurotic persons one often finds this attitude towards life as being merely provisional in an exaggerated degree. Its unconscious strand finds its expression by avoiding the necessity of solving some psychological problem, because their neurotic conflict is based precisely upon their incapacity to solve it.

But in a slighter degree we all suffer from the evils of this idea of a provisional life. We are all inclined to put off for the future the full unfolding of our personality, to believe to-morrow to be of greater importance than to-day. Our natural laziness and numerous psychological fixations compel us to this attitude. For this reason we are here again confronted with an important educational problem, how we may establish in young people so much free activity and artistry in life that they may accept each day as equally important as the others and try to live every hour to its fullest extent and to shape it to their wishes or requirements.

The school, however, favours the contrary attitude exclusively, that of provisional life. It brings this about chiefly because it forces the child to remain in a sphere where it feels itself standing outside real and full life. Since the school cannot succeed in permeating the whole life of the child it causes a fatal cleft within it, so that very many children live one life which we will call A, and another B, during their school-days.

Life A means for them freedom—Sunday—holidays—comradeship—the nice smell of mother's kitchen—Meccano—playing with their dolls—keeping rabbits—riding a bicycle—football—expeditions of exploration—helping father with his work.

Life B indicates school—loneliness—tiresome duties—lack of freedom—oppression—being good—chalk-dust—the tyranny of books—stale atmosphere and a bad conscience.

The result is that children begin to put off intensive full life and regard it as something that belongs only to the future. They accommodate themselves to the endless chain of school-days as one does to an illness, in the hope that after this interval one will be able to resume one's activity once again. Thus the children look forward to the week-end with high expectation—when they will really live. But they feel that this little span of time over the Sunday is far too short to allow of free development. But the consoling expectation of the holidays remains. Still here again in the case of many children, school life has already robbed them of the capacity of enjoying the holidays to the full. They lack the spontaneity for simple phantasy, childish optimism and unbroken impulsiveness to allow them to take full advantage of the longed-for free time. And in this way the blessed holidays slip away without having been made use of, just as the life of an inefficient person slips through his fingers.

Positive life will have to be postponed still further, one imagines, until the time when school-days are ended; then one will be able to unfurl the sails for a voyage of life, then one can develop one's own existence and fill it with meaning. But the habit of living provisionally has by now gained such a crippling hold over the young folks through long use that they can only half live even then. They betray themselves and put off their decisions further and further, until after their training for business or a profession, after they have their first real job, after their marriage, and so on throughout all the various stages of human existence. At the end nothing remains but mourning over the wasted opportunities of making good and the missed chances of happiness.

The school must inculcate these essentially fatal superstitions as long as it is anything else rather than a medium for the development of the valuable qualities of the child, and as long as its spirit is not in full accord with the sum of all true youthful existence.

The old school attitude was to regard youth almost exclusively as a time of preparation for maturity. To be young meant therefore necessarily according to this view a negative condition, something that was unfinished and immature. Childhood consequently was something the significance of which was that we do our best to get through it as quickly as possible. Yet children and adolescents accept these beliefs unconditionally and grow up in a spirit which negates their own existence.

Rousseau and Pestalozzi in the past vehemently demanded that each age should be recognised as having its own occupations, its own beauties, and its own rights. Children should be allowed to be children before they can become men and women. We should rejoice that the recognition of these requirements is to-day decidedly on the increase. One considers young people less in the light of human material for use in the future than heretofore. Youth is no longer considered so exclusively as only a time of preparation, but now as a period which is also full of meaning in itself.

Consequently the new school will strive primarily to be a place of intensive and happy development of life. It will attempt to bring about for every child that each day will be as far as possible a complete unity of existence. This will result in the view that every dissociation which splits up youthful existence into two spheres of interest will be abolished and together with this will be swept away a constant danger for the continuity and psychological harmony of childhood.

CHAPTER XII

MISTAKES

Hitherto we have been dealing with the diseases of the school, the predominant causes of which lie in the present-day public educational system, that is, in its entire intellectual structure. Respecting these evils, we are all responsible for them to some extent, whether we are teachers or not.

But besides these, there is, nevertheless, a long list of school troubles which for the most part may be traced back to fundamental educational mistakes on the part of individual teachers, which might be altogether abolished if only the teachers would change their behaviour towards the children. We will briefly summarise a few of the most prevalent of these.

(a) PARTIALITY

We discover increasingly by experience that children suffer more than adults from injustice which they observe practised upon others as well as upon themselves. The child has not yet learned how to deal with the fact that it is a common human failing to measure others with an unequal standard. In this respect particularly, he expects from us teachers the highest degree of justice, and demands from us its most perfect expression because he has not yet realised our weakness. Such requirements can hardly be satisfied and the tragedy of disillusionment must for this reason play a more or less important part in the history of every childhood.

Many of the injustices in school-life arise from the despotic tendencies of the teacher and are therefore principally the consequence of his inability to renounce sufficiently his own gratification of purely subjective wishes in the work of education. He deals with the virtues and faults of the children not from the standpoint of their own moral code, but according to a standard provided by his *moods* and his personal attitude to life.

Children always suffer from arbitrary behaviour of this kind with great intensity, but especially from that form of injustice which one describes as *partiality or prejudice*.

One may perhaps hear a teacher boast that he is entirely impartial, and that he likes all his pupils exactly the same. One may always reply thus to this speaker, without any danger of making a mistake. "Yes, but that means that you *dislike* all your pupils equally, or your statement cannot be taken seriously." It is almost impossible to find a teacher who does not take with him into the classroom his natural need for affection. Because of this we must necessarily admit that a pupil must be more or less attractive to a teacher. All we teachers are partial to some extent. It is beneficial to look this squarely in the face so that we may act upon the discovery consciously; in order that we may suppress increasingly the emotional and subjective taking of sides in our educational work and at all events remain impartial in our behaviour. This, in point of fact, requires all the self-discipline of which the teacher's character is capable.

Every act of injustice in the school, every time a child is picked out for preference or slight, must have a demoralising effect upon him, and endanger his relationship to the teacher. All partiality must also signify an act of interference to the comradely attitude of the children among themselves.

It is depressing to find how often among the following reports we read descriptions of injustice of this kind, through which the children of parents who were of a lower social grade or in straitened financial circumstances suffered in special ways. We should be careful, however, not to allow our indignation full rein where such manifestations are concerned. Here again it will be a case of recognising the underlying impulses that have been set in action and remaining honest. Do we not all prefer a clean, attractively dressed child to an unkempt offspring of the proletariat who is neglected body and soul? And if a teacher should lose his temper on those pupils whose parents are the least intimately connected with the school, it need not always indicate his entirely asocial point of view. He is only doing what every shop-assistant does, who, when he has got into trouble with his employer, bullies the apprentice; nothing more than an official who, when he has had a difference of opinion with authorities, then goes home, to act the tyrant there.

Naturally lack of self-control of this sort in the school is particularly injurious because the children are so completely in the power of the teacher and because their consequent embitterment puts in jeopardy all the deeper influences of school-life.

It can scarcely be helped that we teachers become prejudiced against some pupils. But these prejudices should not be passed from one teacher to another, so that it becomes impossible for some children to gain any sort of personal consideration or human treatment.

Each teacher is obliged to make enquiries concerning the character of his pupils from those who have taught the children before him. But we should be careful to treat them as though we knew nothing about their antecedents. Every child should be given the idea that it is possible to begin a new life with a new teacher, if he wants to do so. A definitely bad character must never be given from one teacher to another about any pupil. Rather should a good teacher always express his belief in the possibility of improvement.

(b) THE FIGHT AGAINST DEFIANCE

It is an old fault of educational method that one should attempt to fight against the defiance shown by a child with rigorous severity, in the attempt to break his spirit. In the eyes of many teachers defiance seems to be *the* variety of childish naughtiness against which there should be no surrender.

A few moments' quiet psychological consideration should show us clearly, however, that defiance is a very complicated mental condition, which the usual coarse weapons of the school generally make worse instead of better. It is never cured by such means.

The defiance of children should be regarded in many cases as an *instinctive defence mechanism* against our educational mistakes. Frequently it will be the consequence of bitter experiences which the child has suffered at the hands of adults. It is his reaction to slights, lack of affection and domination, sometimes also to senseless spoiling, to which he has been subjected. It is often an attitude of withdrawal from grown-ups, when a child has given these an especially large amount of love or unusual confidence, and then the adults in question have not estimated these gifts at their true value, nor taken them seriously, and perhaps have shown themselves to be unworthy of them.

We are familiar with the fact that this defiant attitude may easily be transferred to persons other than those whom they originally concerned. For example, the defiance frequently appeared first in connection with the father, the defiant clash of wills and negativism connected with it, however, will be readily passed on to his teacher, as well as all other persons who come up against the child with educational claims to authority. But the teacher should take the greatest care not to put an end to his former relationship with a child without further consideration the first time a defiant attitude should appear in class.

The child negates our authority with his defiance; he accomplishes an attempt to put himself upon an equal footing with adults by means of this action. It will indemnify him through pleasurably-toned consciousness of his own power and courage for imaginary or actual deprivation of love and understanding.

Naturally enough it is the strong-willed characters who react to an injury to their pride with defiance. The children who are possessed of a smaller capacity for resistance acquire depressive inferiority feelings instead and subordinate themselves to them without ceasing. Defiance is therefore often the lesser of the two evils and is a relatively healthy defence against anything which seems to threaten them psychologically. It always comprises one great danger, nevertheless. The defiant child always suffers more or less from a feeling of *guilt*. It feels that it is not entirely in the right. The guilty feeling, however, may increase the defiance too much, so that it becomes actual stubbornness which signifies the condition of a child locking itself in, not only against the influence of adults, but also from the voice of its own conscience. Such children suffer immeasurably as a rule and need particularly gentle and patient educational handling.

It will be generally necessary to use a great deal of patience, love and understanding in order to bring about the melting of the ice of this frozen attitude.

(c) CORPORAL PUNISHMENT

Corporal punishment is less frequently part of the daily life of the school to-day than it was some twenty or thirty years ago. There are teachers in all parts of the world nowadays who make it a point of their pedagogical honour to reach their goal without being obliged to lay hands upon their pupils. Yet in spite of this there is, nevertheless, a good deal of thrashing. Every one knows this who is in any way connected with our schools. The material collected by the questionnaire provided countless instances of the fact that in many schools thrashing is still even to-day an essential factor. But before we give any opinion upon the rights and wrongs of corporal punishment, we must first of all take into our consideration the educational significance of punishment.

It is intended to help the pupil not only to give up his fault from the surface but to overcome it from within his personality. To acquire such complete mastery over it, it requires above all unbroken courage, happiness and self-confidence. These are the indispensable factors for this moral struggle, but they are nevertheless actually weakened through guilt provoked by the wrongs suffered by the children. It is essential for us to remove this feeling of guilt before we may restore the individual to his former moral energy. And here we reach the one reasonable educational significance of punishment. Punishment is a means of *atonement* which may cancel inhibiting pricks of conscience.

Punishment, therefore, should be no vehicle of oppression, but one of *liberation*. Where it attempts anything else it will produce an anti-educational effect. For example, when the teacher has aimed at achieving intimidation and terrorism, he is making use of the lowest trend, the instinctual nature of the child and not of his tendency towards improvement, through the strengthening of which alone will betterment be possible.

Anyone who attempts to educate through fear allies himself with the animal instincts of the children and not with their spiritual aspirations.

From this it may be gathered that a reasonable punishment is only possible in relation to a child who is sensible of his wrongdoing and is filled with remorse and consequently a need of atonement. Failing these conditions, the punishment will only have the effect of intimidation and will therefore readily bring about a rift between teacher and pupil.

All methods of punishment which serve the true purpose of atonement are good. For example, in many cases those will be appropriate which require special tasks to be performed in certain directions as an atonement for the faults. Purposeful also can be a renunciation of pleasure or a certain amount of curtailment of the child's liberty.

Is it not possible also for corporal punishment to have this atoning and liberating effect? One cannot give a reply to this question without considerable thought. Whether one should thrash or not is a question of *method*. Whether a method is successful or not should be decided by critics who take up the problem from a psychological standpoint. We must also pay attention to what we may learn from psychological experience and conclusions.

I. It lies in the nature of corporal punishment that in the majority of cases the pupil feels degraded. Degradation produces the opposite effect to that which we wish to achieve. The pupil feels, after his wrongdoing, that the kernel of his personality, his ego, has fallen short of his ideal. He therefore expects instinctively that the teacher will settle accounts with this centre, that is, with his ego, as directly as possible. When, however, the teacher, instead of this, stops short at his body, that is, at the lower and external manifestation of his personality, as though that were the essential part of a human being, the effect produced by this form of punishment is *degradation*.

The same result is to be found when teachers constantly give expression to their satisfaction and approval of a child by constantly stroking and kissing him, or secretly giving him sweets and such-like. Behaviour of this kind has a humiliating and demoralising effect similar to that provided by beating. The children will be degraded to the level of animals to a certain extent by this means.

II. Corporal punishment leads to bodily pain. Physical pain does not, as a rule, produce a happy frame of mind in people. It is a characteristic of bodily pain that it intensively absorbs our attention and to a certain extent automatically mobilises our ego-instinct to defend itself. Anyone suffering pain will be dominated by his impulses and therefore driven into a state of mind that is educationally valueless, which usually continues to reverberate after the direct pain has ceased. Those who are punished in other and more sensible ways—by the imposition of mental suffering, for instance—react much sooner with the moral development of their minds.

III. As we have explained above, punishment only acts beneficially when it is administered by the teacher without emotional impetus, that is, quite impersonally. It must be made clear to the pupil by the quiet, affectless attitude of the teacher, that through his wrongdoing, he has fundamentally sinned against not merely one person but sometimes much higher, *the moral code*, and that in this case it is his duty to atone for it.

Almost without exception corporal punishment gives the child the impression that it is an act of personal retribution. He believes the blows to be the discharge of the teacher's anger, annoyance and irritability.

This is easy to understand. The child constantly observes that adults are most easily inclined to blows if they have lost their temper—when they are annoyed; and in this respect beating is really a dangerous thing for us also. Many teachers who start a thrashing in relative calmness, thrash themselves into anger allied with other emotions. It readily awakens in them the primitive human lust for revenge which normally slumbers deeply hidden within us.

The child will be aware of these released affects in the mind of the teacher, even when, perhaps, for once he consciously thrashes him impersonally and abstractly. The whole scene presents itself to the child simply as a personal conflict between ill-matched opponents. For this reason corporal punishment becomes so frightfully important in the child's eyes. He will believe that grown-up persons behave in this way because they are much stronger and that if he were as big and as strong as they, they would leave him alone! Helpless anger and bitter resentment therefore are the natural consequences in the majority of cases of punishment of this type.

We thus reach this conclusion that no teacher should make use of corporal punishment who has not a solid relationship with his pupils, so that they believe unconditionally in the educational impartiality of all his motives and methods. But a teacher who is blessed in all these respects will easily be able to gain his ends by the use of other means. Those who believe corporal punishment to be indispensable are usually the ones who are least fitted to carry it out.

IV. It is well known that corporal punishment may lead to a pathological displacement of erotic impulses. The new psychology suggests that masochistic tendencies may already be found in children. By this term is to be understood the phenomenon that some people derive sexual pleasure from pain, that they like to be given pain by others, and especially by those whom they love. If this perverse erotic tendency is established, it may in later years lead to severe mental disturbances and tragic inhibitions which may continue throughout life. One should not exaggerate these dangers, but they exist, nevertheless, and there are a great many more persons who suffer from masochistic sexual difficulties than the lay public is commonly aware.

We should not like to state positively that masochistic tendencies can be started in children through corporal punishment. It is known that thrashing usually injures those in this respect where certain tendencies to this impulse displacement are already in existence. We are, however, certain that corporal punishment can be an important factor which favours the development of such germs which otherwise would never have gained strength. Cases are by no means rare where thrashing has increased a slightly masochistic tendency that already was in existence, because it received welcome nourishment from this harvest of pain. It may be the action of the corporal punishment which caused the masochistic tendency to break through into consciousness and remain there for life.

The greatest misfortune for the teacher is that only those children who show well-developed, exaggerated symptoms will be recognised as suffering in these ways. It is a difficult matter for educational eyes to recognise them when the first sign appears of the slightest masochistic symptom. This means in educational practice that we can never be absolutely sure in the case of any child whether we shall not develop in him a masochistic tendency which will be incurable.

These are a few allied unfavourable effects which can be seen in the victims of punishment. Through the habit of thrashing in a school, a number of highly questionable results may be noticed in the fellow-pupils, besides those which we have already described, feelings which are aroused through looking on. Let us consider these dangers.

V. In a great many cases the malicious pleasure and sadistic enjoyment derived from looking, which exist in practically every child to some extent, will find nourishment. The sadistic component impulse, which once again our new psychology has demonstrated in all clearness, hides germwise in everyone. It is one of the functions of education to try to suppress this asocial instinct, which is opposed to all culture, so that it shall not find expression in the actions of human beings. Yet, when we provide gratification for the most primitive tendency of this strange vice and supply it with material to work upon, we foster its growth. Children are not so innocent as widespread and lying sentimentality would have us believe. All of them are inclined now and then to acts of more or less overt cruelty. One can, therefore, never allow a child to suffer bodily pain in the presence of the class without a few of those present deriving a secret pleasure from it and in this way also a certain amount of injury to their minds. For this reason alone it would seem that thrashing before the class is especially inexcusable.

VI. Moreover, the constant fear of being obliged to suffer a similar disgrace becomes a positive torture to many children, who, in point of fact, are almost entirely protected from the cane.

VII. Frequently the comradely relationship between the children themselves will suffer through the use of corporal punishment. The victim is at the same time branded with shame and will be regarded in this light by the others, particularly when such proceedings are common in his case in comparison with the experiences of his schoolfellows. The teacher who strives to put into practice the most fruitful reforms of education in relation to the modern community spirit abolishes thrashing as being incompatible with the new ideals for this reason.

VIII. Very often, however, we find that corporal punishment has a terrifying effect upon very sensitive children because it awakens so much sympathy and resentment in them. One may easily underestimate the children's depth of feeling in this respect and imagine that they only realise the mistakes of their elders in any high degree when they themselves are the direct sufferers. Naturally this takes place principally when the corporal punishment is carried out upon poorer children or those who are intellectually weak. Children at school will often suffer from looking on at such scenes much more than if they themselves had been obliged occasionally to suffer the corporal punishment.

We adults can only estimate with difficulty how much hatred and contempt for a teacher can be aroused in a child, and how much tormenting lack of confidence in grown-up people collectively will arise under these circumstances. A particular state of mental confusion will be produced when, in frequent cases, the children are swayed alternately between sensations of malicious pleasure and those of sympathy with the sufferers.

IX. The school-mates often suffer in other ways besides from watching these occurrences, for the intellectually refined child, being obliged to look on, signifies an aesthetic torment to some extent. A thrashing scene is ugly under any conditions; normal good taste is always offended by it. It is particularly repugnant if girls are being beaten. This idea alone should give those in favour of corporal punishment much to think about. How can anything be good if it causes offence to our most elementary sense of aesthetic requirements?

One may only suggest as a means of decreasing this last-mentioned evil that the teacher should take children who have to be punished out of the class-room and that the administration of the corporal punishment should take place elsewhere. But this would make it almost worse, if this were possible, since the carrying out of the punishment *in camera* would by this means take on a new, highly depressing quality, laden with phantasy and tinged with an extremely painful colour.

These psychological reasons against corporal punishment—and we have not mentioned all of them—must compel us to take the view that thrashing scarcely fulfils any of the conditions of the educational requirements of punishment which we have already described. *Therefore it must be condemned.* These objections to thrashing are commonly recognised theoretically to-day. Thus it becomes a question of equal importance that, if this is the case, why, then, should it be still so prevalent in the home and at school?

Not only do we find desire for power, lack of humour, irritability, bad temper and a deficiency of understanding and love on the part of the father or teacher responsible for this state of affairs—all of these factors very certainly play their part—but the dominant reason is an inherent laziness on the part of the teachers. They will not change their old ways, nor break with their old, familiar habits. And then, moreover, it is usually *so convenient to thrash.* All needs of punishment can be expressed by a box on the ear or the like! One has the comfortable feeling that one is left master of the situation and is now free to continue with the day's work. If the child's misdemeanour is to be atoned for through some sort of imposition, although this is the most reasonable form of punishment, it gives a considerable amount of trouble. The teacher will have to consider the magnitude of the fault and think out a task which bears some sort of relation to it. He will also have to see that it is carried out and perhaps will even have to take upon himself the extra work of correcting it when finished. Corporal punishment is carried out really with much less expenditure of time and trouble.

Besides, we must also take into account the power of primeval tradition. People have always beaten offenders. Why should one to-day forgo this means of punishment now that young people seem to be particularly wild and intractable?

As we have already said, the idea of the educational unsuitability of corporal punishment finds very little opposition in educational circles to-day—theoretically. Yet a fundamental belief in the educational efficacy of this kind of punishment is still unbroken everywhere from the practical viewpoint. Besides, at the same time, the superstition concerning the indispensability of this method of correction is still alive in many places. It is very difficult to root out a superstition that exists concerning a method which has formed part of the iron ration of educational practice of all peoples of the world for hundreds of years. Time and again we are told precisely from the teachers themselves, "One cannot in fact get on without thrashing occasionally. It is impossible to reach the required standard of good behaviour and discipline in the intractable children without it."

And the events of the last thirty years have apparently confirmed the views of these pessimists, since in practically all class-rooms corporal punishment is still carried out. And if one isolated teacher makes it a point of honour never to do it, then ten others will say immediately, "Yes, but he is a particularly clever chap. He has a special gift for his job. You must not expect us ordinary mortals to get through as he does."

But to-day, thank God, it is quite otherwise. To-day there is already a very large number of teachers in every grade of the profession, in schools of all kinds, in the cities and the country, in Switzerland as well as in other countries, who accomplish their work without corporal punishment, and who have, in spite of giving it up, uncontested discipline and the greatest educational success. *Therefore it can be done*; that has been proved a thousand times. The sceptics should never say, "One cannot get through without thrashing," but more correctly in many cases, "*I do not wish to get on without it.*" They should try to bring through to consciousness what proofs they have for the support of their views.

A widespread argument in favour of corporal punishment runs something like this: "One cannot manage in school altogether without thrashing as long as it is the custom in the homes of the children. Many are brought up by it and need it in order to make them respect authority and discipline." What a modest computation of the teacher's educational prowess is expressed in such a statement! And how little faith in the adaptability of the child mind! The parents behave like lay teachers and to a great extent work in close co-operation with them. Still the teacher is a professional pedagogue. He has an educational training behind him. For this reason it seems to us no unwarrantable presumption if he supposes himself able to direct the child in a better way than that in use in the home. It is also up to him to counterbalance domestic errors in education as far as possible and to cancel them.

The abolition of thrashing is a need that applies equally urgently to the home as well as to the school, although the problem in each case is not precisely the same. Yet the spirit of the home will follow that of the school always to some degree, and real progress will only be achieved when the improvement is effected in both. *But the schools should lead the way!*

Fundamentally everything depends upon our attitude to our profession, *what the spirit of education is that we accept.*

Corporal punishment is the requisite of a system of education which is based upon the theory that youth must primarily be controlled and held in a leash; the opinion that the function of education is before all else a battle between the adult and youthful wickedness, idleness and presumption. Certainly to a teacher, for whom material success and the upholding of external discipline signify the most important ideals of his profession, thrashing will be entirely appropriate and purposeful. All those who wish to get through the day's work with the minimum expenditure of nervous energy will thrash. Those who are slaves to their own wish for authority and would rather be feared than loved will likewise thrash. Anyone who wishes to cultivate human beings like sheep, hypocrites, people with feebly developed self-confidence and flexible moral spines will thrash. As a manifestation of all such aims, punishment becomes nothing but intimidation and oppression.

But at the present day new educational ideas are becoming prevalent which have always been in existence here and there. A general recognition is steadily growing that all education should be based upon the principle that a mature person should offer help to those who are immature, kindly and faithfully, to tide them over the difficulties of development; that an older person should act as the guide to younger ones on the road to their common goal. And at the best the senior is only a few steps in advance where knowledge and character-formation are concerned. According to this spirit we should not be the taskmasters, but the friends, advisers and guides of a free and happy childhood. We will not maintain a frosty distance between ourselves and them, but foster a human approach. We shall not require a compulsory and oppressive authority but a far-reaching respect arising from their freely given estimation of our worth. We do not want mass education but solid individual study of each child and extensive individual treatment.

In these more intimate human contacts all pedagogic requirements and possibilities will be comprised. A nearer approach to this ideal is more important than the institution of all kinds of school reforms in method and external organisation. Anyone who carries out teaching in this spirit must feel that corporal punishment is something fundamentally foreign, an anachronism, and a most questionable educational contradiction.

We are surely not so one-sided, however, as to believe we can decide the merits or demerits of a teacher from his views upon thrashing. There is no question of that. It is a far more complicated matter that we have before us. There are some school-masters who never beat their pupils, but who, nevertheless, provide mental torture for the children in their charge which, under certain circumstances, is as cruel and has equally dangerous effects as the prevailing habit of thrashing. We will discuss these in the next section. But corporal punishment still continues, in spite of this, to be an educational monstrosity.

Corporal punishment should be abolished entirely. It acts upon the principle that no one will be harmed by an occasional insignificant box on the ear or a slap. The total cleansing of all class-rooms from the last remnants of the thrashing mania should be carried out in the interest of the teachers. It would increase the all-round friendly feeling in the public and contribute a great deal towards raising the public estimation of the teaching profession. Let us then accomplish it for the sake of ourselves, therefore, as well as for the sake of the children.

(d) MOCKERY, CONTEMPT AND SARCASM

One will occasionally hear teachers boast that they are able to manage their children excellently and to keep them in order through the use of *irony, jest and sarcasm*. Such people sometimes take great credit to themselves that they gain their end without the use of corporal punishment and have found out how to control their pupils with mental methods rather than physical ones.

These teachers, however, forget that every sort of degradation is against the principles of education and that one may degrade with biting words just as easily as with blows. They forget also that discipline that is purchased at the expense of the confidence of the children is valueless.

They may protest that everything depends upon the tone of voice that is used, that a cheery, good-humoured jest does not wound. This in itself is correct. But where is the teacher who can make use of such a method purely from good motives and without any trace of self-aggrandisement? And where may we find in practice the child upon whom such jests may work *educationally*, who will be successfully improved by such means and not made to suffer from a feeling of wounded vanity?

Would not adults, confronted by several varieties of satire, wish to be revenged upon their contemporaries for injuries of this sort? Revenge would, however, bring relief of the tension aroused by the irony and might lead on to further possibilities of improvement. But in relation to a child, mockery and satire are cruel, because by means of them the child will be weakened and humiliated in its natural and necessary struggle for the development of its own self-esteem.

Mockery is never a means of elevating but always of degrading, not perhaps in itself, but because the child by reason of his intellectual immaturity cannot adopt any attitude through which he can meet the adult with his own weapons. Therefore we practically always find in this satirical and sarcastic treatment of young people a trace of despotic tyranny that arises from a vain and cowardly urge to play for one's own superiority.

The sufferings of the individual child under the mockery and scorn of the teacher will be greatly increased by the behaviour of the class. Children have as great a tendency to cruelty as their elders. They are usually only too ready to seize any permitted opportunity derived from the example of their teacher, to add to the burden of their school-fellow by their triumphant self-esteem. But nevertheless it is a dangerous kind of pleasure which the teacher thus bestows upon the class at the expense of one of his pupils. He appeals to the lowest instincts of the children in this way and gives them gratification. He will certainly achieve a cheap success in this way, it is true. It does not require any very high degree of intellect to sharpen one's wits upon a child, and he hardly ever fails to get the ugly response of applauding laughter. The demagogues among our teachers will never be able altogether to renounce such methods of gaining power over their pupils.

Our collection of depositions respecting school troubles contain a large number of reports that go to prove what a devastating effect the mockery and contempt of a teacher may have. In the first place the experience of being laughed out of countenance often leads to a tormenting increase of the child's general instinct of shame which frequently carries with it a fatal shattering of self-confidence. Formerly far too little attention has been given to this danger of school education.

Satirical jokes are as far removed from real humour as silly arrogance is from true wisdom.

PART II
REPORTS

INTRODUCTION

In order to make it easier for the reader to find his way about in the infinite variety of the following reports, we have arranged them in groups under the same titles that stood at the head of each chapter in the first part of this book. Because we could not make use of the first two in this way—namely, those called Daemons and Sufferings—we have begun with those referring to the third chapter of Part I, *Discipline*, and collected under this heading those school troubles of children which seem to arise from this difficulty.

A large number of the reports might have been included in several of the groups. They reflect life in its variegated many-sided aspects; life which can never be apportioned into sections, so that nothing remains over. Readers must consequently allow us to make use of a certain amount of arbitrariness in this selection.

Many of the reports, in the interest of making them more readable and in respect of the scheme of the whole publication, have been abridged somewhat.

The title of each separate report has been chosen by us.

The letter (f) or (m) in brackets after the title shows that its author was a female or a male. The age of the author when the report was sent in is also given.

CHAPTER I

DISCIPLINE

(a) THE MOST CHEEKY CHILD IN THE CLASS (f. aged 39)

I FIRST went to school on April 27, 1897. I cried terribly and my Mother was not able to comfort me. Naturally I was a happy, very lively child. I did not go to school willingly, however. Therefore I was suitably dealt with. I was put in the girls' class in an elementary school and had a woman teacher. From the very first I was terrified of arithmetic. I was scared to death of it and tables would never stay in my head. That brought down upon me many a hearty box on the ear. Try as hard as I might I could never do sums, not even when I got into the higher classes. In other subjects I did as well as I did badly in arithmetic, and my essays were always read out and praised by the teacher. I loved history best of all and I was more attentive during this lesson than in any other.

Now I could not endure the long hours of sitting still as a mouse, and therefore used to entertain the rest of my class by making grimaces. When I glanced round at the laughing faces of my school-fellows I was very happy. But they would begin to giggle out loud, and the teacher used to shout:

"What are you laughing at?"

"Fanny's making such funny faces!"

I got a box on the ear for that, too, more or less earned, and began to cry immediately.

"Yes, you are the most cheeky child in the class."

"Oh, Teacher!"

I raised my little hands pleadingly towards her and looked at her in supplication, because it seemed to me

DISCIPLINE

to be quite dreadful to be the most cheeky child in the class.

"You want to argue about it, too, do you? Out of the room with you!" commanded my teacher.

Once I had the misfortune to sit on her hat. She had laid her great flower garden on my seat. I did not see it and therefore sat down upon the roses, amid shouts of laughter from my companions.

"You did it on purpose, you cheeky child, how naughty you are!" scolded our teacher. She took hold of my head and ducked my face several times in a basin that was full of water.

Hearing and sight departed from me.

"Now go and sit in your place, wet as you are, in disgrace!"

Oh, how wet I was! Someone knocked at the door and in came our school inspector. He was a kind, cylindrical little man. I sat there on the front form and he stood exactly in front of me and addressed the class kindly. Suddenly he stretched out his hand and stroked my head. He drew it back quickly.

"Hallo, what a wet little girl we've got here, like a drowned rat!"

He stared at me in astonishment, put on his spectacles and gazed at me again. I looked up at him shyly, but hoping for his help, and said, ingratiatingly between my sobs and tears, "I sat on her hat."

The teacher gave him an indignant explanation.

"But, child, that was not good of you at all. You mustn't be cheeky!"

There it was again, that dreadful word!

On the very first day when I went up into the second class I was called up to the teacher's desk during a lesson. I had a school-master this time.

"So you are Fanny?"

I nodded.

"I haven't heard anything too good about you at all. I hope that you won't try any of your cheeky tricks on me."

I wept all the morning. It seemed only too true that I was not like the other girls. If they went to the teacher and told him, "The stork brought us a little sister this morning," or "Next Sunday I may be going with Father and Mother for a trip on the steamer," they were answered ever so kindly. But once even I was taken for an excursion to Constance with my parents. I began to tell my teacher about it first thing on Monday morning. But he interrupted me, apparently quite annoyed, and said, "Have you finished your sums? Show them to me!" Frightened, I fetched my slate.

"Everything wrong as usual!" he exclaimed. "You are a first-class dunce."

That was the only time that I told him anything. I used to go to school every morning full of anxious fear for the events of the day. When I got measles I used to pray every night: "Dear God, please let me be ill for ever, and then, you know, I shan't have to go back to school."

At home I used to cry so often in my sleep that once my Mother asked me anxiously, "Frances, dear, why do you cry like that at night?"

"I am so afraid of school."

"You are a silly child! Tell me what you are afraid of."

"Because I'm so cheeky!"

"But you are my Fanny all the same."

"Yes," I answered, "but it isn't very nice at school."

In the fourth class it was worse than ever. We had a very prejudiced teacher. Every Saturday he told a story to the whole class. When he noticed that my eyes just devoured the words that fell from his lips, he said in the middle of the story:

"Go and stand by the door. You can't do your sums!"

My heart beat so hard it seemed to come up into my throat. This was awful. I cowered into the farthest corner behind the door where I couldn't hear one single word.

In the fifth class it was almost as bad. When the teacher started to write down our names the first morning he said to me: "So you are the celebrated person from the fourth class. I have been told in our Common Room how cheeky you are."

There it was again, the same old wound, and my ambition was altogether crushed. It was no use for me to try to be a good scholar.

Naturally I was always the scapegoat. Here is an example of what used to happen.

One day a school-fellow of mine, who sat five rows behind me, was given a sum to do. She made an awful fuss about it. Suddenly the teacher shouted out, "Frances, you are telling her how to do it! Hold out your hand!"

Quite surprised and horrified, I answered, "But I don't know what the answer is nor what the sum is about!"

"Then you will get a double punishment for it!"

This made a deep impression upon me which I could never forget and I became still more shy. In vain did I try to wipe off these blots from the escutcheon of my name and to save my reputation in the school. At home I took refuge, conscience-stricken, in my homework and buried myself entirely in various duties. Then at last, towards the end of my school-days, our own teacher became ill and we had a substitute. He was fresh from the training college. In spite of his youth I immediately felt the greatest respect for him; I felt too that he liked me. He was able to accomplish what none of the other teachers had been able to do. He taught me to understand arithmetic. I made the most astonishing progress. My old wound healed. With unlimited veneration I clung to this new teacher, who was now mine, and went off to school every morning perfectly happy. He was actually very strict, but never unjust nor partial. He treated us all alike. In a few days I was the happiest pupil there. When our old teacher recovered and returned to work, he said to me in the first arithmetic lesson:

"Sit still, you can't do this!"

How astonished he was at my new ability to learn! His unkind remark damped my ardour considerably, but I bravely fought against my shyness, because I had now discovered a great joy in learning. But when I was alone at night I still used to puzzle over it for hours, so that I couldn't go to sleep: why was I so different from the other girls? Ah, then reports were a terrible worry to me! Once I had 4 for arithmetic; for industry and behaviour, 2. Oh, this 4! I slipped out of bed that night where I had been lying awake in fear. I crept into the sitting-room on tiptoe and opened my satchel to have another look at this 4. I had hidden the report nervously between my exercise books. Suddenly I rubbed it out and put a 3 in its place. This 3 got me into quite enough trouble at home. After the holidays I rubbed it out again and made a little hole. The consequences made life almost unbearable for me. I was sent before the school authorities, had to go to school on half-holidays and my school-mates were warned against me.

I became an outcast in real earnest now, and often enough I would be told: "I'm not allowed to play with you!" And these same children would say to me before lessons began: "Look here, *do* do something silly so that we can have a good laugh!"

"All right, if you will let me play with you after school."

Even to-day, after all these years, if I hear a mother say to her children, "You mustn't play with that guttersnipe," I feel a burning resentment. And this is exactly what I had to suffer at home from one mother. Also I lived quite near the school, and when the children were having their drill in the yard outside, I would study the habits of the teacher. One heard nothing but: "That's right, Lizzie! Good, Annie!" etc., and then suddenly, "Young Ackermann, do that again!" "Aha," I thought, "the black sheep. He only has his surname!"

In one of the higher classes a teacher once asked me what my Christian names were.

"Frances Magdalen!" I answered, startled.

"What's that!" said the head-master. "Such a pretty name! What a shame and disgrace!"

I began to pay attention to my school-fellows, and found that it was always the pet of the teacher who used to ask me: "Do climb up the tree just for once!"

This was absolutely forbidden. The same child, however, would tell the teacher about it and rejoice when I was punished. I was always surprised to find what hypocrites they were.

I tried to get away from school as quickly as I could. Much later I began to learn all I wanted to by myself, because I had a strong tendency against anything that was systematic. But I never did any more arithmetic.

A school-fellow asked me, when I was in my seventh school-year: "Fanny, you might write some verses you have made yourself in my album!" I wrote the following poem in it.

> O Schule, wie bist du mir doch verhasst,
> Denn meistens werd' ich da geschasst
> Aus allen Plätzen warm heraus.
> O Schul', was bist du für ein Graus.
>
> Es regnet da Prügel mit Riemen und Stecken,
> Weil ich die andern nicht darf verdrecken.
> Ackermännli hier, Ackermännli dort,
> Ackermännli, des Lehrers Prügelort.

Ackermännli kann des Nachts night schlafen,
Es träumt ihm gruselig von räudigen Schafen.
Der Lehrer nennt es den "Bock" zum Spott.
Ackermännli denkt: "Einmal lauf ich dann fort."

Eines Tages blieb Ackermännli der Schule fern.
Einsam zu wohnen, das war sein Stern.
In einem Rebhäuschen fand man das Kind,
Die Füsschen erfroren, vom Weinen fast blind.

(*For translation, see p.* 133.)

One day, when I was about to leave the class-room at the end of school, I heard a voice that said: "Young Ackermann, stay behind!"

The teacher seized me by the ear.

"Little wretch! It would be better if you learned to speak good German than go about writing stupid rhymes. I will write your report in verse, you cheeky little beast!"

So now I had to expect a poem in my report as well as those dreaded figures. I was so harried that the prophecy that had been made about me became only too true. I am quite sure, however, that my school-days were the cause of my nervous heart trouble. Because of this I have only to meet any teacher in the street and I get terrible palpitations. If I were made an example of before the class it was a death sentence. I was often annihilated, but I seldom complained at home. Schools and authorities were heavy chains in my captivity. When someone belonging to my circle of acquaintances once said what a pity it was that I was so reserved as a girl and went so little into society, a lady who was present, one of my former school-fellows, replied, "Yes, but even at school she was never quite normal!"

(*b*) BLOWS ON THE FIRST DAY OF SCHOOL (f. aged 42)

I remember my first day at school quite well. It was the worst experience of my whole school-days. My father, who was my best friend throughout his life, I only knew

DISCIPLINE

as white-haired with a beautiful long beard. With no presentiment of danger before me and full of a glorious feeling of unlimited freedom, I went to school. It was a boundless disappointment to me that the teacher in this school in the country town of M., near Zurich, had only a little black moustache. Immediately he fell in my estimation, for he was no real man. We were a mixed class of boys and girls, and in a row behind me I found my little, rather humpbacked friend W. I had not seen him for some time and was very delighted to find him in this strange environment. Next to him sat the teacher's own daughter Betty, whom I liked very much. We had a great deal to talk about, especially because I had not seen my little friends for some time, and I had come here from home without any instructions about behaviour, etc. Nobody had ever said to me: "Just wait until you get to school," or anything of that sort.

We talked to each other from time to time. The teacher admonished us several times. We made our first strokes on our slates, and, quite naturally, showed these to one another. We began chattering again and the teacher and the school were entirely forgotten. I was taken gently by the ear and guided back to my lessons, but ah! we got talking again soon afterwards. All that we had to say was so important and the little bit of writing we were set to do we had already learned at home.

Then our good teacher's patience gave out, and from his desk out came a long lath, fairly broad, and each of us three got a smack across the cheek. I remember nothing about the pain—it is doubtful whether there was any— but I was seized with indignation and righteous resentment, and made up my mind never again to enter such a school nor come to such a teacher, who was not even a real man. When we were let out of school I passed him without a word, looked at him straight in the face and, trembling with mutiny, left the school. I went a long way round so as to take as long as possible over the walk home. As, finally, I could do nothing else but go home, I arrived at the house eventually, injured and ashamed, to find my mother, who was always rather severe, standing on the steps. She already knew of my evil deeds. Her unkind reception was even worse than my punishment at school, and the fact that my beloved school-fellows had run straight to my mother to tell her about my first day at school strengthened my determination never to go there again.

But things turned out differently from what my unfettered freedom had pictured. In the afternoon I went to the forest: with my mother I was never on very intimate terms and so did not discuss my intended desertion with her. Then my father came to me, my best friend, who always understood everything and who forgave everything. He gave me reasons and new points of view which more or less reconciled me with life once again. I never noticed how quickly I changed my mind. Going to school soon became a pleasure. I have very happy memories of this first and second year of school with this same teacher, Mr. Sp.

One of the worst impressions of my sixth school year was concerning a terrible hour of punishment. About eight children came late for school because we had been helping a school-mate to look for a lost purse. The teacher simply would not listen to this excuse and the whole row of us had to hold out our hands while he laid about him left and right in anger with his cane. I still shiver when I think of this unreasonable and apparently unjust punishment and remember very well how furious I was and how sorry for the others. The teacher lost all my respect.

Any teacher who does not treat his little pupils kindly is not capable of teaching them, as far as I can judge from my experience of normal children. To be a teacher means to be an educator, a psychologist, and first and foremost to be a *good* person. All our teachers are by no means *good* people. Naturally we realise that none of us are angels, and cannot be. But we do want our teachers particularly to be picked men and women. For this reason it is in the first place especially necessary that our training colleges for teachers should be under the direction of psychologists, of good people, who have courage and sympathy enough to direct unsuitable candidates into another profession. Very many go through the training and know quite well themselves that they are not suitable to be the leaders and advisers of children, but have not enough courage to start training for something else and, as they think, waste all the time and money which they have already spent upon their training for the teaching profession.

Dr. L. R.

The little poem on p. 129 can be rendered:

> Oh! School, how much I hated thee,
> Since I was always chased away
> From places where the others play.
> Oh! School, how you tormented me!

> There rained on me beatings with straps and with sticks
> Because I was too foul with the others to mix.
> Little Ackermann here, little Ackermann there,
> Ackermann, the teacher's thrashing sphere.

> At night little Ackermann, cannot sleep,
> He dreams in terror of sorrows deep.
> The teacher called him "Scapegoat" for fun,
> Ackermann thinks: "Some day away I'll run!"

> One day Ackermann left school afar,
> Lonely to live, that was his star.
> In a wee hut they found the lad,
> His little feet frozen, his eyes most sad.

CHAPTER II

PLEASURE IN ACHIEVEMENT

(a) I PREFER A HARD TEACHER TO THE SCHOOL FORM
(m. aged 27)

I AM surprised that there are people who have not been happy at school, and that this question should be so important. I was not aware of it. I believed myself to be alone in my aversion. I have never considered the possibility of expressing my disapproval of the methods and effects of education. Modestly I always thought I myself had been in the wrong.

For the first year I went to school gladly enough. In course of time, however, I came to prefer working in the various ways that life offered one in the free time away from school. What we learned at school did not seem to me of sufficient importance; much of it I found unnecessary. A great deal was sheer torment.

I learned easily enough. Without it being my fault I was a good pupil and often held up as an example. But it was like this: I rejoiced triumphantly when many of my comrades who expended far more industry and zeal upon their work had reproaches heaped upon them because fate had not bestowed the same talent upon them. These reproaches, however, although they had nothing to do with me and did not come my way, at the same time wounded and embittered me. In my third school year I made up my mind with the utmost determination to leave school for good and all in the middle of the year.

My parents agreed, although unwillingly. I preferred a hard teacher to the school form. I went out into life, real life. I became a cog in the wheels of a town. And if I went to bed at night dog-tired, I was filled with the happiness of knowing that all my strength had been given to the service of the machinery of the town, and realised that if my own tiny bit were not carried out it would leave a gap; I knew that some day even I should be useful.

And even if I found this life a hard one, full of worry and disillusionment, I would continually comfort myself with the thought: This life had been chosen by myself, shaped by myself, and would be made worth living through my own will. That perhaps was the kernel of the matter. On the one hand had been the school with its compulsion, on the other was life and its freedom, or, better expressed, behind me was the school with an outside foreign compulsion and here was life with an inner voluntary compulsion.

I remember well a remark made by one of our teachers during a botany lesson: "It is a pity that so little interest is taken in nature." This reproach, although not actually directed towards me, made a deep impression upon me. What did this otherwise excellent teacher know about Nature? He meant the names of the plants and the total destruction and investigation of the buds and flowers.

Are we, then, to assume that everyone is hostile to nature who is not acquainted with the names of plants, who is ignorant of the names of the mountains, but who, nevertheless, will be delighted with the shapes and colours of flowers, who can lose himself in dreams and sink into silence when the sun kisses the snow mountains and when it sinks into the great yonder and into the deep? In moments such as these are not the dissection of flowers, geological research and the like, discordant with the rest of creation?

I believe that everyone, every pupil even, has his own joys, his interests and his hobby. Should not the school give more attention to those things which interest the individual scholars? Should not the authorities there try to find out where this interest lies and in what ways it can be followed out? Should not they attempt to do more for the young people in directions where they are rather backward? Why should it always be necessary for the scholar to be made to fit the way of the school and not for the school to adjust itself to the pupils?

R. A.

(*b*) SITTING STILL HOUR AFTER HOUR (f. aged 33)

You want to know from what people suffered most at school. The question is by no means easy to answer, because much of that from which we felt oppressed at school seems so insignificant when one comes to look at it more closely and is connected with our personal sensitiveness.

When I look back on my school-days, which, after all, do not lie very far behind me, it seems to me that the compulsion of being obliged to go to school was the chief trouble. For children who have been allowed freedom for six years, who have had no limitations put upon their use of time, going to school, sitting still hour after hour on the school form, must necessarily strike them as *compulsion*, at least during the first year. If the teacher should happen to be a friend of the children, who knows and understands the tendencies of little people, he will be able in course of time to win these little minds, and make them like school, even though sitting still should bother them now and again. Yet how many teachers are there, unfortunately, who are acquainted with all varieties of child-development who try to force them to punctuality and attention with severity and thereby suppress the best in the children, which is the confidence which they should feel in their teacher.

It seems to me that the first requirement which should control the school is mutual confidence between pupil and teacher. But, most unfortunately, this confidence is often remorsely destroyed by the first impressions of the school, before the child knows the teacher. I well remember the time when it was decided to what teacher I should go. It is true that my first teacher was not a school-master of the old type who compelled us to learn with merciless severity and his cane in his hand. In spite of the fact that I was a good pupil, I still don't like looking back at that time in my life.

As soon as the lot had been cast, I looked up all my companions with whom I used to play who had already been at school for a year or two, to get some information about my teacher. What I was told, however, was this: "Take care, you know, he is very strict. I wouldn't like to go to him; everyone is awfully afraid of him." Even the mothers of former pupils and those who only knew him from hearsay gave me their condolence, and alarmed me thoroughly. I was terribly shy and now became far more nervous from what I heard from all sides. With the greatest misgivings I started on my first day at school. It was not so bad, and the teacher did his best to thaw us a little, so that I went home quite happy. But already on the second or third day we reached the usual state of affairs, and when a school-fellow was punished because of some trifling fault, all my budding confidence was destroyed and I saw the teacher only in the light of the school tyrant.

The good that the teacher sought to bring about with his severity I could not understand. I could only see in him a school-master who punished every unsatisfactory lesson with his cane, or censured it with such a satirical remark that we feared this far more than his blows. It was useless to complain about it at home, since my parents had the greatest respect for this teacher, because they saw how quickly he got us on and how awfully fast we learned in his class. That we only accomplished this out of fear, and not from love of learning for its own sake, would never have occurred to my parents.

It must be admitted that we were in advance of the other classes, and were, so to say, *the model class*, but no one saw the worries that had brought about this result. Our chief fear of all was on account of his reports. In this respect our teacher was quite remorseless. Every act of disobedience was registered in black and white in the mark-book. What that meant to us children one may imagine when one realises what great importance our parents attached to these reports. I know with how much fear I carried home the little book when, instead of the usual 5–6, I had only a 5 for some particular subject. The consequences were not to be avoided, even when it had not been altogether my fault. I kept this fear of reports throughout my whole twelve years of school-life. Kind as my father was, in this respect he knew no mercy. When I had a report that was not quite as good as usual, not really bad in any sense of the word, it seemed to him to be the same as a personal insult to himself which had to be avenged. He would never have believed that the teacher could ever have been wrong, and could have given a report that was not just. The report was to him just like the receipt of some payment. I suffered particularly from this anxiety about reports in my last year of school. It was not the fear of punishment that worried me, but the ambition to be a very good pupil, and at times I accomplished my aim.

At that time I used to do my best to cultivate pallor and anaemia for weeks together, and I was often so tired that I simply could not grasp the sentence or the figures which I heard; it seemed as though the pressure on my brain entirely obliterated the power of thinking. At the time I had no idea what produced this effect! I had a very reserved nature, and therefore never complained about it, but my pale, weary face must have shown the teacher that it was not my fault that there were some days when I could not reach the same standard as on others. But it never once struck my teacher to ask me in a friendly way why I was so unequal in my work. A kind word would have given me confidence to tell him how the pressure on my head hindered my work. Instead of this he would continually frighten me still more with the words: "From time to time you only work with half your ability," and in this way he would poison the days when I could work with my full strength.

I think that in matters of this kind the direct acquaintanceship of the teacher and the parents would achieve a great deal, and many misunderstandings of this sort might be cleared up. The teacher would be able to understand and advise a child during his years of development far better if he had an opportunity to discuss the child and his peculiarities with the father and mother.

Another point caused me a great deal of trouble, which was that the teacher, and, besides the teacher, my class-mates in the secondary school, would only recognise their own opinions as correct. Particularly in the German essay lesson I suffered from pedantry of this kind. Each essay would be discussed for hours on end; every sentence repeated again and again, until it had been given the form which met with the approval of the teacher, and then he used to be annoyed afterwards that we all gave in practically the same essay. Neither, however, was he satisfied if, in spite of the preliminary drilling, we allowed ourselves to give expression to our own thoughts.

Once he left the subject of the essay entirely to us, and I sat down with the greatest pleasure to a theme chosen by myself, "The Seasons." What couldn't one think out about this, what could one not picture! One could allow all one's phantasy to flow freely! Trembling with excitement I waited for the moment when our exercise-books would be given back. I had the firm conviction that I had put my very best work into this essay. How bitter was my disappointment! My book was thrown down on the table with the words: "You did not write that essay yourself. Only a grown-up person writes like that!" If only my teacher had tried to get into touch with my parents once, he would have known that they would never have thought of giving me any help with my school work. I shed bitter tears about it, not because my work had not been praised, but because my teacher could have entertained such a suspicion about me for one instant. Had he only allowed us sometimes to do work of this kind unprepared in school, and not always laid the impression of his own seal upon every sentence that we wrote, he would have arrived at a different opinion concerning many of his pupils.

In the third year of my attendance at the secondary school I came across a teacher who gave us greater freedom in this respect. How I enjoyed those composition lessons! Every one of those essays gives me pleasure even now, and I often take them out and feel astonished at the vitality which streamed through them as from a bubbling spring, smile over the lofty sentiments and the burgeoning phantasy that are to be found in them, and even if the teacher whom I had then would sometimes put a question-mark in red ink by the side of some one sentence or other, which did occur from time to time, it did not worry me. Life is in fact very like school, where one may find question-marks in all colours.

During my last year at school I paid a visit during the holidays to a school where a friend of mine was working, a young Pestalozzi in the best sense of the word. What I saw and heard in those two days in his school made such a deep impression upon me that, in spite of my own unfortunate recollections of my own school-days, I once more put my school satchel happily under my arm and took my place in school. The most valuable impression I gained there was the mutual deep confidence between the scholars and their teacher in spite of the fact that the teacher had among his pupils difficult girls, who in many cases had wandered from school to school, where they had always come into conflict with their teachers, who had given them a bad character when it was arranged they should come to his class. But then they had gone on to this acquaintance of mine and had stayed in his class. If one of these young folks, who generally came from an unhealthy home environment, and then had been tossed about from one teacher to another, being often beaten by them, came to him, he would stretch out his hand to these embittered, frequently defiant or precocious children, with the words, "So you are my new pupil! We will see what we can do in the way of establishing a feeling of confidence between us. I will trust you and you shall trust me. We will help one another and be friends."

That would often work a miracle. The children would listen, incredulous at first, and then, when they looked at his kind face, they would put their hands into his, and would never be disappointed in him afterwards. This work of his was difficult very often, far more hard than that of other teachers. How many weeds there were in these children's characters which had to be taken away with a gentle hand! How much had to be accomplished before the child felt a real confidence in him! It was frequently a terribly slow process, but it came to pass at last when they realised how sad it made their teacher if they again went astray. He never used the cane, and when he found the children did not do everything he wanted them to, he did not set to work upon them regardlessly, but talked to them as a kind father to his children, got into touch with their parents, and often was able to show them how they had failed in their upbringing of their children, or how they should train their children in order to make useful people of them. Or he received from them good advice himself, made himself acquainted with the home relationships and afterwards found out a sure way of getting into touch with the rebellious children.

In his class, nevertheless, there were no children who were more privileged than others. His class-room was never dominated by merciless silence and absence of movement. "Children must be allowed to move," was his motto. "We adults would find it just as difficult to sit motionless hour after hour." As long as the lesson is not disturbed, they should be allowed to move about in their places, and if they should look out of the window sometimes, what does it matter? On the contrary it gives us a hint that the lesson we are giving is not interesting enough to rivet their attention, and we therefore should do our best to make our instruction still more interesting.

M. S.

(c) COMPELLED TO SIT ETERNALLY UPON THE HARD FORM WITH FOLDED HANDS (f.)

It is really high time that something serious should be done about the education problem. Nowhere do we find people so loud in their complaints and objections about the schools as in Basle. But if one should make the suggestion, "Good, then let us parents co-operate and do something about it," one receives this answer, "Oh, but then, as long as our children are going to the school we cannot say anything; the children would be made to suffer for it"; and then they will add, "M. is out of it, thank God! Other folks can burn their fingers trying to pull that coal out of the fire!" That is always the attitude of older people.

What is the chief reproach we should like to bring

PLEASURE IN ACHIEVEMENT

up against the schools? It is more a question of the teacher than the pupils. What is principally lacking is, on the whole, *happiness*. How can any work grow and develop without happiness! Or perhaps you know a State school in Basle where the children go and are happy, where they enjoy every day of their school-life? I do not!

And yet I can state with perfect conviction that both my children were terribly delighted with school when they first went to the infant class. At the start they went gladly enough—and now? If I were to ask them, they would answer with rare agreement, "The best of all is when we are free to come home and in the holidays."

What is the reason of this?

The endless compulsion, the long hours of sitting still, which are so unnatural for children, are largely to blame for this state of affairs. One may notice how difficult it is for the first or second class of children to sit on a hard form and listen. It would be difficult enough if what the teacher had to say was always interesting, but in the majority of cases it is necessary for the teacher to repeat the lesson over and over again, until all have grasped it. This is naturally very boring for the more wideawake children, and they give their attention to something else, which brings down upon them scolding or punishment.

We think also of this point: the children are obliged to sit still for a long time at school, and when they eventually do come home, instead of being able to play and run about in the fresh air, they have a lot of homework to do.

In the higher classes the children have scarcely any time at all to themselves, especially for daily games in the open air, which are so important for the sake of their health. In England they have arranged things otherwise, since daily athletics or games form part of the usual time-table, and England certainly brings up its children to be efficient young people!

There is another thing which leads to a great deal of conflict in the child mind. At home they are taught the supreme importance of truth and honesty. "Mother, you don't understand," I heard as a reply to a question of mine the other day. "At school one has to cheat, crib from the others, etc. Everyone does it; if you don't you're called stupid, get bad marks and never get on." Here, then, is a double moral for them to assimilate; it is an integral part of the educational system.

The chief thing seems to me to be that one allows the children to work too little by themselves. They love to stand alone, think for themselves, discover for themselves. One puts before them too many ready-made thoughts and opinions of grown-up people which they are obliged to learn by heart. There is altogether too much theory and too little practice. The children need pulsing, teeming life around them.

The intellect is educated at the expense of the emotions and the practical abilities of the child and forced to develop at too great a pace; this makes the children lacking in harmony and happiness.

M. D.

(*d*) THE TEACHER HAS TAUGHT FROM THE SAME BOOK FOR TWENTY YEARS (m. aged about 36)

From what did you suffer most at school?
Answer: From boredom.
Cause of the boredom: Bad teachers principally.
I believe that the teacher is usually more to blame than his teaching material.

Second example

At our Gymnasium (name given to boys' secondary day schools throughout Switzerland and Germany), there was a botany master whose lessons reached the height of boredom. For more than twenty years this man had dictated precisely the same stuff, word for word, to his pupils, and let them copy it down in their exercise books. It covered the scientific construction of plants, their metabolism, etc., without ever coming to any nearer approach to the actual, living plant world. One never got the least feeling of a love of nature or of pleasure to be derived from the study of this subject—this teacher could just as well have been teaching us about commercial arithmetic, book-keeping or the like. In the same way he gave us lessons on Zoology, anatomy and so forth. Our young heads were stuffed with unending facts, without the living pulse of love of the subject being put before us to give us a notion of the rich variety of life and add some interest to his instruction.

Why did not this teacher simply get his lessons printed? Probably because he could not then have got through his lessons simply by means of this dry dictation, and because he was morally bound to offer something to his pupils. This method of his was the easiest way out of the difficulty. For him the profession of a teacher was nothing beyond a means of earning his daily bread.

When the Weissenstein, just outside our window, could be seen in all the glory of its winter raiment, silver and glittering under a deep blue sky, it was not surprising that our boyish hearts, that were consumed with a love for ski-ing, longed to be out there where one could career around on these snow-fields in the happiest mood of teeming joy of life and health, instead of sitting there in his class-room where our teacher gave us stones for bread.

Even to-day I have an inextinguishable hatred for this teacher and all others of the same type, which is just as vivid as during my school-days.

On the contrary, we had an excellent mathematics

master. Before I went to him I was backward in arithmetic, but this teacher was able to make me understand it through his clear, simple instruction, his contact with the individual pupils and his habit of never being satisfied until the matter was quite clearly grasped, as well as his love of his subject. Thus I went to his classes with pleasure and happiness, and I think that these are the reasons why the memory of them has remained so clear in my mind and also because I profited so much by them and finally derived real pleasure from solving arithmetical problems.

Yet history, which was one of my favourite subjects, never gained any encouragement at school. The Gymnasium did not try to foster this interest in the smallest degree and offered me nothing in this direction. The teacher, a well-informed man on the whole, constructed his lessons upon a plan estimated to show his pupils his own stupidity rather than the history of world development. There was no pleasure to be got from his classes; we derived but one impression from them, such as the idea: "I am infinitely more clever than this teacher. How foolish it is to have to come to school!" Instead of giving us an extempore and vivid lecture he would say, "Next time down to the end of page so-and-so!" Then generally in the next lesson he would take us over some slippery place till we came a cropper, much to his delight.

Some of the others had a better opinion of him than I, but many shared my view. This experience which I have just described will prove that my affection for historical study and anything historical never bore fruit while at school in the very least.

In this way I reach my conclusion that the chief trouble of one's school-days is not the subject-matter of the lessons that is put before us. All of us would have listened gladly enough, especially to anything connected with our favourite subjects, if only it had been presented to us in a comprehensible fashion; if only the teachers, the few who treated their job as a method of earning their living and nothing else, had not been so cold and lifeless. I still consider these men as thieves who made an infinite number of the hours of boyhood, which could never be brought back again, hard, dry and impoverished, instead of rich and happy, as these hours would have been if only they had let us go for a walk! That would have been far better, because we learned absolutely nothing from these lessons. Anything that does not come into being out of contact with life and love contributes nothing to life. And I am glad that all this dead school knowledge, as it were, was forgotten directly after I passed my school-leaving examination. Fifteen years have slid away since then as in a dream. I was seven years at the Gymnasium, which were unbearable.

I regard it as a grave sin of omission that we had no opportunity for practical work. Since then I have developed a fondness for it and am very sorry that at school there was no chance to learn any sort of practical work. During his school-days the pupil is far too immature to be kept solely to one-sided work, and in this way he is never able to learn what talents he may possess, nor to discover clearly in what direction his gifts and interests may lie. I myself, particularly, only learned this late in life—but that is the way of things.

Furthermore, we had far too much homework. One should bring one's knowledge home from school and not the other way about. Then one would have more free time, especially for gymnastics and sport or games, which I consider to be at least as important as any of the other main school subjects. Half the day in the classroom ought to be enough, and anything that cannot be got into that, one should treat as mere ballast and superfluous. This cursed cramming of useless knowledge! Thank God that one forgets all such rubbish pretty soon!

W. M.

CHAPTER III

INTELLECTUALISM

(a) THE IRON FIST WAS THE ORDER OF THE DAY
(m. aged 37)

THERE is nothing upon which I look back in my previous life, excepting perhaps a few examinations, with greater horror and with physical shuddering, than my school-days between the age of 15–16 years. Shall I give you a picture of my mental condition then? It was years of weary pilgrimage through an arid desert where one only found an oasis here and there, the life-giving influences of which I can still see in my development to-day; a pilgrimage through forsaken, wind-eroded wastes with a mind that was consumed with unquenchable thirst, with hunger that could find no gratification for its mental powers, longing for a guide and a friend who could lead me!

Gottfried Keller, who also came into severe conflict with his school when young, has perfectly described this state of mind in a young, defiant man, with a few terse, vigorous words in his poem, *Schlafwandel*:

> "Von der Gewohnheit Eisenfaust
> In Schritt und Tritt gelenkt. . . .
> Verlornes Jugendland!"

School was my *Foreign Legion*, and with tears I learned the joy and the wild hatred of this beautiful poem by heart during this time of my life.

Out of this wilderness used to echo in my subsequent life Voltaire's curse, *Écrasez l'infâme!* but now hurled against the School and not the Church.

If only I could have once poured out this curse without inhibition on the whole school, I should have been able in the future to have had a clearer and more accurate conception of life and have been able to estimate it more correctly. This is what compels me, in spite of my usual dislike of writing, to take my pen in my hand and give vent to this ancient mental burden of mine.

1. *The State Syringe of Knowledge*

Every peasant woman knows that each root of beans and each cabbage plant need separate treatment if they are to thrive and grow. If I should open the light of my early vegetable frame too soon, my seedlings will get nipped with the frost and die; if I should fertilise my vegetable garden with an insufficiently mixed artificial manure containing too much nitrogen, cabbage disease will soon prevent any proper growth of the plants, although I may spray them as much as I will. In this way my school was nothing but a relentlessly working *State syringe*. Anyone who has been plunged into this ceaseless, horribly regular, warm shower-bath may easily wonder how it was he was not drowned in it. Thanks to a very tough constitution, I got off lightly with a slight chill!

Now it is by no means difficult and always rather paltry to make fun of one's school-days and one's teacher, but mockery is far from my mind. It was not usually the teachers who were the chief sinners against the Holy Ghost of our Youth. Yet they were generally connected with the iron fist that dogged our every step. They suffered as much as we, which I was able to discover from personal experience later on. The iron fist was the basis of our education, our daily ration, to which we had all to submit. Like an already long familiar, boring film, this damned ration was reeled off daily, hourly, before our starving eyes. If it had only been a film! It was an endless patchwork, more aggravating than *Blatzli-Bajass*. The swindle that was carried out (and still is) when it came to *science* passes all belief. I renewed my acquaintance with this bugbear in many forms later at the University, but then I was better prepared to deal with it. The knowledge I had already acquired, and I was by no means a bad scholar, might have been described as a pile of chaff in comparison with my later experience. Without any kind of distinction, the differential calculus, historical dates, chemical elements, lay side by side and one on top of another like a regular witches' kitchen. Everything was packed into a distended darkness as though it had been thrown in with the largest shovel imaginable.

How unspeakably difficult it was to get oneself out of this misty labyrinth into the light of day. That it would probably never have been accomplished without the help of an experienced friend was shown by the fact that one was obliged to throw the whole of this knowledge-ballast overboard in order to get the little ship of my life afloat again. Many of my former companions were absolutely suffocated by this poisonous fog. Anyone who cherishes a hope of obtaining modern education from foul soil like this is past praying for.

How absolutely insane was a daily ration like this!
Here is an example of what I mean:

8–9   History: Julius Caesar in Gaul.
       After five minutes' recreation we went on to the next subject:
9–10 Simultaneous Equations.
       On the top of that we were served out with
10–11 The Style of Hebbel in his *Nibelungen*.
       We were then dragged along to
11–12 A botanical lecture on Pteridophytes.
       After a two hours' break we were kept busy from
2–3   with simple examples from English syntax.
3–4   was taken up with the law of Ohm,
       and at long last we landed up in our final lesson for the day at the
       West Indian Islands.

This chameleonlike, futuristic ribbon rolled along with nervous restlessness year after year before our eyes. The universal picture that is current of the young man of to-day, whom a school-leaving examination hallmarks as mature, is just like this: he has washed in every sort of science but his skin is not yet thoroughly wet.

2. *The Umbrella*

We young fellows, full of the joy of life, naturally shielded ourselves as best we might from this daily application of the syringe. Umbrellas forward! How cold otherwise had been these prescribed portions of food that were thus served out to us without such self-help; how arid and stale would have been our unproductive homework without jokes and by-paths! A carefully guarded tradition of the higher classes of the secondary schools came to our assistance, whereby every conceivable kind of forbidden help was passed on from class to class. How simple and very foolish did we consider the most good-natured of our masters at that time!

I will show in what a refined way this defence system worked that was handed on by tradition by giving you a little example of it. Our French master, a native of one of the French cantons, regularly gave us three pages of words to learn for each lesson. This language-merchant had a somewhat suspicious nature and therefore would place his most promising pupils in a row in front of the rest of the class and make us ask them questions about the words learned for that day. If one of them had the top button of his tunic done up it meant, "I have only learned the words on the first page; all questions about these, please!" If the second button was pushed through its corresponding hole that meant, "Please ask me questions about the second page!" etc. The system worked beautifully.

I was no infant prodigy in English, in spite of a perfect master. The composition lessons, which occurred regularly each fortnight, were an absolute torture to me. But from four to six of our group of sufferers found a willing helper in another of our comrades. Not only could he bring the miracle to pass that in these two hours devoted to essay-writing he could produce his own composition, but also four to six others, all quite different, but written upon the same subject. He sat in the back row of all. As soon as we had received the subject for that day's work from our teacher, this friend and helper of ours would wait for our orders, which would be sent along to him in silence from form to form. According to verbal agreement we paid him a fee of one franc a page. We were perfectly satisfied with our bargain and the proceeds were spent in drinks all round at the neighbouring "Crown." Certainly it was a most flourishing business!

The most questionable factor in the whole proceeding, however, was that this habit of deception spread through every subject taught in the school. Before long we used to feel a great deal more satisfaction in deception than in honest work. The cheating was valued according to the amount of deception practised and the danger run in carrying it out, and for that reason it would be carried out even when preparations for its success took more time than the actual work would have done that was required from us. All respect for the school vanished and its place was taken by a sort of cynical boasting. How much disaster we thus thoughtlessly brought upon ourselves we only discovered years later!

We were also able to carry out something else by the use of by-paths of this sort, because they helped us to get through the exaggerated amount of homework we had to do. Whereas my brother, slightly younger than myself, who was then taking a course of commercial banking, got to bed by ten o'clock at night, I had to struggle at a neighbouring table until past midnight with my homework, which consisted for the most part of pure memory-cramming. For this reason the fifty dates of Goethe's life still remain in my mind as an unpleasant memory. The eight-hour day was a thing unknown for us boys, who were all at puberty. It meant that for six or seven hours daily we laboured on the school-form and for another two or three we worked like oxen at home. These endless hours of sitting at work obliged many of the pupils to take to spectacles, toughened the skin on the backs of 100 per cent of our scholars, and, unfortunately, also the cortex of the brains of all of us.

The monotonous sitting, which was only broken by two hours' gymnastic lesson during the week, was the most complete introduction to slacking. Our limbs were neglected in favour of exaggerated brain gymnastics, and our muscles weaned to weakness. Even to-day this is probably not much better. We shall see the absolute degeneration of our population before the school-masters open their eyes to this fact.

Until then cheating will go on in the schools!

Dr. W. R.

(b) "I CAN'T DO SUMS" (m.)

My first school year was a source of joy and happiness to me. Because my parents had a school in the country and I was a bright youngster, to whom learning was no sort of difficulty, great hopes were set upon my future. But already in my third year a striking weakness in arithmetic appeared in me, and when, one day shortly before an examination, ten multiplication sums out of a dozen given me as a test came out wrong, it brought down a thrashing upon me and I was kept in. I felt the spectre of the school before me, wearing the aspect of the spectacled face of a teacher which followed me about with a remorselessly punishing mien during my waking hours as well as in my sleep, my work and my play. I still remember how I suddenly turned round when lying across my teacher's knee during the execution of the punishment and begged him to let me off the rest, because I should certainly get punished again at home! An uncontrollable fear had overcome me at the idea of being beaten before the whole class of boys and girls that made me tremble in every limb and fibre of my being. It was no use. This man, from whom I had once, when he came to see us, received an apple out of his pocket in exchange for a kiss, showed himself without any pity on this occasion and went on thrashing me. After that the fear aroused by what I had always dreaded actually taking place made me forget the pain and I went on crying quietly. My boyish memory then suppressed the experience of my childhood about the kiss and the apple, and the incident led to an estrangement between this man and myself, so that the news of his death, which occurred soon afterwards, appeared as a deliverance.

As the result of this occurrence I suffered perpetually from the notion that I could not do arithmetic, and, as well as I can remember, neither my parents nor teacher took any trouble to find out what was the matter. I did my arithmetic homework with difficulty, but correctly; when it came, however, to a test, when we had to work alone and under strict supervision, I always fell to pieces. That continued until I was old enough to go on to the Central School. This meant now that if I did not improve in my arithmetic I should be refused. I was then taken in hand. During those long frightening winter evenings, I was obliged, with the assistance of my father and a length of rubber hose-pipe, which lay beside the arithmetic book on the table all ready for use, to go over all the rules, in fear and with tears, that I had never been able to grasp in my former school classes. The cure was not carried out in vain: at last I achieved an unexpected proficiency in grasping and working out complicated arithmetical problems; even those exercises about mixing different sorts of coffee and little vine plants gave me absolutely no more trouble. In consequence of this I headed the list in the entrance examination of the State Central School, and felt an indescribable pride and a godlike sensation of victory when my name was read out first on the list.

My new conviction that I should now always be good at arithmetic did not last long, however, because in the Central School I had to encounter new, unknown territories such as Algebra and Geometry, one after another. The abstract figures and letters of the alphabet that appeared in them seemed to me to be nothing but question-marks and picture-puzzles, and the old fear of figures once more began to keep me awake at night. The teacher who was in charge of the mathematical section was the Director of the School. Once upon a time he had been a good teacher, they said, but for the last thirty years he had done nothing but write upon the blackboard geometrical figures and problems without asking one question or requiring one answer; then made one of the pupils read what he had written on the board, and dismissed us with the remark: "We will repeat that!"

If he were in a good temper it was his habit without exception to ask us this question: "Who has understood that?"

Once only one of us ventured to raise his hand because something was not clear to him. Then the Head shot from his desk like an incarnated devil and flung himself at the startled boy. "That's because you didn't pay any attention!"

We were therefore obliged to keep all our hands lying

on the class-room table, because we felt instinctively that it might go badly with us were we to behave with strict honesty. Could anyone be surprised if no one again had the courage or the confidence to ask for the counsel of this teacher? Was it any wonder that we deceived and lied to this short-sighted man, who had become hard of hearing as well as bald, whenever we could and cultivated the fine art of mental acrobatics in cheating and prompting one another? One day, however, the old fellow must have got wind of what we were doing because he set us to work out a test-paper and walked up and down between the rows like a policeman, and, so that no one would be able to evade him, he also set the most intelligent of his pupils to act as invigilators. Those who were not firm in the saddle came down upon it, and had to expect, after being kept in for two hours, a report note that would get them a punishment. I was among these unhappy scapegoats, and, because our Head knew my father well, I particularly had the doubtful honour of being obliged to carry home a memorandum to my father that ended with the words, "I beg you to keep an eye upon him."

Once more I encountered dark days when my father sat beside me in the evening and, with blows and many a box on the ear, initiated me into the mysteries of the binomic law. What an appalling horror that binomic law was for me in those days! At last I knew it in my sleep, forwards and backwards, could explain its origin and its use, but what *it actually was* still remained a riddle to my childish understanding. How often before I went to sleep I tried once again to analyse the a^2 and the b^2, and then fell asleep full of fear lest I should not be able to remember it in the morning, and I had terrible anxiety dreams which, in the morning, seemed about to come true when the eyes of my severe teacher looked round for their victim behind his spectacles. In this way four troubled sad years passed away. I used to come home with bad reports and stern warnings respecting future promotion. I was locked in my room all day on bread and water, and had to endure the hardship that my father and mother never gave me a kind word and regarded me as a lost soul.

Then I entered the Training College and gained my teaching certificate with a 3 in mathematics! It has now become my favourite subject, because I have a more extensive understanding of that than of any other.

F. N.

(c) OVERTAXING THE MIND (m. aged 71)

If I send in an answer to your question I shall do it in order to help give increased publicity and call attention to some of the dangers that threaten our children—our children into whose hands we confide the future, and for whom no sacrifice can be too great for us.

In our School we had, on the whole, quite good and kindly teachers. Only once did a teacher punish me for something which I had not done. My assurances of innocence and my protests availed nothing. I was helpless before his condemnation. If only a well-intentioned school-master realised what devastation he created in childish emotions with his false accusations he would investigate occurrences of this kind more thoroughly.

My troubles began when I went to the Central School. Our bogy-man was a teacher from Bavaria. He seemed to have missed his vocation, since in the crude fashion of a non-commissioned officer he treated us, his poor victims, with boasting and blows. Every time we had to go to him for a lesson we used anxiously to ask the other pupils, who had just left his clutches, if he were in a bad temper, because much depended upon his changes of mood. Things would become misty before our eyes when he shouted at us, and woe betide the guilty one who, because of fear or stupidity, did not know the answer to his question.

"Bend over!" he would shout, and the punishment would begin.

"You idiot!" he would yell, and often at the same time hit us across the face with his signet-ring by way of encouragement. Once only did the heart of this tyrant soften. It was winter and the weather was damp and cold. We boys coughed and croaked until the walls rang with the echoes, so that he hounded us all out of class-room, to our great joy, into the "Temple."

At that time our worst torture was the enormous amount of homework we were given to do, that torment of all the pupils of the Middle Schools. Because our reverend school-masters believed that in this way they would stand well in the sight of the authorities, and also in the good graces of the examiners, if they made us poor victims the models of thorough teaching and well-assembled knowledge, it happened that we were overburdened with work to take home. Instead of having a happy boyhood, we had to endure an existence loaded with exercises. To overload a donkey is considered to be cruelty to animals, and one hopes that one of these days the intellectual overburdening of children to lead them to a higher state of culture will be superseded by more humane ways of obtaining mental security. Happily I was not always a pattern scholar and got through my work by various short cuts. Sometimes a boy is obliged to be free as a bird and scramble about like a squirrel. One can see by watching boys out of school what an urgent need they have to exercise their physical strength, to make use of their muscles and to stretch their sinews. Formerly a large number fell victims to our one-sided education! I never regretted a single day that I spent wandering about the woods and fields.

INTELLECTUALISM

We give far too little attention to the fact that some pupils are like late autumn fruit, and only ripen intellectually later than the others. I remember well enough, and it is now a fairly long time ago, when I moved from the elementary school to the Central School, how much trouble it caused me to grasp mentally the large number of abstract conceptions which suddenly burst upon my attention. With what difficulty one struggled with grammatical rules, and those of mathematics and geometry, everything that one understood later easily enough, because each one of them contributed something towards the understanding of the other and awakened our interest.

What a different story it is in the case of the boys! Life teaches one to grasp things that are similar in our environment through rules, and we learn to perceive their necessity by our observation of objects, until in time we are able to realise better their fundamental laws. To-day particularly, the wealth of scientific knowledge requires us to seek for unifying rules, which are subject to common laws, by means of which those who thirst after knowledge are enabled to grasp the concerns of the universe better than ever before. How much memory-cramming might be done away with if we could simplify our knowledge! If one wants to grasp the world one must make it small and if one does make it small, then it appears large to us for the first time.

The procedure of our school was quite the reverse of this, however. Rules came before experience. It was expected from these undeveloped, weak brains that they would be able to comprehend stores of knowledge that still lay wrapped in mists of twilight, by means of abstract concepts and deductions, to be able to grasp laws the supremacy of which the child did not know, and to learn about things which lay in the far-off, blue distance. If, in addition also, this terrible memory-cramming is required by the pedagogues—who, of course, know a very great deal, but do not possess the key to the hearts of the children, do not love them, have no patience and are no longer in a state of mind to be able to feel in sympathy with them—the tormented children will suffer as well as their teachers. For that reason it is doubly necessary that those school-masters who are more knowledge specialists than teachers should be transferred as quickly as possible to some other vocation.

I know that educational methods are now happily better than they were and that the former thrashings are being decreased, but there is still a great deal to be done. I am also aware that in a great many cases the *teacher* is in no way to blame for the overburdening of the children, but the school curriculum, as well as the demands of the higher authorities; in short, the spirit of the times. Manual work would make the understanding of a great many scientific branches of their studies considerably easier for our young folks. One should take them out more often into the country, increase their physical strength, which would make them strong in spirit and in mind and awaken their interest in the universe. This would expand their minds and they would be able to grasp things better. The time-table should be simplified, because a *thorough knowledge means a better knowledge.*

One more thing. Why do they not give more attention to nervous children in school? Their number is increasing alarmingly. Heredity, life and education endanger the nervous condition more and more and what one might demand from a coarse lout is not suitable for a highly strung intellect from whom one can steal away all courage for life through wrong treatment, so that one may cause him to suffer from anxiety for the rest of his life.

A. S.

(d) I NEVER GOT A GOOD REPORT BECAUSE I WROTE BADLY (m. aged 36)

Like most children I had my peculiarities. For that reason it came about that in some subjects I was a good to very good pupil and in others, on the contrary, between a good and a bad one. In consequence of this I had to suffer a good deal when I went on to the secondary school. For example, I was by no means gifted with good writing. I do not know why; perhaps it was because I had to help my father a good deal in his workshop. I was very good at arithmetic, however—I had inherited this from my mother. But because I wrote badly I never got a good report. Even if I should have written a good essay I had bad marks for it on account of the bad handwriting. In physics and chemistry, where I could have answered more than anyone else orally, I got bad marks also owing to the untidy diagrams and drawings.

However, that which caused me to feel most unhappy was the attitude of the mathematics master. He would often put a bad mark in my exercise book by the side of two or three pages of correct solutions to problems, and write against them in red ink, "Bad arrangement." For this reason in my report I had always a far worse mark for arithmetic than I deserved. Therefore in school I suffered more on account of my bad handwriting than for anything else. Recently, when I was looking over some old things of mine, I came across some of these remarks. A happy smile passes across my face because to-day I have to do a great deal of arithmetic and nobody writes remarks by the side of it. I myself am personally responsible for my arithmetic and my typewriter sets it out very well. The most important thing is to get the correct result.

The development of civilisation necessitates that

changes must occur in every sphere of life. This applies to schools also. Everything changes: methods of learning, teaching material, etc. One thing only does not change, *the art of the pedagogues*. And for this reason one should give more attention to the point that I wish to make here. Only real teachers can ensure success and this is the main thing. What can be done about it, because one knows well enough that educational talent cannot be taught? One way would be this, and it would ensure a great improvement for the pupils, that we should seek out the men who are born teachers and make these our school-masters. It might be carrying things too far if we were to put this into practice immediately, But it is our duty to do all in our power to make it possible. The first step towards it would be to change the rules which govern the relationship between the teacher and his position. It is a great pity, both for the people and the school, that it is not possible to remove a master once he has been definitely appointed to a school, even if one knows that he is a bad teacher. When a teacher comes to the end of his studies and takes his examination, nobody knows with any degree of certainty if he is a real educator or not. Only practice will show this. But before that he is generally appointed and remains a fixture, even when the vocation is ill chosen for him and both the parents and the children know that this is the case.

When anyone working on his own responsibility choses a wrong trade, he must change saddles, if he does not want to tighten his belt against starvation and finish up in the workhouse or some such institution. For most other callings suitable ability must be shown in advance before a post can be obtained. After the post has been gained, the proficiency will be tested from above and below, from outside and inside, and only acclaimed when it is proved to be good.

It is quite different, however, in the teaching profession. Their work is only controlled to a very limited extent, and there is very little risk of their losing their post from lack of ability, but only through bad behaviour. If one were to remedy this state of affairs it would be for the benefit of the schools. I do not say this in a spirit of envy, but from a sense of justice. Why should one give the same reward to the work of a bad teacher as to that of a good one? Why should we accept anything but the best work possible from a teacher? The schools would be better served if only men of first-class ability were appointed to vacant posts and if they were properly paid. The unsatisfactory ones could be sent on to other professions for which they were more suited. For our schools we do not want school-masters, nor intellectual virtuosos, but *teachers*. Thus where our schools are concerned we should pay greater attention to quality than to quantity. As educators we require only refined and noble persons, possessed of extensive self-knowledge, who are in a position to be able to direct the inherited talents and natural impulses of others upon the right lines. We do not want teachers who compare all their pupils with themselves, and only put those who are intellectually gifted into the foreground, but men who hold the opinion that every person is worthy of honour and respect, who can carry out his own work with some adequate amount of ability. Anyone who teaches in this spirit will be more successful in drawing others together than those who are always on the look-out for pupils who can break a record. In this way they will do nothing but increase the struggle between each individual and his contemporaries.

W. S.

(*e*) IT IS SHAMEFUL TO BE A BAD SCHOLAR (f. aged 40)

Recently I was compelled to fetch my little daughter from school with an umbrella. She is in the third class of the elementary school. Since at a certain spot along the road two ways met, by either of which she could come home from school, I stopped for a moment to consider which of them my little girl usually chose, in order not to miss her, in case she was already on her way back. I looked first in one direction and then in the other, but could not see Mary among the few children who were coming towards me.

"Good morning!" a friendly voice said suddenly close to me, and as I looked round I found a pair of kind, good-tempered, but rather sad eyes fastened upon me. "You are looking for Annie Mary, aren't you? She is still at the school and is waiting there for you."

I thanked the child for her kindness in giving me this news and took a picture out of my basket which the woman at the little shop where I get my household stores had just given me for my child. This child, whom I did not know, modestly refused it. "Oh, but that's not necessary!" she said. And when I quickly put it into her pocket she put her little hand into mine to thank me, just as if I had bestowed some large reward upon her. Then I went on to the school with the greatest possible haste. Besides my own Annie Mary there were several other children there too, who were waiting until the rain should leave off. Unfortunately, this did not look likely to happen. Therefore I invited two more, who went the same way as ourselves, to come under our umbrella. In spite of the downpour, the three went along chattering about what they had been doing at school that morning. I interrupted them presently and told them that a nice little girl had very kindly given me the information I wanted, so that I had not to wait, and that

I would like to know who she was. I described her frock and pinafore and then received the answer from all three at once: "Oh, yes, that was Martha So-and-So, the second stupidest child in our class!"

This explanation was like a stab, especially as I had been so much taken with the child's behaviour. I told them instinctively that they should not immediately jump to the conclusion that she was less clever than they, and that it was not her fault that she could not learn as quickly as they could. Also that it often happened that the children who were rather backward at school often passed the clever ones later on when it was a matter of practical experience. But they listened to my argument with a considerable amount of incredulity. Possibly this was the case because we are always trying to give our children an incentive to learn by telling them that their subsequent success depends upon it! For this reason I said no more upon the subject then and allowed the three chatterboxes to return to what they had been talking about before. I myself, however, turned my thoughts back to my own school-days, and discovered, to my shame, that the ungifted children in our class had fared no better.

Honoured *Schweizer-Spiegel*, or, rather, honoured Mr. Schohaus! This is a great mistake that the school makes, that although it appears to make no difference between the rich and the poor children, it does make such invidious comparisons between the clever ones and those who are not clever. The school should take all the more pains with this last-mentioned group. Their childhood will be ruined through the school otherwise! An intelligent pupil will be valued highly at school whether he comes in patched trousers or with holes in all his clothes, and one who is not gifted will be taken no notice of, even if he comes dressed in velvet. The one whose mind and outward appearance are equally well equipped is doubly to be envied, but we should also sympathise with the victim of the opposite state of affairs. One should give special attention, in my humble opinion, to the teacher regarding this harmful state of affairs, and see to it that because of these two conditions the education of one child is not turned into a festival and that of the other into an absolute hell.

There are, of course, some pupils who, in spite of their lack of intelligence, have a great deal of ambition. I do not ask for special consideration for these. Usually they do not come off badly, and particularly to-day, when bodily strength counts for more, on the whole, than intelligence. Away from the school they will often take the part of leaders to their comrades. But I am sorry for those who modestly allow themselves to be pushed into the background because they are conscious of their weakness. If they should also happen to be outwardly unattractive children, their cup will be filled to overflowing. Their school-fellows cannot estimate the secret sorrows of such children, but the teacher can do so, and must do so likewise. For this reason, according to my opinion, it is very important that one should study the characters and the sympathies of the students in the training colleges, as well as their intellectual capabilities. Should I be in a position to help a district to choose a new teacher I should put no weight upon his certificates, but take especial care to watch how he treated his ungifted pupils. If he had sufficient love and patience to deal with them, then everything else would be all right.

M. P.

(f) EXAMINATION FEAR (f. aged 27)

Your mention of anxiety dreams gives me an opportunity to reply to your questionnaire. It is now six years since I left school, and since then I have had many experiences that were certainly of a more severe nature than my school reports and the results of my examinations; but in spite of that, in my dreams, I always return to one scene with every possible variation.

As a school-girl I am standing in front of my class at school. Some examination is taking place. I feel the strange, cold eyes of the visiting examiners fixed upon me from all sides. I am required to give some information upon some subject about which I have never learned. I am trying to think it out, but no possible answer will come into my mind. Overcome with confusion I glance at the examiners, who are summing me up with astonishment and disapproval. I can feel that a horrible blush is mounting up and spreading over my face and that the eyes of the examiners gaze upon me still more coldly and ironically. At that point waking up generally releases me from this terrible situation.

If I should turn my thoughts backwards to my school-days, it is actually the examinations which seem to have embittered them for me. I had a great many of them to work through: the final examination at the end of the nine obligatory school-years, the entrance examination at the secondary school and the teacher's training college, as well as the one for the teacher's certificate.

I am sure that my former school-masters and mistresses would never be able to grasp how these examinations could remain in my memory in such an unpleasant fashion. I was reckoned a good pupil and I only came into conflict with those instructors who used to teach us in a boring and indifferent way, and I let these see my total lack of interest without any disguise. The final examination, which was in itself altogether harmless, I hated as an unworthy spectacle, and when I saw that the teachers whom I respected and loved would drill us in preparation for this so that their classes would do more brilliantly

than the others, it made me sad, because my former warm feelings for them suffered a marked diminution in this way.
                                                             K. M.

(g) THOSE WHO CAN'T DO GYMNASTICS WILL NEVER BE ANY GOOD! (f. aged 38)

Your questionnaire, "From what did you suffer most at school?" has not only awakened memories of my own school-days, but also others from my professional life, which has brought me into constant proximity with hundreds of pupils and other persons over a number of years, without actually being in the profession of a teacher myself. It has brought to my notice that sorrows and joys recur afresh in each generation and that those things which appeared to us as unbearable, provide equal unhappiness for the present generation. I have selected the following examples from the experiences of myself and my fellow-sufferers.

Very few scholars are equally gifted in all subjects; one will be brilliant in languages but weak in mathematics; another is good at nature study but has no memory for dates in history. I was myself well endowed with ability for all kinds of scientific study, also for the so-called artistic subjects; but drawing, gymnastics and singing were a positive torture for me, although I took the greatest possible trouble to satisfy my teachers. Instead of recognising my perseverance, however (this would happen in the gymnastic lesson), if I was not able to climb up the ladder someone would shout: "You will never be any good!" During the singing lesson, when I sang out of tune, they would say: "You spoil it all!" and in the drawing class, if my colours and outline did not resemble those of our copy, I would hear the verdict: "You will never do anything right the whole of your life!"

That used to hurt. Later, in my professional life, I would hear time and again of children and young people who complained that teachers would judge their pupils according to their talents in this one-sided way instead of encouraging their industry. The teacher of a special subject is usually so obsessed with the importance of it that he is convinced that anyone who cannot master his province will come to shipwreck in later life. He is not sufficiently conscious of the fact that such derogatory remarks can awaken feelings of inferiority in his pupils against which they will have to struggle for many years. How much better it would be for them to recognise the industry and good will of their pupils, so as to encourage them, and to put a high value upon their marks for perseverance in their reports!

B. B.

(*h*) DAILY HOMEWORK UNTIL 10 P.M. (f. aged 16)

My godchild, Elsa, attends a secondary school in Zurich. From the age of twelve to fourteen she was devoted to her teacher. She had good cause, too, to be satisfied with Elsa, because she was a dear girl, talented and industrious.

However, when she reached the third class the situation altered obviously. The homework increased so enormously that she was obliged to work until about ten o'clock each night in order to get it finished.

The girl became increasingly nauseated with this heavy amount of homework and her former devotion to her teachers diminished. One desire possessed her, and that was to be released from school and from her teachers.

There is but one explanation of the cause of this unreasonable cramming in a secondary school. Not only do the present-day schools in Zurich demand a very high standard, but many of the teachers gratify their own vanity at the expense of their pupils, and require more than the minimum in order to shine with the reflected glory of their success.

One day Elsa announced that her teacher had said her class was behind in French because the pupils of another teacher had already reached page 53 of the book upon which they were at work. Then she was obliged to do overtime at French for a week and every day had to do one hour's homework at French only! Upon another occasion the teacher told her she was backward in algebra because the pupils studying with someone else were already working at equations. Thenceforth began a perfect orgy of algebra. Each evening calculations were made until late at night.

And how much are these Head-teachers respected by the school authorities who are so cursed by their pupils and their relations? Could not someone bring to their notice that a permanent delight in learning is much more important than a few crumbs more or less of French? No! On the contrary! These ambitious Head-teachers obtain the best reports after the visits of the school inspectors, while the reasonable teachers are not regarded in the least as models of things as they should be! As long as we have school inspectors of this sort who judge the ability of a teacher according to the number of pages in the text-books that have been stumbled through, just so long will things go badly in our schools.

A. S.

(*i*) SCHOOL BALLAST (f. aged 36)

The word *School* has an uncomfortable sound in my ears. For twelve and a half years it was a veritable hell for me and throughout the subsequent golden time of academic freedom and work, as well as in the present-day struggle for existence, it has remained a perpetual reminder of hell.

INTELLECTUALISM

The struggle with the curriculum! It is inhuman, how much the schools try to cram into the little heads of their pupils, and how often is but little of this endurable or digestible! That it is far better for the digestion of young people to give them something that they eat with pleasure is familiar enough—upon that point we find plenty of evidence from investigation. The compulsion to study so many subjects in the present-day school has a brutally cruel effect upon our children. It fills their brains full to overflowing and stifles them. How, then, can any quiet deliberation, consideration and grasping of the matter so learned possibly take place! Everything is done in a hurry and the superficial artist, accomplished in learning by heart, comes out best, whilst the pupils who work thoroughly and with deeper concentration are left behind! However, in this way good luck comes from their misfortune, because these *thorough scholars*, who have come to grips with the malevolent crags of learning and cultivated a persistence necessary to scale them, have become accustomed and steeled for the stern battle of reality. They have acquired true knowledge and therefore far outstrip outside the school in practical life the superficial knowledge-merchants and win a victory over them, in spite of all the school reports that were gained.

The struggle with the teachers! I am aware that they have a difficult profession and we others say often enough: "I should not like to be a teacher!" But many teachers are no real educators, but the victims of their choice of a profession or of their lost patience, their inadequate payment, their unfulfilled aspirations in their calling, their overburdening with *"other things"* as well as of their own oppression by the superfluous curriculum which they are obliged to carry out.

This was the state of affairs for us in chemistry: with unprecedented energy we children plunged into this subject. But who gave us any idea of the wonderful relation of the laws of nature, who explained to us the power of attraction or repulsion possessed by some of the elements? Who made clear to us how one could bring into existence quite new and different substances by the putting together of some elements and the separation of others, and who was able to thrill us with the idea of the high practical value of these deeply fundamental facts for use in everyday life? No one: *no time!* Perhaps if our chemistry master could once have suspected how our young brains struggled in silence and secretly when we worked at our experiments during the *practical*, and how all science was dominated by the one thought: "It is to be hoped I don't fail!" he might have helped us. Why were we so strenuously and inhumanly crammed and martyred by him as young students of chemistry? Did not the crippling atmosphere that surrounded his pupils hour after hour oppress him as well? I should be horrified to have such a barrier between my intellectual world and that of the children entrusted to me.

I will talk no longer about individual persons, but conclude with the most bitter complaint that we pupils had at that time and which the students of to-day raise as well. Nearly all teachers believe their own subject to be just the most important. And they pay not the slightest attention to those things that are required for actual life.

Is the school there to help us with life, or does life exist to support the schools?

Dr. F. S.

(j) THE MORE LEARNING, THE LESS KNOWLEDGE (m.)

May a school-master also voice a complaint? I had the good fortune to be a so-called *good scholar* in the elementary and secondary schools as well as at the Training

College, and for this reason I can look back over this time without horror.

That, however, which often entirely spoilt my appetite and that of others for some subject was the carrying out of all instruction in a spirit of arid knowledge-cramming, the presentation of a skeleton of names and figures (especially when it came to scientific subjects), where one missed only too sorely the living covering of flesh; a smattering of incomprehensible knowledge, preferred by the curriculum and the examinations, and particularly the enormously high value placed upon learning in comparison with that put upon knowledge.

The most worrying of all was the feeling that the pupils existed for the sake of this acquisition of much learning, a vessel for the reception of *valuable* contents, each taxed to the utmost of his capacity instead of the worth of this intellectual nourishment being estimated, and its degree of digestibility adjusted according to the intellectual strength of the individual scholar. To make use of a banal example: Knowledge and pupil stood in the same relation one to another as the fertiliser and its bag, instead of the fertiliser and the starving little flowers. In short, one strove after the goal of subjects rather than the aim of acquiring education.

At that time I promised myself that when I became a teacher I would deal with the matter from the other side. But I had to discover that one knows more than one can carry out, in exact proportion to the education of my colleagues, that is, that one knows well enough what the pupils should achieve, but one experiences a great deal of trouble in finding out the best way of ensuring their accomplishing it.

Equally depressing is the discovery that the larger proportion of grown-up people want nothing else from the schools but that which they suffered themselves in their youth, in spite of the fact that they find out daily from experience that this kind of education does not prepare them for life, and that for this reason the *good scholars* fail time and again when it comes to actual life, and contrarily, many about whom it was said: "You will never do any good with your life!" become good business men as well as good citizens and useful people. But in spite of all this they cling to *the good old days*, and regard as renowned those schools of the past where *learning* is still insisted upon.

Why should this be? Is it simply the tendency to cling to the past? Is it envy that the young folk of to-day should be given something which they did not have? Is it fear to give power to the godless youths of to-day that they believe to be without piety and respect for authority, through true education, that might be more mighty than that of our old-time learning? Is it the method of the ostrich which will not acknowledge the *worthlessness* of that which in their own time they themselves acquired with so much industry and sweat, tears and thrashings? Or is it *true belief* that its possession was something especially valuable, because it cost them so much? Who knows the reason?

The prevailing opinion acts as a tight boot upon all those who are in any way connected with the school. The situation may be illustrated thus. An educationist from Berne at a recent gathering of Swiss teachers in Zurich was able to damp down all enthusiasm for Glöckel's school in Vienna simply by expressing his opinion: "It is all very beautiful and excellent in its way, but it would not be practicable for us here in Switzerland." Therefore this means that something which is excellent and beautiful cannot be carried out by us! And this is the state of affairs from which we teachers suffer the most.

C. S.

CHAPTER IV

MIS-EDUCATION

(*a*) SINGING AS A TORTURE (f. aged 48)

LAY folks have no conception how much the schools ignore the new discoveries and experiences of modern psychology, and for this reason I should like to call your attention to one of these problems which is certainly familiar to all parents, namely, that of *corporal punishment*.

The cane still retains its old power in spite of our twentieth century, which has been called the *Child's Century*, regardless of the new knowledge obtained from psychology, and in spite of the widespread teaching of Pestalozzi. It is used even among our smallest children, often out of all proportion to their offences and without shame. I will illustrate this opinion with a few examples, convinced that I had the misfortune to come into contact with teachers who rewarded good work with a good mark and bad work with the cane, regardless of who had carried it out and under what circumstances; that is to say, what ability the particular child had of bringing the work to perfection, either at that moment or at any time at all.

From the age of seven years to ten, I was a good and conscientious pupil, but had no talent for singing and was even without any feeling for rhythm. My teacher, who was considered a pattern of her profession, attempted to make us all equally efficient, even when this was not physically possible, and thus she even tried to achieve it by blows. Hence every singing lesson was a dreadful experience for me. First of all she always singled out those who couldn't do things. She would shout a note and if I could not sing it after her—and I could only seldom get it right—she would pull my hair. My eyes would fill with water and I was then obliged to take the little green exercise book in my hand and sing the notes in it while I beat time to them. I was never able to do this, although I was obliged at each beat to hit myself in the face with my own hand, the teacher controlling my arm. But then I had to be made to suffer a little because of my defective talent. Yet each time it happened it seemed to me that I should never forget it.

The teacher had explained to us when one wrote *fiel* with an *f* and in what cases with a *v*. At the conclusion of the lesson she dictated two little sentences to us: "The tree bears much fruit (*viele Früchte*)," "The boy fell (*fiel*) into the brook." We had to write each sentence seven times and she had threatened us that anyone who wrote one little word wrong would be hit over the fingers once; if we wrote two wrong words, we should get two strokes, etc. When the exercise was finished we were sent out into the play-ground while the teacher corrected our work. When I went to sit down in my place once more, I saw on my slate, marked in white chalk, the figure 14. I glanced quickly at the slates to right and left of me; there were little, tidy o's, but behind me, yes, the utterly stupid Rosa Krähenbühl, she also had a 14. I suddenly went all hot and cold down my back! Had I then mixed them all up and got none of them right? I was scared to death. And then she came and stood in front of me, stretched out my right hand and struck me seven hard blows on it, then seven on the left hand, so that I cried aloud with the pain.

The teachers had a habit of often sitting in the corridor to chat together during the Pause. When the class-room was left without any supervision it naturally did not remain quiet as a mouse and the teacher would often open the door quickly and send me up to the blackboard to write down the names of the chatterers. When she came back she would look at the board and anyone whose name was there received strokes with the cane across her hands. If the list of names was very long she would begin with the first, and all knew that their turn would come after a time. Once when the teacher did not come in for a very long time I wrote down "Teacher" among the list of the gossips. For that she dragged me about the class-room by my plait until I could not see or hear and my mother kept me in bed afterwards on account of a severe headache.

Thirty years later

I have two children who attend a secondary school in the country. If at lunch-time there seems to be a depressed atmosphere I ask if everything has not gone right at school or if one of them did not know a lesson. Yes, everything was all right, but the teacher was in a bad temper again, and it was dreadful. He chased Rudi round the class-room with his cane, and when he himself crashed into a table, he knocked Rudi out of the room. But Peter got it still worse. The teacher wiped the dirty, evil-smelling blackboard rag all over his face and then hit his head against the blackboard several times, so that it cracked.

My younger child is in the junior class and a good pupil. On the same form with him sits Werner, the son of our neighbour. He is an inattentive little fellow and bad at arithmetic. "So," says my small son, "he often gets the cane. The teacher says he cannot pull him together. Mummy, what does that mean, 'pull him together'?"

Little Werner troubles me. Bad conditions at home have contributed to his sad little life; why, then, should he find hardness and tyranny in the school too instead of patience and understanding? Two wrongs will never make a right!

(b) LACK OF UNDERSTANDING (m.)

I went through a very hard time in my secondary school. The school then stood out as a threatening, sinister cloud in contrast to my sunny days. What a faintness smote my heart when I got a whiff of the school, and with what speed was I endowed when I had to go down those long and severe-looking corridors! This building was no home to me and I felt no love for it. It choked me for six years, and the feeling would often nearly stifle me that I was in bondage to all these reverend professors in their frock-coats.

I remember one of the teachers particularly, of whom I was much frightened. We had to do technical drawing with him. He would get very angry and rough at the slightest lack of attention on the part of any of his pupils, for which he blamed them immediately. He shouted and doled out a box on the ears; and I can still see his wild, fixed stare and his tightly drawn-in lips. I was terribly afraid of him and it was the greatest martyrdom for me to go to his class. I tried to appease him in every possible way: I brought him, in an almost laughable fashion, flowers, strawberries and other things besides to the school. He seemed to understand the joke too, then, and was more merciful with me and with the others. But it was always alarming to be with him; even his smile was frightening, although it gave me some release.

At that time, for a few years, I took almost unnatural trouble, was reckoned as one of the best and most promising scholars and suffered extremely under the school conditions. The teachers were as gods to us whom we must obey blindly. One was obliged to surrender one's ego and be exactly what the tyrants wanted us to be. I am convinced that to-day also this is the greatest torment to a child, the compulsion to be dragged into some other sphere than that of his natural inclinations.

The most difficult years of all for me were to come later, however, when I entered the training college for teachers! From the very start I felt oppressed to such an extent that all my personality seemed to vanish, and this increased so much during the four years I was there that I finally left the school shy, reserved and unusually suspicious. I had no longer any opinions of my own, but was afflicted with such uncertainty that I seemed unattractive to a great many. I possessed a false attitude to everything and it was very difficult for me to reawaken my own character from this period of wrong values.

How had it happened? Whence comes it as a rule that students should suffer so much? The cause is nothing else than an absence of understanding of the child mind. And for this reason the blame lies altogether on the side of the teacher. He fails to get in contact with them, he fails in his handling of them, in his patience with them and in his relationship with them. The teacher carries out his duties, earns his living and beyond this troubles himself very little about his pupils' affairs or about the young mind which should be expanding like a flower, for which it needs the sun.

For example, in the first German class we had to recite poetry. After we had finished the teacher would make remarks upon the recitations and then we had to give our criticism. I was used to a fresh and bold style and was among those who came forward extremely seldom with a recitation. One day when I was giving my opinion to the listening class, I suddenly felt something chilly in my neighbourhood that froze the words in my mouth. It proceeded from the other students, who, not daring to speak themselves, regarded anyone who did raise any opposition as if he were a criminal. And the teacher? He looked at me with an ironical smile as though he wished to say, "There, I knew from the first you would not have anything sensible to say!"

That confused me; I stumbled and stuttered, became red and embarrassed, saw around me nothing but hostile faces and may easily have said something foolish. The teacher put an end to my remarks with a wave of his hand, and from this first lesson onwards, because of this little, apparently unimportant experience, my whole destiny for four years was pre-determined.

It was this same teacher who, at that time, in the first few weeks of our course, gave us a good many lectures upon ethics. For example, he represented ambition as something so low and so vicious that, for fear of becoming ambitious, I crept away inside myself entirely, in order just to win the approbation of the teacher. I was so sensitive to the influence of anyone who came in contact with me that I gave in to his wishes without any reservation.

These are two apparently ridiculous incidents that have remained in my memory, and one may perhaps find them scarcely worthy of attention. And yet they were the two moments which determined the estrangement that overcame both myself and my character, through which finally I got on the wrong path and that provided the more cruel disappointments for my youthful mind.

Naturally each teacher cannot help such things occurring and he often does not know anything about them. He was, nevertheless, one of the best teachers, the only one who tried to lead us unselfishly, who got into touch with us and tried to awaken our sleeping depths. Yet he did not know how to set about it; in many ways he was too paltry. Thus, during our last year, for example, he tried most zealously to wean us from what he considered *bad games*, draughts and chess. He tried to put us off them by making ironical remarks. It was not at all surprising that afterwards they were played with renewed enthusiasm, because then we were able to get a half-sweet, half-frightened feeling that we we doing something forbidden and rather daring.

I could give many examples of trifles of this kind. And yet he was the only teacher who showed the least inclination to take any interest in our intellectual life. I will say nothing about the others, because they did not make the least attempt to get intimate with their students and had certainly not the smallest idea about the thousand tender, awakening inclinations and intellectual needs that arose from numerous, important personal occurrences which the students experienced. They fulfilled their duties; gave out to us the prescribed material; would often make a good joke, or were in a bad temper, doled out their sympathies according to the mood of the moment and played their parts well as school-masters. The way they carried this out in the spirit of good citizenship was quite praiseworthy.

Now what was lacking, who was to blame? These teachers were not alone to blame for this state of affairs, not in the least. They had been made like that and above all they got on quite well from being like that. The defect arises from their selection and their training. What importance have most things in themselves that one learns there that each student adjusts himself to with repugnance in certain subjects? All cramming of knowledge is only an external rind which resembles that of an orange, if one may make use of such an illustration, attractive and possessed of a delightful colour. Yet we throw it away immediately. One gives far too little attention to the educational profession. All other callings that are considered to be of importance require a relatively long study. And in this one a man is considered ready for service when he is but twenty. At that age one has not the slightest idea of life, one has no experience and most of the fresh, young new-comers have an ingenuous but great opinion of themselves; they are fundamentally earnest enough, but have no idea of the difficulties of their profession. One may talk of *the great responsibility*, but this is now considered an old, outworn idea, and who wants to take it seriously?

I have now, after three years' practice, learned to know what it means to be a teacher. How often do I enter my school with the greatest feeling of repugnance! And I have only one reason for this: I feel that I am not what I should be. I see also how difficult it is to have a vivifying effect upon my pupils and to transfer all my beautiful and deep aspirations into reality.

And that indeed is what we all lack, the power of carrying out ideals. There are a thousand fine books written and read, but they are not put into practice. And what else do we require than new practical methods? Is one not sometimes almost reduced to desperation at the present time that such an outcry will be raised in praise of some athlete who, like a dog, runs himself almost to death without aim or object? This man is considered a pioneer; but in the case of a hospital nurse, who sacrifices her whole life to her work, who is always among broken people, and is always there, when life whines and cries and becomes extinguished into darkness —no one mentions her when she dies.

O. F.

(*c*) THE OX IS MISSING! (f. aged 53)

With a few exceptions I can look back at the first two years of my school-life readily enough. During those two years, however, my pleasure in school was entirely spoilt, thanks to the readiness with which the teacher used to cane us; lesson-time was actually fear-time.

A little example of this *charming* treatment, which was doled out to us when we were in the first class of all, still remains in my memory. The school, where I first went in fear, but afterwards happily enough, was in a little village among the mountains near Zurich. One day we children had to count up the domestic animals. The little class stood in front of the first form. We named all of them that we could think of, but yet the teacher was not satisfied; there was still one more. Our strict teacher then asked each of us one after the other. He began with the smallest boy and got no satisfactory answer. A blow with his violin bow across the head might help matters, perhaps. So he tried it. He went on up the class, one after the other. He gave me a dose of the same medicine—his beautiful violin bow broke across my head. He was very annoyed on account of his accident, but he did not seem to notice the mockery of it. The elder pupils also received a scolding because they had not been entirely able to control their laughter.

The ox had been left out! Yes or no?

Then it happened that the third class changed its teacher, to the joy of the whole school. Soon the former compulsory pupil became an industrious, happy one, a proof that everything lay in the hands of the teacher.

E. M.

CHAPTER V

EXPENDITURE AND RESULTS

(*a*) STRIKE WHILE THE IRON IS HOT (f. aged 28)

Elementary schools twenty years ago in the chief town of a small Swiss Canton

In the first class I once had a teacher who used to tie my hands together with his handkerchief and then, together with the whole class, gloat over my frantic efforts to free myself. I was a very vivacious child and in my anger would rage at him without the least respect, bite the handkerchief with my teeth, put it over the hooks on the window, or those on which we used to hang up our clothes, in the attempt to tear it. But instead of making things any better it would only bring me further punishment. I would be kept in while my teacher teased me and tormented me for his pleasure.

I hated this teacher and the school. Yet my parents used to believe that my hatred was connected mainly with having to sit still on the school-form, since this was never a strong point of mine. Finally other children also told them about my suffering and they brought the case up before the school council. But they took little notice of children's chatter and exonerated the teacher. In the second class I had a teacher whom I adored, and with him I learned easily and happily, as much for the sake of what I learned as that he left me in peace and I was able to feel respect for him.

My little brother only left his parents with the greatest sorrow in order to go to school in his first year. He was on the whole conscientious but very slow, and he took any blame very badly. The teacher, who had noticed this, gave him the greatest consideration possible and never scolded him, even if he had only made one row of I's when the other children had covered their whole slates. He used to encourage him, talked to him and had a wonderful understanding how to get the best out of the boy, much to the joy of our parents. But the teacher got some lung trouble, was taken to a sanatorium and did not come back again. It was touching to see the little boy's grief and how much he missed him. A grumpy old Vicar came in his place of whom he was terrified. He went to school every day in terror, always made some mistake and was beaten for it. He became highly nervous, his friends often had to bring him home because he would have attacks of trembling which he could not get rid of as long as he was at the school, and on account of this he was taken away.

Under more skilful handling all this disappeared. He is a chemist to-day and will often relate that none of the many subsequent school years and courses of instruction ending in examinations had cost him so much nor had brought him into as much trouble as those few weeks with the Vicar.

Secondary Schools

I did not suffer at all in the German language class. I played all manner of tricks, was punished, and was considered lazy and refractory, although I showed no deficiency in my learning. My essays would show marks 3, 3-4, even perhaps 4, as against 1, which was the best mark. The subject might be, for example, *Strike while the Iron is Hot*.

Section i. Literal aspect. A. The Iron. B. The Smith.
Section ii. Metaphorical aspect. A. The Proverb. B. The meaning.
        C., etc., etc.

When doing it we were obliged to repeat the views of the teacher in chorus, so that nothing more remained for us to do at home than to write down what we had prepared. Anyone who remembered word for word what had been prepared received the highest mark, 1. That, to me, was far too uninteresting, and gave me no trouble; therefore I naturally got a 3 or 4.

In the second class I had another German teacher. On the first morning he came into the room and wrote up on the blackboard, "April 23. Suggestion for Essay to be read aloud. Free subject." Then he turned to the class. "During the next hour you will all give me the title you have chosen," and then began his lesson. Oh, what an inspired feeling that gave me, how exciting that was! I was all fire and flame. In a fortnight's time we had our essays returned; my subject, *My Favourite Animals*, mark 1. I became one of his most attentive and best pupils and respected that teacher throughout all the remaining three years of school-life, and I do so still.

Whenever a teacher understands how personally to come in contact with the children he will have a great victory and provide a blessing for them at the same time. It is a colossal task for the teacher, and it requires consideration, a fair allowance of psychology, no schoolmasterishness and no large classes.

H. M.

(*b*) TOO MUCH HOMEWORK (m. aged 15)

There are many readers of the *Schweizer-Spiegel* who say they cannot send in because they are still attending a secondary school and therefore do not wish to write about the darkest side of their school-life. But my opinion is that it is precisely we students who are able to give you the most pertinent answer to your question, "From what have you suffered most at school?" because all our unpleasant memories are still fresh in our minds, whilst those of the adults are mainly those which they remember from their childhood.

According to my view the large amount of homework that is given to us is by far the greatest evil that the school provides. At present we have one teacher in our secondary school, who is a great enthusiast for sport and games. Therefore he takes every opportunity to tell us we should be out in the open air as much as we can. Yet at the same time we have so much homework that to do so is absolutely impossible. We have to begin upon this work the moment we leave school and go on until it is time to go to bed, in order to get it all done. I agree that a little homework is necessary; but cannot this be reduced to a reasonable amount, so that we could have a little free time left to us after school-hours? Our masters give us homework not only because it is really necessary, but because it is the custom to do so and because it was done in their own school-days. If only this homework could be reduced so that the pupils who lived near the school had some free time left for their own disposal the greatest mistake of the schools would be abolished and they would no longer be such spectres of fear to the children.

H. Z.

CHAPTER VI

THE RIGHTS OF PERSONALITY

(*a*) FEAR AND BOREDOM (f. aged 36)

I FIRST went to school full of beautiful expectations. No one had frightened me about it. I was already acquainted with my future teacher. He seemed to be a kind man and was always surrounded by a group of his pupils. I went to school rather later than I should have done because my brothers and sisters had had scarlet fever. I do not know whether the following experience occurred during my first or second week, but in any case it served as my introduction to the school, and left a lasting impression upon me.

We had to learn to write; that meant that we had to make slanting lines with a pen in an exercise-book. A small boy who looked like a little dwarf—he actually was one, I learned later, as were also his six brothers and sisters (and they were all mentally defective)—filled his whole exercise-book with round scribbling, as little children are so fond of doing, instead of straight, slanting strokes. On account of this misdemeanour the teacher kicked him like a football up and down the narrow passage between the rows of forms. The little boy had tucked in his head. He looked just like a football, too. This incident alarmed me and provoked a feeling of absolute helplessness which did not leave my mind for three years. I did not think of criticising the teacher, because he never seemed to be a real human being to me. For example, I could never imagine that he drank his coffee in the morning and went to bed at night like other people. He represented Fate itself. In his outbursts of fury, he resembled the grimacing deities of many of the primitive tribes.

If I should recollect those early days I connect my life with a very great many moments of severe anxiety. It would begin in the morning; one had to shake hands with the teacher. If one's thumb slipped, which was easy enough because his hand was so much bigger than ours, instead of remaining exactly at the top, he would always be angry.

Oh, what a wilderness it was in our class-room! The second sensation that overcame me, besides fear, was *boredom*. Upon the wall hung a print that one could roll up on a stick like a map, *The Pig as a Domestic Animal*. That was the most boring thing I have ever seen in my life. It was as different from a living pig as the teacher was different from a human being.

I belonged to the not very clever children and had considerable trouble to learn to write. When we, for example, learned to make an l, the most stupid boy in the class, who was really a sort of tramp, and I had to make this figure on the blackboard, to the general amusement of the class, as a punishment for our clumsiness. After a time which had seemed to me unending, the teacher said, "You can sit down now!"

I turned round and had already taken two steps when he called me back with a jeering voice. My companion was released, but I was to go back and go on making l's. I was quite alone before the enormous blackboard that all of us were in awe of. It seemed as though the piece of chalk in my hand were on the side of my enemies, and, to my misfortune, would make nothing but crooked figures, at which I was shocked myself when they were done. At last I was allowed to go back to my place because everybody had got tired of the show.

These three years were the most unhappy of my life. I would often hold my nose when I went to bed at night in the hope that I might suffocate.

But the situation changed when I got into the higher

classes, 4–6. I began to criticise the new teacher and notice how prejudiced he was. The punishments became lighter the higher the position of the child's father. The child of the richest father of all was entirely protected from all punishments. If, for example, every child in the class was to be caned for not knowing something, these children in question would be left out. I now belonged to the group of clever children and also had nothing to fear on account of my family. But perhaps because I had suffered so much personally during my first few years at school, I was embittered by these acts of injustice which I now had to experience in the rôle of a looker-on. Once more I saw the same sort of football scenes, but they no longer had the effect upon me as a horrible, unavoidable destiny, as an earthquake. The teacher was no longer a god of thunder, but a man, and I saw that he poured out his wrath only upon the poorest, who naturally were not his best pupils. He would only kick two wretched boys from time to time, fairly seldom, it is true. How low these two were in his estimation could also be observed, because he also made them, as their chief punishment, and on account of their dirtiness, sit beside one another on the same form. I was also made to share this disgrace once too.

I began to hate this teacher terribly because of his injustice. I would create the most horrible revenge phantasies, and upon many, many evenings when I had finished my lessons, a friend and I would play a game that consisted of thinking out a suitable hell for him, complete with tortures, one of which was, for example, that red-hot lizards should tear out his hair.

My troubles came to an end in the secondary school, because there I did not take the teachers or the school seriously any longer, and regarded the teachers especially more from the humorous side.

Dr. A. H.

(b) YOUTH SHOULD BE RESPECTED (m. aged 31)

MOTTO

> "Et que vos enfants suivent nos leçons
> C'est nous qui fassons,
> Et qui refessons
> Les jolis petits, les jolis garçons."
>
> BÉRANGER, 1819.

The chief evil in the Swiss schools is, according to my opinion, that the character of the pupils is systematically suppressed and ruined.

Elementary School, Classes I–III, in a district of Zurich

If a pupil should ask a question that is not a convenient one for the teacher to answer, the class is made to shout, as if on a parade ground, "Stupid question!"

The result: The pupil in question never dares again to express an original idea; he will be systematically humiliated during the three years and in most cases finally becomes quite stupid. For trifling misdoings, especially if it is a case of poor children, punishment takes the form of pinching, pulling their hair or ears, etc.; a large number of refined tortures, in short. The teacher in question was a very amiable, little old gentleman with a small pointed beard, a church-goer, and well known and liked among the parents as a nice teacher who was never brutal to the children. His favourite song, which we had to sing every day, was this:

> "All goes well with me, very, very well with me.
> Because Teacher's heart loves me,
> Because Teacher's heart loves me,
> It goes very, very well with me."

Classes III–VI

An energetic teacher, a great gymnast, and with whom one learned something. I still feel ashamed, however, if

I think about it, how one used to look on while the children of poor families, girls and boys, were cuffed round the room with kicks and blows like footballs, lifted up into the air by their hair, etc., amid peals of laughter from their school-fellows. I still wonder how it was that there was never a fatality.

Public School (Secondary, for boys)

I attended the first two years of the secondary school course, with the intention of going on to a technical school. I wanted to become an engineer. Here I was regarded by the teachers as an outsider, and they called me "Engineer" in mockery. Otherwise my experiences were much the same as during:

Four and a half years in the Technical School

When I entered the school I arrived with other new boys, partly from the country and from other cantons. The spirit of this institution was more or less that of a Reformatory. But woe to anyone who rebelled at such an insult or the injustice of it all. The professors were omnipotent, and the whole future of the students lay in their hands on account of marks and reports. The young people were threatened about this every day of their lives. They knew exactly what it would mean for them if they were expelled; public-school education would be henceforward closed to them. If the State schools had power enough to do so they would forbid them to go to any private school which prepared for matriculation examinations. Each year a few scholars were ordered to leave as examples to intimidate the rest. Even if the porter made the most crass accusations against these young folks of eighteen, they had no redress. Comradeship was not encouraged as dangerous to authority. In the French schools one knows that prizes and medals are given for good work, and at the same time that there is also one prize for comradeship, awarded by a secret ballot amongst the pupils themselves. These big classes of boys, who at the commencement of the course were full of vitality, shrank between then and the taking of matriculation to a little handful of sad, downtrodden fellows.

Results: Compare two young men of eighteen, for example, one Swiss, from a State school, and an American. The Swiss probably has the rather better education, but is nevertheless quite unstable, without any self-confidence, ashamed of himself. The American, on the contrary, has been trained to be a man. He has also made some good friends among his school companions. Whereas the one goes to meet his life afraid and weakened, the other begins his fight fresh and full of happy courage.

Two of my class-mates of this school committed suicide about a year after their matriculation.

Youth should be respected and not despised.

W. G.

(c) APE, GO TO AFRICA!

What caused me the greatest suffering at school was the herd-treatment. From 1909 to 1917 I attended a school in a large town in the Canton Solothurn. There, at that time, until a change was made in the year 1912, each school-master and mistress had two classes, in each of which were more than thirty pupils, so there were more than sixty in each class-room. It was certainly quite impossible that they could know any child personally or even have any intimate knowledge of the best way to treat them so that learning might be made as easy for them as possible. As it was then, as one may readily understand, the teacher gave the first consideration to the clever pupils only and then to the best-dressed ones; the others, however, even when they were not stupid, had very little attention. This neglect was felt by every child, and must have been regarded by them as the partiality of the teacher, or as injustice. In point of fact I was not one of these outcasts because I was much too nervous, and for that reason very industrious; also I should never have been able to endure constantly recurring set-backs.

In the 3–4 class we had a teacher who was already an old man, who had, besides his school work, several other irons in the fire. Owing to this he would generally arrive late for school and brought with him an extraordinarily bad temper. Woe betide any whom he caught chattering or up to any boyish tricks when he did get into the class-room! A great many pupils were afraid of him. Every morning we had exactly two hours' mental arithmetic without intermission. We were seldom asked questions in order. First of all he would ask those whom he would feel sure could not give him the answer. Then he would say immediately, if one or other of those he had shouted some question at could not give the solution promptly, "Ape, go to Africa!" Africa was, as a matter of fact, a corner of the room on the right of the teacher. The pupil would then have to stay there until the arithmetic class was finished. Often the whole class nearly would be in Africa. At the end, therefore, he would shout, "Now, you apes, go back to your places!" I thought this Africa business was a terrible thing and therefore worked every calculation immediately with feverish anxiety.

At home, even in bed, I could not go to sleep for a long time because of fear concerning the following morning, and went on doing sums to myself until late at night. I used often to wish, in fact, that I should never wake in the morning, so that then I should not have to go to school any more.

I had also a great fear of his little cane. Anyone who

had once felt it on his calves or his hands, or even over his head, used to heap curses on this cane, together with the teacher. If he ill-treated a poor victim in this fashion the whole class would keep as still as a mouse, and all the children's eyes would gaze collectively at their teacher in terror. Sometimes one or another would begin to cry out loud even before he received his punishment.

Every morning, on my way to school and when I reached my place, I would put up a prayer to the good God that He would help me to give the right answer to all my sums and put the teacher in a good temper. The consequences of these two exhausting years of school-life were not outgrown for a long time and I had to spend a long time in the fifth class of the school.

The next few years of school were much more peaceful again, and the Central School itself was a far happier place for me. But still in this respect it was the same—there were still too many children in a class and the teacher paid too little individual attention to them. How many pupils found the school a torture on this account and had their young lives embittered by this means, because children are just and wish to be treated justly? The saddest thing of all, however, is that the teacher permits himself to beat the children entrusted to his charge, and often indeed punishes them in most unjust ways; without first investigating the reasons—why some homework has not been carried out or has been destroyed in the school—he sets out to thrash them. Many of them then become quite obstinate and lose all respect for their teacher.

My little sister also, who was rather delicate and therefore found learning very difficult, considered school a great torment. She was always confused and never knew what the teacher said to her. At home we made a great mistake by constantly urging the poor child to learn, and each of us tried with kindness or severity to explain her school-work to her. But she allowed everything to pass over her head without paying any attention to it, and talking to her did no good at all. She would never complain about what happened to her at school; she told of none of her experiences, and gave no account of her sufferings as her sisters and brothers had constantly done. She was so embittered by the school that she was simply stupefied. Only later on, when she had left school for a long time and she had developed surprisingly to our minds, both physically and intellectually—because as a child she had always been a little, pale-faced weakling—she told us what a miserable time she had in school in the classes 3-6. It was specially hard in her fifth and sixth school-year, when she was with a teacher of whom it was said that he knew only too well how to beat his pupils. He believed, even in the case of my sister, that the only way to help his pupils was to drive the learning into them with the cane and with cuffs. No day would pass without her receiving blows or scoldings, or being pulled by the ears or the hair. And when he was busy with a thrashing he lost all sense of direction—it was all the same to him where his blows went—on the children's heads, on their backs or the nape of their necks, and they came very, very hard. This treatment was the cause of a great deal of nose-bleeding from which my sister suffered. But she never used to complain, because she was so ashamed about it.

She seemed to me like a courageous little martyr when she told me one evening that her teacher would often tell her she was the most stupid member of her family; none of the rest of us had been so stupid. "I believed everything that he said to me, but it did not make me any more clever. Every box on the ears that he gave me made me hate him the more. But now he is very ill and old, and I don't bear him malice any longer." With these words she shook off the old school memories. If only the teachers would carry out their responsible duties with more love and treat the children as human beings, the school might become a delight for every one of them.

H. B.

(d) THE STINKING CARCASS (m.)

From what did you suffer most at school?

Here is my answer: "You stinking carcass, get out of my sight!" said Dr. — to me when I had done my Greek translation badly.

When I went out of the class-room, I allowed myself the pleasure of murmuring in the teacher's own style: "You grunting swine, stay there in your sty!" which was promptly repeated in a loud voice to the teacher by a fellow-pupil, who cannot have understood what I said. You can picture the result for yourselves. Moreover, the matter can be summed up thus: that because of this incident my stay in the last class but two in the Secondary School of the town of B. did not last much longer.

This final striking experience illustrates very clearly the entire aspect of my school-days, as well as the relationship of the school and myself towards one another. It seemed to me to be extremely unjust that the teachers, like gods, should be allowed to behave exactly as they liked with their pupils. I defended myself against them with all the means in my power, and I do not know who suffered the most thereby, the teachers or I. I made the most general eventualities of life as difficult as possible and was regarded by most of them, if not an absolute idiot, then as mentally defective or as a good-for-nothing. The episode which was described above took place in a Greek lesson, my favourite language, and then because of a mis-translation! I must say in connection with this that even to-day, more than ten years after this experience in this school, I still turn to Homer with pleasure for my recreation, and read ancient Greek with the greatest ease. I have always had a great interest in languages, but that is not of much account in a school where one has to translate according to the wishes of the teacher. "Take care, worm, or I will tread you to destruction, because I am that I am," seems to be the maxim of our school existence, and under this code most of us used to suffer considerably. Thank God that life has wiped out the oppressive picture of my school-days from my mind.

H. Z.

(*e*) STARCHED, EXAGGERATED AUTHORITY (m. aged 46)

From what did you suffer most? The answer strikes me as being short and sharp: from the *Authority of the Teacher*. It is, and was without any doubt, the *power* of these rulers, and on that account I trembled through four classes in school until I reached my last year, terrified under the tyranny of these terrible gentlemen! In this last year of all, however, when we had passed the age of fourteen, the bondage was suddenly raised, our new teacher treated us like human beings, and for the first time it seemed to be realised that we were of the same nature as our school-master. From that hour I went to school very willingly. And it was still more surprising, from this day forward, that I noticed that the teachers treated us with a certain amount of respect. I was one of the best, if not quite the best scholar, whilst during all the eight former years that I had spent in the school I had never been able to achieve more than the position of a very average pupil.

It is perhaps valuable to state that this oppression was exercised by the entire teaching staff, even by the good ones, although in their case it was several degrees

THE RIGHTS OF PERSONALITY

less than that practised by those people whom I still regard as devils in human form. In this connection I think of a teacher whom we had in the fourth class. Even now when I shut my eyes I can see him standing before his desk, thin and tall, a cane in his hand; he was hopping from one leg to the other, licking his fingers with his lips, and a horrible vicious grin was spread over his face. Before him, however, stood a little boy who scarcely reached his waist. The next moment he had picked the child up, flung him over a chair and commenced to thrash him unmercifully. I must say that I myself was never beaten in this way, but in spite of that, this often-repeated picture has never vanished from my memory from those days until now, and if I should say the word *School*, I get the same feeling of fear for an invisible, uncanny oppression, and at last the recollection always emerges of this sadistic —— villain, I should like to write. But if I consider the matter calmly to-day there are even times when actually I like this same teacher himself, whose discipline was the hardest I experienced during all the years I was at school, when I remember that there were occasions when he treated us with a certain amount of friendliness.

That may be true enough, but among my recollections of my school-days there are practically no rays of light, which fact now seems all the more painful to think about because they show what these school-years might have been, what possibilities lay in them for affectionate relationships between teachers and pupils to develop; even the students might have experienced among themselves in another atmosphere a great many more intellectual friendships.

My school-life took place a generation ago, in a little town in Eastern Switzerland, which was once famous, with Basle, for having the best schools in the country. I am convinced that much has changed, and has improved since then, but it is certain that there still remains plenty to be done, and that our children in the schools experience no greater injury than that derived from the *starched*, entirely false, *exaggerated authority of the schoolmaster* and his severe, tyrannical discipline. That both are absolutely superfluous I once proved in a country school near Berne. A class of twelve-year-old girls and boys worked in a most surprising manner, and yet there was not a trace of *discipline* nor of *authority* to be felt; one could feel nothing but an uplifting love of the children for their big comrade and teacher, who was, they felt, so good to them and who did so much for them.

J. B.

(f) BAD HANDWRITING (m. aged 30)

At the commencement I must own that I lack the usual worried attitude of absence of knowledge upon this subject, because I have myself been a teacher in a village school for several years.

What the cause was that I ran straight away from a lesson howling on the first day or hour of school, and could only be brought back again with the greatest trouble, I do not know precisely any longer, as little as then, when I naturally was immediately stormed with questions from parents, aunts, my teacher, etc., why I had run away. I only know one thing—that the reason that I gave then was not the correct one; I had run away because I was afraid of the thing on the wall (a relief of Palestrina). That had been in a small town!

When it became necessary for us to write out, on the following day, an essay which we had prepared, I had always to go through a bad night; I was scared about having nightmares, and yet, in spite of them, I wished that the night would never come to an end. In the morning on my way to school, I wanted to vanish at every street corner, to run away from what was to come! But I was good; the school-door, the class-room, were reached in their turn. I got out my exercise-book, blotting-paper, notes, and I wrote (that means I painted), crampedly troubled, each letter of the alphabet as our teacher liked to see them. Naturally in this process I left out letters, because I was already suffering from writer's cramp, and also with anxiety that I should not get done. At last I came to the full-stop at the end.

Like a criminal who awaits the discovery of his crime, I would slink home because the books would only be corrected later! On the next day would generally come the horrid moment about which I always secretly hoped that perhaps it would not be quite so bad as usual this time! Then I would take my exercise-book into my hands and stare at the page that was lying open. From corner to corner across the entire, painful exercise, in striking contrast to my frequently wavering lines, were drawn the free, dashing pen-strokes of the teacher, with uninhibited lack of consideration for my feelings, and underneath short and imperative were the words, "To be written out again!" I then stayed in and wrote it again, with the same amount of trouble and fear as before, and under the firm conviction that I was surrendering two precious hours of my freedom.

Just as in the last years of my life at the elementary school, where good handwriting was essential, written work during the remainder of my school-days was the cause of my worst educational troubles. Whether it was German, history, mathematics, or foreign languages, it was always totally impossible for me to manage to write correctly and according to orthographical conventions, which often made the fruit of my labours entirely without result. Even if I had made adequate preparation for some written work, and found an *elegant* solution for some problem, it would often happen that in writing down the result in some place or another, a wrong figure would stand before or after a comma. For example, in a logarithm that I had worked out perfectly accurately I wrote down the figures wrongly. Thus, instead of 0·69897 I would write 0·69798. Such mistakes were also made by some of the other pupils too occasionally, but in my case they would happen constantly (I now know why), and they brought me literally many a crossing out of my work.

Or when in a French lesson we all sat with our heads bowed in meditation over the table, trying to remember what the rules and their related exceptions were that must be thought of in connection with the set sentences before us, it would happen that the teacher, to whom it was also important that we should not give in exercises that were too bad, would say, "Don't forget what we wrote out last week; but be careful and think about the exceptions that we underlined with red ink!" Then a good number of the pupils would seize their pen-holders with a feeling of relief. Finally I began to write too, but with a small degree of relief only, because with the best will in the world I was not able to remember under which of the exceptions the red lines had been drawn.

If I should try to fit in my school experiences in relation to this questionnaire, and regard it from the point of view of all the little and big cruelties and acts of tactlessness on the part of my school-mates, who were anything but gentle, during my first years at school, I find that my fear connected with written exercises in school was closely related with the crippling feeling that, although I might with the very greatest industry in some subjects achieve a *good*, I could never under any circumstances get a *very good*. The school was mostly to blame for this.

Later, when my school-days were a long way behind

me, I discovered the reasons which had been the cause of my want of success, and also the ways in which I might have been helped, and I was astonished that psychology could achieve such results, particularly in the case of improving a bad memory, of which one has now read in numerous publications of the past twenty to thirty years. School-masters simply seem to ignore them entirely, at least in practice. But that is no business of mine to discuss here.

H. v. M.

CHAPTER VII

HUMANITY

(*a*) THE TEACHER AS GOD (f. aged 26)

ALWAYS, whether we were leaving school or whether we were coming in, Mr. O. was already there, always clothed alike in his suit of Jäger material and his black cravat. It seemed to me quite impossible that, like other men, he slept, ate or drank. His only meal seemed to be one apple daily, which he carefully cut up with his little pen-knife and ate during the Pause. In my opinion it seemed that as soon as school was over, Mr. O. disappeared into some unearthly world, similar to himself, in order to return once more in the morning to us frightened pupils in his dustless, superhuman correctness. The idea that at night he would undress and get into bed, and go to sleep like other people, seemed to me to be absolutely grotesque; or to eat, or drink a glass of beer, be ill: it was not to be thought of! When we saw him eating the customary roll and beef upon a school excursion, that seemed to be an act of almost religious significance. And that he could talk apart from the object of transferring knowledge, seemed highly improbable, and if he by chance said anything that was not connected with education I believed it to be some pedagogic catch said in order to prove my wisdom.

If I saw him in the street, I could not believe that he was going for a walk like anyone else, but imagined that there was some ulterior motive behind it that had to do with the school. Perhaps he was going to buy some chalk for the blackboard! I never saw him take off his coat; I could never imagine him without his clothes. If he washed his hands under the little tap that was in our class-room, it seemed to be an action that had quite another significance than if we or our parents had done the same thing.

One day, when the end of the world had been predicted, I felt an unreasoning joy that then he, too, would be brought to nothing and that there would be no more school, although I was by no means convinced that this catastrophe could swallow him up like the rest of humanity. It did not surprise me in the least when he survived it.

O. G.

(b) AFTER SIXTY-FIVE YEARS (m. aged 70)

I am already at the end of the seventh decade of my life, and have recently finished writing my autobiography. It seems to me that certain aspects of this description of my life would be suitable for answering your question.

"I suffered mostly from the brutality of the teachers and their lack of understanding of the child mind, especially those who were concerned with my religious teaching."

There was also something else. I will quote two instances, which have never entirely vanished from my memory all through my long life, therefore they must have made a most permanent impression upon me. The first occurred in my earliest childhood, when I was five, the second is taken from my eighth year. The former took place in the school at "Häfeli," the second at the State school of those days.

From the Infants' School, 1866 (*Häfelischuel*).

Each week we used to go for two long walks, upon which we were obliged to walk in pairs holding on to a long rope, through which wooden rods were thrust which served to divide the rope off into equal sections. Our teacher used to be accompanied by two of her friends on these excursions, who helped her with the shepherding of her little flock. We went through what then seemed to me the miles of Häfeli streets, and finally arrived at a large meadow outside the town where the two powder-mills stood. Here we would play games, jump about, dance and sing, and then partook of a picnic tea.

I do not know what I had done amiss, but when we were collected to make the homeward journey I was not allowed to hold one of the sticks and take my place with the other children, but was made to stand up against the wall of one of the powder-mills in front of them all.

"And now you are going to stay here, and we will all go home!" was my sentence.

I can still see, as though it had happened to-day, how the long serpent of children slowly vanished through the dusk of the evening, and how the three adults followed behind them, and did not even look round at me again. I was seized by an infinite fear. It seemed as though the whole world had abandoned me and left me to my fate. I saw the night sink down in that endless meadow—and I became petrified at the thought that I might never again be able to find my mother. Then my childish heart broke and I sobbed, with the tears running down my face.

They had all gone away; it seemed to me they must have gone miles. I shouted aloud, I screamed, I could not move from the spot; it seemed as though I was held by iron claws to the wall of the powder-mill. Then the teacher came back and fetched me. "You won't do that again, will you?" and I said, "No, no!"

But I still do not know even now what crime I had committed. I believe I had been blamed by a naughty boy for something someone else had done, either himself or one of the others, because I know that as a child I had really never done anything naughty; I was too good, naturally.

Hasty, unjust punishments have a terrible effect upon the mind of a child. It is better not to punish at all, if one is not sure who is guilty, or a far deeper guilt falls on the head of the teacher on that account, and the child loses his confidence in justice.

From the State School, 1869

At that time corporal punishment was in full bloom in the boys' schools in Switzerland, and I still remember to this day, with the same feeling of resentment, the fiendish joy with which, beyond all doubt, the sadistic teacher let his long cane whistle over our heads from his desk or upon the backs of one or other of us. But especially I remember the devilish expression on the criminal face of this teacher when he would tan the breeches of some poor youngster, and went for him with a cane which the condemned had been obliged to bring with him himself from the shop in the town, often several hours after the misdeed, "to tan his hide for him," in the carrying out of which he would use his whole strength, which was considerable.

I can still not understand that such abortions like this teacher of ours, and others like him, can ever have been trained to educate our Swiss boys. Every school inspector must have been able to recognise at the first glance that such creatures would be bound to tyrannise, but could not be expected to help their young Swiss pupils to cultivate the required sense of freedom and awaken their self-respect.

These scarecrows never did anything to me, because the thrashings were only doled out to the children of poor folks, which was a further scandal for the Swiss pedagogues of that time. I often ask myself the question,

What ass can have stood at the head of the State schools of my fatherland at that time?

But in spite of all this I had such a heathenish fear of this teacher that I soon told my mother about it, so that from time to time she would send him, by me, a pound of the finest Suchard chocolate. That tamed the brute.

How blessed are the school-children of to-day that they are no longer drilled according to that foolish pattern, one just like the other, but are now provided with teaching material that must make their hearts dance for joy. All these appliances are so beautifully thought out.

When I look through modern school books I envy you them, how charming and handy and clearly is everything laid out for your acceptance as though upon a dish for presentation! But I consider you still more blessed, you school-children of to-day, because you are no longer, as we were, living in *the stupid century*, as a French author has called the last, the nineteenth, led to the school-form like calves to the slaughter-bench, filled with fear that you cannot overcome for your torturers, who turned many merely naughty boys into bad, really fundamentally wicked fellows, and brought up cunning, lying, revengeful, envious, even criminal children in this country of ours.

Ch. P.

(c) INDIVIDUALITY AND THE SCHOOL (m. aged 35)

My wife went very willingly to school and liked being there. She went to a private school that had the privilege of preparing for matriculation until shortly before the examination. Even to the present day my wife is friendly with her former teachers, and remembers her school-days with the greatest satisfaction. This question, therefore, has nothing to do with her.

It is quite different in my case, however. I only went

to school willingly upon very few occasions. Usually I looked upon it as upon some boring beadle, hating it often from the bottom of my heart and suffering extremely from it. When I had taken my matriculation examination I left my educational establishment with a sigh of relief, as though a burden had been lifted from my back. I had been attending a State classical school, where I had learned Greek as well as Latin.

Here you have examples of two extremely different opinions of school on the part of children and young people.

Whereas my wife was quite well aware without any particular deliberation why she loved her school, I am obliged first of all to discover the separate causes of my school troubles with considerable difficulty.

Let us take this as our initial premise: the school was not the cause of my school troubles.

I never suffered at school from the matter that was taught, cramming of knowledge, overburdening of my memory, oppression and such things at any time. Perhaps the possibility of trouble lay in the time-table. I could always find ways of avoiding the demands put upon me by the school when I had something else to do. So also could my school-fellows. The tactics of parrying was carried out with more or less success almost as a reflex action by every scholar in the case of individual teachers whose requirements were too stiff, or which did not meet with our approval for some reason. In addition to these, no examination spectre stood in the background for me. Precisely during my school-days did the praiseworthy system of credits come into existence, so that for the lazy pupils that much-wished-for possibility existed to be able to slide through the examinations. The power of the school had only a very limited control over us.

Especially did the usual school oppression provide an atmosphere of dishonourableness in my eyes, and the boredom that one found in instruction was frequently infinite. But even here I cannot find the source of my "hard fate."

With more cause I am inclined to make individual teachers responsible for my troubles. I can remember clearly enough many injustices, malevolent actions, and tricks that arose from school-masterish attempts at revenge which upset me and embittered me extremely. I do not want to give an account of these really hateful histories here. It will be enough to state that I had full opportunities to become acquainted with the human inadequacies of the personality of a few of my teachers. And yet not even this kind of school recollection really provides the answer we are seeking to our question.

My troubles at school are only to be understood when one takes my psychological condition at that time into consideration. I was no model pupil. On the contrary, a really difficult chap, who brought the kernel of his subsequent school troubles with him the very first day he entered school. Had I been different, then my school experiences would also have been different.

The relation of the school to my troubles was limited to this, that so many of the teachers failed me educationally, treated me wrongly because of their own moral discrepancies, and thereby made my school conflicts incurable. I had not really presented them with an impossible educational task.

According to my opinion in most cases it was a matter of childish school troubles which arose only on account of an encounter with some sort of childish and school-masterish inadequacy in the past. The school as such did not play a very great part; it might well be that what one calls school really is the influence of good and bad teachers.

Hints that we can gather here and there about the educational difficulties of intellectually significant people seem to contradict this view. They seem to me to show no intrinsic lack of reverence for intellectual superiority. When one comes to consider them closely, the school troubles of great men frequently seem to have concerned their genius less than the inadequacies of their characters, which stimulated and rubbed up the wrong way those of their teachers.

Moreover, we must always remember that the school as an institution is arranged to suit the average intelligence and, in addition, represents an altogether clumsy instrument for education. And for this reason precisely, apart from the educational qualities of the teachers, it does not easily succeed in dealing satisfactorily with natures which show unusual traits of development. And in the same way this is just as applicable for those who are gifted below the average as those who have more than normal abilities. *Dr. X. Y.*

(*d*) THE ROUGH COUNTRY LAD (m. aged 71)

It was many years ago when I went, as an eleven-year-old country boy of average ability, from a village school to the central school near Z. In one of my first geography lessons, the teacher, who was in his fifties, put a question to me that I did not understand, and I answered him with "Eh?" as we used to do in the village. Instead of explaining to me as an educator of youth might have done that this was an unsuitable reply, he applied two lusty boxes on the ear, scolding me the while, and made me ridiculous before the whole class. As a country lad I had to suffer a great deal in this school. This was my greatest hardship. It embittered me throughout all the four classes against the teachers who taught in them. I think of it at times still with considerable anger. Might not the teachers in a town school bestow more understanding upon a rough country lad? *A. P.-B.*

(e) ONLY CHILDREN (m. aged 20)

Last October someone sent me your paper from home. When I was looking through it, Dr. Schohaus's article on schools caught my eye. "Hurrah! Here is exactly what I have been wanting for a long time," I thought; "here is someone who, after he has left school, does not find it too much of a bother to pull out into the light some of its deficiencies, and who has courage enough to give some publicity to those things from which 99 per cent. of all people suffered in their childhood."

When I was still at school—and it is now three years since I left—I always made up my mind that when I was free of the domination of teachers I would see to it properly that my grandchildren would not have to go through the same as I was obliged to.

My chief trouble during the eleven school years that I lived through consisted in this—and it happened principally in the school which I attended in a town in central Switzerland—that the teachers always considered the pupils as so inferior to themselves and treated them as though they were creatures of very little account. We had a geography master who, one might say in passing, was a cipher, a nobody; unfortunately he still carries on his existence as a teacher, and was a good example of this type. If one should ask him a question, he would smile in a superior fashion and give an answer in a voice which seemed to say: "It is a pity that you are such a fool." Once, it is recorded in this school, he had given utterance to the following sentence: "You are only pupils; I am, however, a captain in the Swiss Army, and carry a bright sabre!"

Unfortunately he was not the only one of this sort; in our school there were several like him, who could never give the pupils their true worth. It must also be the same in other places, or Hermann Hesse would not have written in his novel, *Unterm Rad*, the following sentence: "A pupil who is dead is regarded by the teacher in quite another light than one who is living; he will then be convinced of his worth, and the impossibility of bringing back his life or his youth, for which formerly he (the boy) was often made remorsely to atone." It was just this superior attitude of the teachers, this condescending behaviour, which oppressed my mind in my school-days. I saw myself as a queer little chap, without intellectual value and without personality. And yet, every normal child in his own sphere of life is just as great in thought, mind and heart as every grown-up person; he only lacks the knowledge and experience which age will bring him. But does this give the teacher any right to look down on the pupil? Is it anything to do with the teacher that he is older than the child and, in consequence of this difference, must of necessity know more than he?

No, the teacher should not feel superior on account of his greater knowledge that the years have brought him, but be a friend to the pupil, and pass on as much of his knowledge to the pupil as possible, and the better the teacher is, the more will the pupil profit from him.

Somewhere Rabindranath Tagore writes:

"If you really desire to be a guide to the youth of your generation, you must refrain from all feeling of superiority. You shall be an elder brother to him, prepared to travel the same road with him towards wisdom and with aspirations towards the highest."

But to be a guide in Tagore's sense is more than most teachers of the present day aspire to. And why should not a teacher be a guide?

Since I first went to school I have had the idea that in our schools there should be a council of the pupils, as there is already in some towns; and, moreover, that this council should have the power in cases of necessity to require that a teacher who is regarded as generally hated should have to leave the school, and I am sure that the pupils would not exercise their privilege unjustly. They know well enough if a teacher is good and when he is incapable, and a good teacher is popular with all his pupils. A council of students of this kind with extensive duties would certainly be a suitable factor for the solution of many problems. Another matter that should be dealt with by it would be that of the amount of school-work required from the students, because it frequently happens that they have, together with their homework, from twelve or more hours' work daily, as well as often on Sunday too, while the hours of work that an adult is called upon to perform are limited to an average of eight!

When will the longed-for reforms be carried out?

(*f*) AS THE TEACHER IS, SO IS THE BURDEN! (f)

I grew up in Basle and there attended the elementary, secondary and girls' high schools. I did not belong to that unhappy group of creatures to whom school appears as a reformatory. Actually I did not suffer in any way, although I went on attending school until I was nineteen. But in spite of that, these schools cost me considerable trouble and tears about which I still cannot smile. I am very sensitive, receptive and capable of being inspired. I could regard no teacher and no study as being a matter of indifference to me, were they either revered or abhorred. And in connection with that one may say readily enough what used to give me the greatest pleasure in learning, apart from the teachers. Fortunately there was always at least one of the teachers to whom I could attach myself, whom I loved because of his lessons. And I would do so much work in connection with these subjects that I would usually neglect my other study in consequence. Thanks to this state of affairs I was always one of the best scholars of this particular teacher, and his lessons became an increasing delight. I forgot the other subjects during these classes, and learned to love the school. Unfortunately, however, these teachers were in the minority. I hated the rest of the instruction that we got, and I enjoyed the Pause as much as the others, when I could give free rein to my personality and abuse one teacher while I praised another to the skies.

Naturally you will ask me what made me so fond of one subject and hate the others so much. The answer I discovered for myself quite clearly when I was fifteen. Any teacher could hold me in thrall who was himself interested in his subject and absorbed in it, or at least could present his material so that his hearers forgot that all he said had to be learned and remembered.

I still remember well the lack of interest and the dullness with which I got through geography lessons when I was about thirteen years old, and in a spring written examination was not able to name the three most important towns in China. And a couple of months later I could not drag myself away from the astonishment and the delight that I derived from reading Sven Hedin's *From Pole to Pole*. I then knew Asia better than the Canton of Basle.

During the first three years I was at the secondary school, French was utterly repugnant to me, because it was trickled out to us by an old, dried-up school-master who, after some forty or fifty years of teaching, had no longer a spark of inspiration left in him. So it went terribly badly with my French at that time. I did not really dislike it so much, but I would never have been able to put any courageous work into it if the old teacher had not been replaced the following spring by a young one. I have never forgotten how, in one of the first grammar lessons that he gave us, he quoted some excellent joke that had made an appearance the previous Shrove Tuesday carnival, over which the town had laughed for a whole month. It was his trick, his speciality, always to know what would best catch the children's attention or what would awaken their interest. He would always bring up some town or world novelty, some interesting piece of news, if he noticed that our attention was beginning to stray. He told us about exhibitions, fêtes, records, discoveries, even about foreign politics, and even more wonderful than that, he let us discuss it and would never laugh at our childish opinions. If we could not say all we wanted to in French, then he would let us say what we wanted to in Basle German. These conversations did not come too often, because our time-table was too full to allow it. But I am certain that not one girl in our class could refrain from giving her attention to his lessons for very long. He was our friend. Very soon ours was the best French class in the school at our level of proficiency.

I think that these two examples will explain sufficiently what made the sunshine and the rain during my schooldays. According to my opinion, the teachers should pay more attention to the attempt to lessen the distance between themselves and their pupils by including, and not excluding, the actual interests of the children themselves. I am also aware that a younger teaching staff provides a fresher atmosphere.

(*g*) THE BLACKBOARD BECOMES A PILLORY (f. aged 20)

Several years have passed since I took my flight from a secondary school in a little village in the Canton of Berne, with a tragic farewell and without taking my final examination.

I never had any affection for the school, although I cannot say that I was afraid there or even hated it. The last two years suddenly changed everything for the first time. They became horrible for me, not at the time only, but they continue to persecute me in my dreams, so that I awake suddenly with terrible cries.

If only you knew what you did to me, you reverend teachers, whom I loved and honoured like a father!

I was a delicate girl, often very ill, and it once happened that I received a doctor's certificate on account of overfatigue and anaemia. My percentage at that time was only 43. That seemed to my mother a sufficient reason for taking me away from school a week before the beginning of the holidays. It appeared to me that after I came back from those holidays my school-mates and teachers wore different faces. Before that I had never noticed myself standing in high favour with the teachers. I was now obliged to recognise the terrible fact that I no longer existed for them—that meant except when they could expose me before the whole class—in which case they would remember me quite often.

They would begin with trifles, they would scoff at me because of the lace on my dress, my hair-slide and a little chain that I used to wear and suchlike. They would hint that I was the only town girl among the other pupils. These had respected me as long as I was in the teacher's favour, but from this time onwards an alliance against me was established between the teacher and these class-mates of mine. I could say nothing whatever without a mocking smile appearing upon all their faces.

But the worst was still to come. Once when our teacher was giving us a lesson, and all were sitting there without a single movement, as he liked us to do, I shifted my position a little. He immediately told me in a furious voice to leave the room. I remained sitting quietly in my place, because I was in no way to blame. When he repeated his command for the second time, I got up and timidly asked why he had told me to leave the room. That was evidently too much for him! His face became as red as a lobster, and he chased me out furiously. I had to remain in the open hall of the building for a whole hour in the intense cold of the winter. I knew I should never be reinstated. In this circumstance my school-fellows found a fresh reason to despise and persecute me.

For weeks and even months after that no one spoke one word to me. In the Pauses between different lessons when they were all playing or walking together, and I came along to join them, they would break off their game or turn away and pretend not to notice me. There were some who were the favourites of the class; there were none of them who had courage enough to take my part, although I presented them all, including their leader, with chocolate and honey biscuits, only to bring myself more into their favour. They took my dainties gladly enough, gave me away in class, but would never give me a hint if I should happen to be in need of a little help.

The worst torment of all for me was the arithmetic class; it had always been one of my most difficult subjects. With the greatest industry I was just able to follow the lesson, and that was all. But with this transformation in my fate at school, I went to pieces utterly in this subject, because my teacher, making use of my weakness, would now give us every day, for a long time together, written arithmetic tests, before which he would always turn to me and say: "To-day we will once more have a test, won't we, L.?" From that time onwards I hated him. Perhaps it was out of defiance, but I could not now get one single sum right. Therefore each answer that I gave in would, to my great humiliation, be received with ironical smiles.

There was a teacher, a man, who had feelings, or should have had them, and yet could not see that he was sowing hatred instead of love! Is he there only to give instruction to the children according to pattern? Should he not rather be their friend? No; he seemed to possess none of these qualities, otherwise he would not have had the cruelty, after everything else that he had done to me, to humiliate me mentally as well.

We were all obliged, in turn, to work out an arithmetic problem on the blackboard; that meant that each of us every day would have to work at this sum on the board until it was perfectly done without any mistake, within the hour. At that time it once took me three weeks. The blackboard became a pillory for me. When I looked round, hoping to get a little help, I would see, instead of the faces of my school-fellows, a single, grinning devil's face. And so it went on day after day.

Can you imagine that anyone could do useful work under such conditions? Had this clever and efficient teacher not seen my infinite terror, or did he not want to notice it?

I became more and more ill. I was afraid to go to sleep on account of the anxiety dreams which I had that were all connected with the school. In these dreams my class-mates would persecute me, strike me with choppers and laths, spit in my face and kick me, whilst the teacher always looked on smiling at what they were doing to me.

The consequent nervous breakdown finally set me free from the school, because I was taken away from it upon medical advice.

I wonder when the happy time will come when I shall also be freed from these anxiety dreams which still continue to persecute me.

My most earnest wish is that a great many teachers will read this confession of mine and learn from it what far-reaching results can arise from the heartless mockery they take as a joke.

L. F.

(*h*) "AH, S. AGAIN, NATURALLY, THAT CHILD!"
(m. aged 35)

I can best answer your questionnaire by giving some account of my school troubles from which I suffered when I was at the middle school. If I am not able to refrain from a few unabreacted digs at education, you must forgive me, because I am one of those who were longing for your questionnaire, since the school had ruined the most fruitful years of their lives.

Between 1909 and 1911 I attended the middle school in Z. Professor R. taught us mathematics. My mathematical ability was nothing astonishing. I belonged to the average group. To work out problems in algebra and geometry we were often obliged to go up to the blackboard. Many of them did not mind this, but I always became uncertain and confused up there, being the focus of the eyes of the whole class, as it were, on the platform, and my thoughts just waltzed round. Then suddenly I would not be able to think what to do next, and would turn red and stammer. How they would stare at me then and laugh, and the teacher, with some coarse joke that pleased him immensely, would send me back to my place. The whole class would then stretch out their hands, each hoping that the teacher would call him up in order to be able to shine. (I never thought of it in any other way. If another stood up before us and could not get on and came to pieces, I was always sorry for him then if it suddenly went right when someone else had to show how it was done.) It still echoes in my ears how R. called me down, when once again I lost my head at the blackboard after making a muddle of what I was trying to do there for some time, which I would certainly have been able to accomplish well enough had I been able to think it out quietly. How he would pull to pieces and depreciate the true state of my knowledge, which I could justify to myself. It was a wonder that they put up with me at all in the class! After an answer of mine that was altogether wrong, he shouted, ironically humiliating, "Ah, S. again, naturally, that child!" It is really a deep insult for a boy to be called a child, but children must seem particularly simple and stupid to a professor of the middle school.

R. was our form-master, and would sometimes go with us for excursions. I burned to be able to give him a better opinion of me by some side track; for example, because I was fond of nature, because I had amusing ideas, etc. But the trouble I took to gain this effect never won his respect after all. He was always surrounded by a troop of pattern pupils who generally made use of the tactics of devotion. In all these three years I never had an occasion to approach my teacher as a person and not as a student, which was one of my most serious troubles.

Another teacher accomplished this; he was our German master. German was my favourite subject. My last essay exercise-book showed upon the average 5 marks per essay (6 was the highest mark), but beside the essay would always be a question-mark. The teacher did not believe that I did my homework myself and would ask me who was its author with twinkling eyes. He did not investigate it any further, but his final view of my ability was demonstrated by giving me a 3-4 and a 4 for industry.

When I consider which among my teachers in this school caused me the greatest suffering, then I see a group of very inquiring and representative gentlemen before me who simply wanted nothing but model students and considered a programme-breaking nobody as a disturbance. Perhaps they would have been more successful as politicians or military commanders. (Some of them did, in fact, become such later on.)

I carried out the requirements of the upper school more satisfactorily, because they simply got rid of unsuitable hangers-on, or, better still, did not accept anyone who failed in his entrance examination. But if a pupil had been with them for three years, is it not a real crime to let him down eighteen months before his matriculation, without getting more intimate with him or his parents, investigating the causes of his failure and giving him some well-meant advice? What use are all the educational reforms, the most beautiful and most well-equipped school buildings, if the spirit of Pestalozzi is missing; if the student finds this to be nothing but an elderly, sentimental fairy, who bestows upon the reverend professors chaplets of laurels to crown their dissertations? The relationship between teachers and scholars seems to me, according to my own experience, to be the outcome of accident, quite impersonal and without any feeling of affection. I believe that nothing but a warm sympathy on the part of the teachers would finally silence these troubles and complaints against the school.

I will conclude this answer to your questionnaire with the following résumé: I suffered most at school from the fact that I was not regarded as a human being and was despised as a pupil.

H. S.

(*i*) JUDGED AND CONDEMNED (m. aged 34)

The experience of my childhood which has led me to write this report lays the blame, or rather the neglect, upon the shoulders of my teachers. It was connected with the sexual enlightenment of children, about which there is so much written at the present time, which leads to so much discussion and about which there is so little actually done. The difficulties are great, but the fear is still greater to give this too early and so to work some injury.

I lived in a large industrial centre in the neighbourhood of Zurich during my school-life. In the sixth year of it I made a very unfavourable statement about one of my fellow-pupils, which accused him of a sexual offence that at his age would have been quite impossible for him. But who does not know the secret ways of those years of boyhood, when one begins to hear more than is good for one! It was certain that I was neither bad nor depraved, and what I had said was but hearsay. I cannot have had the least idea what it meant and cannot have had any notion of the far-reaching effect of my words, nor their smutty significance. Is it possible for a boy of twelve, in any case, to think more smuttily than a grown-up person? Many teachers should give this a little more attention in a case similar to that of my own.

Still the punishment to which I was condemned was not to be avoided. It was terrible and I was absolutely annihilated. As an outcast, and a low fellow with his ears boxed, and utterly condemned, I was dismissed from the school-room, humiliated and an object of scorn, long before the others.

To-day, after many goings astray, this experience has lost a good deal of its acuteness. But how, indeed, would I have behaved in such a case had I been the teacher? If something of this sort had happened in my class-room would I have been able to treat it as a disposition of providence, and have made use of it instructively rather than punishing the offender?

How much longer it was after that time before I heard anything serious upon the matter of sexuality? That did not occur until shortly before my Confirmation. I was an apprentice in a little village in Sihltal as a mechanic. There, one day, our pastor came into the class-room. He had already given a course of lectures in the Zurich University, although he was still very young. When he came in he said: "Now, my dear fellows, to-day we will discuss a very serious subject. But anyone that laughs will get a box on the ears before I throw him out." That was clear enough and spoke volumes, but no one did laugh. He then sat down in front of us, looked at us with his kind and yet imperious eyes, and then at last we heard the truth. He spoke to us honestly and yet in a wonderfully reticent way. Was he really our pastor whom one ought to regard with a shy respect because he could see through us so penetratingly? No, he was a dear, kind-hearted human brother, ready to be a true, honourable guide to us. He has remained my ideal to the present. Where can one find this kind of excellent manhood among the educators of boyhood? If only there were more like him, then our topsy-turvy educational system would lose its hardness.

H. F.

(*j*) I LEARN THE TRUTH FIRST AT THE AGE OF 23
(m. aged 28)

To-day we are living in an age which is in many ways different from the past. Psychologists, doctors, writers and others have felt it their duty to write with their hearts' blood to express vehemently the truth, and not to consider the opinion of the world. We may regard all these as the fathers and teachers of humanity. How long will it be before the other fathers and teachers will be fully conscious of their office? I write "fathers and teachers" intentionally, because I wish to stress the serious subject of the co-operation that should take place in the education of the child.

But I will try to make what I mean quite clear. In my own early childhood I learned from a shameless older companion to discover my strong instinctual powers not in the best sense but from the other side and to abuse them. Instinct was power, because it spurred me on to pleasant actions with the formal sanction of the world and my environment, increased my ability and allowed me to breathe freely. Then suddenly instincts became weaknesses, which I was obliged to hide under the forbidden cloak of lies, and which hindered my capacity for work. They provided me with doubts, and thoughts that constantly oppressed me. Instincts now became foolishness that was hard to understand, which hindered me, and yet provided me with an opportunity of having happy, lively hours together with my friends; they now became a perpetual burden, which turned the radiant, carefree child into a gloomy, phantasy-laden dreamer.

Yes, and who was it who taught me to stoop in this way? Who taught me to think in this shamefaced way, covered with blushes, about atonement, unchastity and crime? My parents, the teacher, the pastor? Oh no, they would not have had sufficient courage! They would have thought their children were pure; their pupils, their Confirmation candidates, were the exception. Did my school-fellows see to it that my phantasies should be diverted into new paths, hinder my pleasure in my work and my happy participation in instruction; enlighten me? Oh no, most of these half-grown-up youths, even when they are twenty, still do not know where babies come from. I was crippled with unspeakable fear in case my shame might be discovered; terrified, lashed with a thousand whips. I would look into the mirror a thousand times with troubled eyes to see if I should see there any betrayal of my symptoms to the knowledge of all. My fear also prevented me asking for help. The perpetual attempt to gain some roundabout explanation failed to succeed because of the spectre of Guilt. I did not consider myself worthy of the love which was bestowed upon me by my parents and teachers.

This bogy persecuted me for a long time. In every corner, in the tiniest crevice, I saw my own distorted image. In my twenty-third year, I now say and write, I decided upon the following plan of gaining enlightenment and turned to a dear friend. He gave me books written by brothers of humanity with their hearts' blood. The bowed sapling once again stood upright. Once more everything in the world took on a glorious light; I felt I could shake off my old nausea: I breathed freely once again and could say "Yes" to life.

Something remained, however: my grudge against the fact that the most holy knowledge was made a jest of by parents and the schools, and that, contrarily, schools and parents prevented one from learning anything about the most glorious beauties of life.

P. G.

(k) HANDS UPON THE TABLE (m. aged 30)

... Another unpleasant recollection has continued to have an effect upon me after many years. As it often happens in the case of adolescent boys, we used to indulge in self-abuse during these last years at school without most of us knowing what we were doing. Then with sexual enlightenment it became a shameful thing. The thing came out thus; and a great investigation was set on foot—a judicial enquiry—finally with one of the parents before the president of the school council, who first talked over the occurrence with the father or mother without the pupil being present, then well-meaning words on the part of the venerable gentleman and the parents, and at last the promise never to do anything of this kind again, and a bad report into the bargain. In consequence of this happening the classes would be constantly interrupted later with something of this sort: "What are you doing there with each other?" or "Hands on the table!" and bad work always gained some such comment as, "Yes, what else can one expect!" I suffered terribly from this sort of thing and its results as well as others. Naturally we knew well enough that a great injustice had been done us, although the great burning question remained unanswered, and all our knowledge of sexual affairs was limited to what one heard in the streets.

Two, three or more of us would often talk it over and decide to ask our teacher for some explanation. But the hostile attitude of most of them, as well as that of the pastor also, robbed us of the necessary courage. Years later even I refrained from reading an excellent book upon this subject because I feared I might find some reproach in it concerning the habit. I knew from talking to others that I was not the only sufferer. To-day I know that the best opportunity for explanation had been allowed to pass by on the part of both teachers and parents. It was more culpable of the teachers, because only a very few of the parents have more than a superficial knowledge of these matters, especially parents belonging to the middle and working classes. Besides, as is usually the case, this instinctual behaviour concerned the greater number of boys in the class, and therefore enlightenment would have been more in place had it come from our own teacher. However, each of us had to get over the difficulty as best he could and in every case it did not by any means turn out particularly favourably.

No one will deny that influences and complexes of this kind which we have just described have a very far-reaching effect and are most highly dangerous for young people. I would also like to add that more than once we heard of a flight into a foreign country or a suicide spoken of in connection with this affair.

R. F.

(*l*) ONE FROZE IN CLASS (m.)

"As we forgive them that trespass against us!" These words from the Lord's Prayer must be also applicable to those who made our intellectual development more difficult during our childhood and adolescence. Therefore the questionnaire of the *Schweizer-Spiegel* ought not to be a depository for unabreacted emotions. Yet for the sake of those who still make their pilgrimage to school to-day and to-morrow, I would like to express a few thoughts on this subject.

The boys' school which I am about to mention is one of the oldest and most highly esteemed. It has directed the life's path for many who later on became great lights in the scientific world. So I will say nothing about any deficiencies in intellectual education to be found there, but begin at a different point.

Two of my teachers there have since committed suicide, both quite young men, bachelors. One, who was a doctor of philosophy, taught us religion. The other, with a degree in biology and zoology, took our class in Nature Study. Two others, also bachelors, who were exceptionally gifted teachers, and specialised in classical languages, developed increasingly into eccentrics who shunned their fellow-men, began to suffer early in life from the lack of voluntary contacts with the world and life, as well as with their colleagues. Both had a troublesome old age.

Psychologists of the present day would have reckoned both our French tutors as belonging to the introvert type. One of them failed to find the right solution of his difficulties in the path of matrimony; the other hid his troubles by a lack of intellectual *rapport* between teacher and pupil. As a native of French Switzerland he never got on very well with the boys and took to the only possible adaptation that was dictated by necessity, that of a chilly, semi-academic attitude which at the same time was really a regression.

I cannot proceed further upon that line. If so, this would become an answer to the question, *From what did our teachers suffer?* But naturally this whole atmosphere was not without its influence upon us. It is clear that the setting free of the intellectual life from the collective mentality, the dehumanising influence of this one-sided development of the intellect to the destruction of the emotions, under the mental direction of sarcasm which turned also into an ironical attitude towards oneself, a cold enjoyment of criticism that was practised upon everybody and everything, may not have been apparent to us boys at the time. But it had its effect nevertheless. It was not accidental, therefore, that once we class-mates had matriculated we saw no more of one another. The school trained us as fully equipped individualists.

We may thus state the causes of the misery from which we suffered. From top to bottom there was no affection. The two religion lessons which we had during the week, which were given to three of our eight classes, were quite feeble attempts to bring the spirit of Christ into a proper relationship with proud humanity. It was not to be achieved, however, and because the spirit of love was absent entirely, everyone in that school *froze*, as much in the teacher's common-room as in our class-rooms. The teachers knew one another too little, and did not feel themselves called upon to get to know us either. They wished for our intellectual ability only and we gave this to them. They were the guides neither of our development in deep personal matters nor of our more superficial interests. It is therefore clear that the human being needs love. Physical training which is to lead to self-control must be brought about with pleasure and be maintained with emotions. That which was in use there, carried out with intellectually considered exercises for the use of apparatus and military drill, was nothing but the logical sequence of the whole system.

A. M.

(*m*) TOO MANY KNOWLEDGE-MERCHANTS AND NOT ENOUGH HUMAN BEINGS (m. aged 50)

What I suffered from most at school was the lack of affection in the relationship between teachers and pupils. I still feel the lack of this sunshine after the lapse of some forty years, and it makes my subsequent orientation to life more difficult. I was aware of an absolute unapproachableness on the part of my teachers in the elementary school, their spirit of oppression seldom disappeared entirely. I can still remember their commands: "Sit still! Pay attention! Write! Read! Draw! Bend! Jump!" etc.

These commands, nevertheless, brought us knowledge and we remained tolerably healthy. Yet one is aware to-day that child-life cannot be given its full rights by these means. Knowledge, strength and ability do not in any way fulfil the fundamental aims of life, or mankind would be put to shame by a motor-car, since these machines are far better equipped both for speed and endurance. The true goal of life should be co-operation, community feeling, harmony, kindness, mental life. I believe that this frequently stressed fundamental aim of life was never very intimately connected with my school experiences, and that in my school-days far too little attention was given to it altogether. In this fact probably lies one cause of the prevalent lack of co-operation and the reproach that we hear upon all sides, that of late, in spite of enormously increased education, we find a superabundance of the all-against-all spirit, rather than one which tends to harmonious unity.

Our relationship with our teachers was one of cold,

neutral politeness. In my elementary school, for instance, I observed among my teachers a godlike attitude, let us say, in a stale, heathenish sense, which was not to be compared with any kind of human behaviour I had known before. At times I suffered considerable anxiety that I might be observed by them whilst carrying out certain lowly bodily needs, and became ashamed about them. When we were not in school, we practically disappeared entirely from our teachers and only began to play if we felt sure of being well out of sight. These things strike me to-day as being unnatural and often are quite in opposition to the essential aim of education as well as that of existence. The teachers stood for us as men with whom we discussed various methods of arithmetic, geometry, mountain ranges, history dates and suchlike; never, however, vivid human experience. They were, as far as we were concerned, *too much knowledge-merchants* and *too little fellow human beings and comrades.* To-day these things seem to have improved; yet a certain amount of estrangement to life and a trend that is contrary to the teaching of Pestalozzi still seem to keep their grip upon the schools, nevertheless.

According to my opinion this arises from the method of education itself. A too narrow standard of individual treatment, the systematic ruling of a programme of opinions and standpoints, a total lack of familiar habits, are and continue to be its main characteristics. According to Pestalozzi, the home (not the school) is the original model for all true, natural education of human beings. One thinks of Pestalozzi briefly as the founder of schools and a friend of schools; anyone who pays attention to him without prejudice will find in him, in a certain sense, the most confirmed and well-equipped opponent of the schools, who demonstrates the limitations and the secondary significance of these institutions. We know that he was opposed to all false education, to over-strict school government, to a too great devotion to subjects in themselves, as he was to an attempt to take life by storm; also that he himself suffered shipwreck on the rock of these same tendencies, and that he could not endure the profession of teacher as it then was. These tendencies of his, which some consider to be signs of his weakness, are, in point of fact, the evidence of his greatness, and arise from his personal characteristics that have always attracted serious, progressive men; bound them to him, warmed and educated them. That which Pestalozzi sought and looked for had nothing to do with separate spheres of life, but with humanity as a whole. He had and gave publicity to an aim in life that should transcend all other traditions, organisations, conditions and peoples; we find him possessed of a method of dealing with all things deeply and comprehensively, worked out from the point of view of human nature, and he considered the school as a means, subordinated through the time in which he lived, to his end, but never as the most fundamental and most perfect means of education in itself.

Th. B.

(*n*) SEXUAL ENLIGHTENMENT (m.)

Before me lie a packet of letters, pages from a diary and two Pestalozzi school calendars, many of them pasted over with strips of black paper and sealed with that touchingly refined care which only children make use of, if they regard some experience of childhood as brought to a close, and wish to guard it jealously from the eyes of grown-up people, so that they should never hear it mentioned again. One learns later that such secret packets seldom lie undisturbed and one is inclined from time to time to attempt to break the seal. We remember our experiences at first most vividly and with painful clearness. But later on we feel how far our life has advanced and that it is now time to abandon the past. We have outgrown it without being aware of the process. New problems have come into our lives and claim our thoughts and wishes, farther and farther retreat the troubles of our youth and soon seem to have lost all their significance. The affairs of our daily life and our environment compel us to adopt a technique for our lives cut according to the general pattern, and from the youth who tries to construct his own world in the strength of *his own pure heart*, in passionate protest against the rest of humanity, is developed the citizen who remains unmoved as long as he is not shaken out of his own peaceful avocations and regards everything with suspicion and prejudice that is foreign to his own narrow environment. At best he will have developed a broad mind through his many experiences, by means of which he will excuse and understand everything if he would ever find it necessary to formulate an opinion.

The first and generally also the only deep conflict with the world takes place when the growing child finds his physical strength beginning to take visible form which for the first time makes life an experience for him; that is indeed rewarding. The adult citizen, as long as he is not professionally or otherwise connected with the young boy, considers his recollections of this time collectively under the category of the *Sturm und Drang* period. He does not bother any longer about things which no more concern him. He will ridicule the past with a certain amount of deprecation, realising that knowledge which he gained later through experience finally helped him to overcome his troubles, so that he now stands firmer upon his feet than ever before. The consequences of his troubles have provided him, now they are overcome and forgotten, with a more beautiful present, even should it be in some ways limited by certain hard conditions. He never considers giving himself any higher aim in life, such as that of making his experiences of use to others. Anything which is no longer a direct personal problem for himself does not count. Why should others have an easier time than he had? One can see how well he got on!

In the meantime, in the same schools, which he formerly attended, in the same forms, under the same conditions and with undiminished vehemence, the same silent and secret tragedies are played out, which the adults never discuss because of their equally silent and fatal conspiracy. It would seem that such an especially interesting topic might demand the interest of the public.

One can formulate the problems of puberty simply enough under the following heading: *the relation of sexuality to the environment*. It is an instinct which later on more or less dominates life, because of the demands of this instinct. It overcomes young people and afflicts them when they do not know what to do about it! The fundamental experience of youth, especially for those of the male sex, is the first experience of this instinct in action. The child in him is now a thing of the past. For the first time this person feels, on the one hand, how much he resembles the rest of mankind, and yet at the same time how completely alone he stands. The essential changes that take place in his body, and which are experienced in a passive way without his understanding them, disturb, oppress and confuse the child. Images long buried in his unconscious mind arise, providing anxiety and terror; questions, sinister and secret, present themselves, but are suppressed by feelings of guilt and repressed so that they poison the child's sleep. Observations made concerning his own body and from the realm of the human and animal worlds take on a new significance without helping him to solve this great riddle. The whole world that was formerly clear to him becomes hard and dark and the child's laugh is changed to a contemplative reserve.

He has comrades. He feels drawn to them as he never was before and yet at the same time repelled by them; they seem to know something and yet give away nothing but distorted and ridiculous fragments which have no deep significance. But Nature continues her course, follows her goal remorselessly and often brings human beings to destruction in this way, since she has not yet considered it necessary to adjust herself to the requirements of the standards of life in civilised countries. She completes mankind from her point of view without giving him the means or showing him ways in which he can make use of her work.

The experienced, mature and in some ways cool passions of adults cannot reckon from their superior distance with the conflagration which is destroying the soul and body of the developing child. Never again in life will such an all-embracing situation be encountered, and never again will the person suffer from such a vehement breaking-through of the powers of nature. How magnificently might it be turned to advantage if it could be directed into the right channels, to the further development of the young body and be made use of for maturing the storm-tossed young mind!

But frequently the best, most intelligent and most wide-awake go off in another direction, unless a particularly efficient guardian angel takes up a position beside them who will protect them from their own love of exploration and their comrades, who are too ready only to pass on their knowledge to another boy in order to lessen their own guilt and their feeling of isolation. Like a plague, the habit spreads from child to child, and once it has taken root it is often struggled against for many years with an unhealthy conflict which drains off the best abilities and causes the child to become so one-sided that all the other aspects of life can gain nothing but a very subordinate significance. The intellectual development ceases for the time being completely, all the powers of earth and heaven seem to enter into alliance to play a sinister game with this uprooted soul, that is not only of great influence for subsequent life, but also bears weight in the formation of a philosophy and finally brings many a good character to nought.

The parents, who must be observers of these struggles if they are not entirely deficient of all good feelings, usually remain indifferent. Left to themselves they will make no move to take part in the conflict, so that their position need be shifted from that of the looker-on and comfort. They are often afraid to go back to a problem which they have now passed, without having been able to solve it. It may be that they wish to protect their children from a falsely understood freedom which, in their own youth, they painfully had to go without. In any case, however, because of one thing or another, an enormous cleft arises between them, which separates one generation from another. And the nearer related one person is to another the more certain it will be that he will be neglected, and his problems be regarded as negligible.

The child passes the greater part of his life in the school. This institution has not only taken up the duty of providing him with general information that shows itself to be of more or less doubtful significance, but it has also taken over the training and guidance of the child in so far as his own home does not carry out its duty in this respect. In the school we find the various forces which govern human behaviour have been set in conflict with one another. The sexual instinct may be considered as one of these, because as a rule its effects become manifest before school-days are ended. Therefore the school should also include this question of enlightenment in its round of duties, and particularly in connection with the conflicts which arise through onanism, in order to deal with them satisfactorily. It should prepare the child beforehand, and not leave him without protection before this terror, exactly where it should get in the first throw of most necessary explanation. Although it may renounce this responsibility, which could be accepted by giving some general explanation, this does not mean that it remains entirely neutral or that it refuses to take any interest in it. It should certainly belong to the obvious duties of the teachers to win the confidence of the children committed to their charge; neither should they consider this difficult because of their function as teacher. The school-master, because of the training he has undergone, as well as because of his natural tendencies, should have sufficient tact, talent for co-operation, as well as a capacity to adjust himself to their needs and sympathy to make it quite simple for him to discover just the right way to handle each case. In that way children could be freed from their unhealthy entanglement, their guilt could be traced back to its real source and the feeling of inferiority destroyed. It is not the physical consequences that are to be feared in the first place as much as the mental depression, which will, before long, drag everything else down under their weight of oppression. One does not wish to add to the children's feeling of guilt but to furnish them with a reverence for the wonderful provisions of Nature, by means of which information they may gain self-confidence and think of their bodies as temples over which they possess no right of prostitution. This, then, being the true state of affairs, each child should know some person who will receive his confession and promise him new courage to overcome his trouble.

At the present time, however, the second party in this honourable alliance of powers, the home and the school, whose duty it should be to stand by the child but who deny their privilege, is certainly by far the most guilty factor. It has the most simple means of doing so through its representatives, the teachers, and thus of taking part in the adolescent conflict by means of explanations, providing adequate enlightenment and bringing this period of life into relation with the rest of development, so helping to ease the boy's burden. But it takes advantage of none of these means. It seems quite incapable of doing so. The average teacher is neither a friend nor a helper to the child, seldom even his adviser. He seems as callous about the matter as the schools; he allows the best opportunities to slip through his fingers and limits his dealings with the problem, although quite without any beneficial effect, to the giving of bad reports, punishments, etc., which concern nothing but the external manifestations of the pupils. He becomes annoyed at their lack of concentration and over the increasing distance between himself and them. Meanwhile the child, terrified of the night and each fresh time he has to go to bed, struggles with the Pythagorean law and with his study of algebra. The child's life is now lived upon a different plane. Secret tragedies full of indulged passion wax and wane; and in total silence, cut off from any wisdom the school might supply, scarcely realised by any third person, he carries on his guarded, hidden life.

My reproach against the schools is that they take no part in this conflict, that they look on at the needs of many of their best pupils, unwilling to do anything to help, and in spite of knowing better, co-operate in the conventional silence of all institutions of the universe, in that they undertake in no way the duty of trying to break down the barriers that surround the child in his darkest hours, and to bridge over the chasm that separates him from his fellow human beings! As long as they withhold their attention and goodwill from this most burning of all problems of childhood, which needs them so urgently, I shall maintain my reproach.

W. G.

(*o*) THE AUTOMATIC OFFICIAL (m.)

Friendship with a teacher seems to me something of a strange idea, and I have a feeling more than accurate knowledge that personal dealings with them are things of the past; instruction has become entirely systematic. Anyone who carries out instructions gets on all right, but those who do not keep step are "fired" after a year's probation when they are, in fact, too young then to be sent away because of their own views and educational enthusiasm.

A fresh teacher for each lesson and each subject, practically all of them an automatic State official who receives his wages from time to time, who carries out his daily work with his pupils without exerting himself too much, giving more consideration to his own ease than helping the backward ones to catch up with the rest.

This is where I lost my own foothold; no serious advice was given to me, never an earnest word that had any real meaning, no encouragement. The lack of co-operation of my teacher, who saw my destiny approaching, frightened me—a dull indifference overcame me, and I surrendered myself to fate. I was weak in French, the deciding subject, and I was considered actually as stupid. They did not know anything about my willingness to work, which, had it been awakened, would have surely developed. After a bitter year at school I was "fired" from this institution. Who knows the mockery that an *outcast* has to suffer? Who can grasp the wrongs also which are suffered, and the horror for such an institution which has turned one out, instead of trying to reinstate one. I appeared to myself at that time as a capable person with broken self-confidence, hindered from progress and lost.

I will not blame the teachers whom I had then, because it was through this occurrence that my life turned out all for the best and I never regretted it later. But my standpoint is that the mistake must be made known. All of them decidedly lacked something of the spirit of the country school-master. It would have been a good thing if the instruction could have been a little more personal and that they had not felt annoyed on account of the trouble and patience they had to expend on the weaker pupils.

P. S.

(*p*) LACK OF AFFECTION (m.)

I can answer your question briefly, very briefly, and say: "I suffered from the psychological superficiality of the teachers. They were all too little fathers to us, and had too little knowledge of human nature; there was too much teacher about them and not enough of the educator."

Let me give three examples of what I mean. Like all little six- or seven-year-old fellows, I went to school for the first time full of reverence and confidence. I regarded the teacher with respect. He seemed to me even more important than my father, or my uncle, or various other authorities. For this reason I regarded him in the same light as I did these others. The boy who sat next to me, the son of a factory owner, by name Manfred K., took the matter in a lighter vein. For him the teacher was merely a man who was paid to carry out a certain job. In consequence of this Manfred was a better scholar than I. He was able to grasp things more easily and to retain them better than I. While he, for example, did an exercise in half an hour, I would work at it for two hours. Then my patience would give out and I would neglect everything.

Other days I would naturally be afraid that my teacher might look at my work with special attention. When that happened, my teacher scolded me and held up Manfred as a model (he cannot have had the least idea what a poor estimation he had of him) and I was obliged to stay in after school and do my exercise again. I sat on in school whilst my comrades went home in the best of spirits. After I had already three hours of lessons behind me I still had to concentrate upon this same exercise which had already given me nausea the day before.

I carried out this command with the greatest repugnance. At last! I thought, and went up to the desk where the school-master still sat and wrote. I showed him my exercise-book and secretly hoped for a few kind words, perhaps by way of reconciliation. But my teacher had seen that I had already put the rest of my things in my satchel and wanted me to increase my patience. The writing was still not good enough. "Here and there the letters are not well made; go and look how these letters are made in printed books!" Then I was overcome with uncontrollable anger. "Just to make me take everything out again!" I said to myself.

I once had a teacher who had the custom of calling his pupils who belonged to the better families by their Christian names, whilst he called the rest by their surnames. This was certainly not done with any unkind motive on the part of the teacher, yet it occasioned no little embitterment amongst the last-named group of pupils.

We felt ourselves humiliated. For me especially, because I was very sensitive upon this point, it was a reason for increasing my suspicion.

Here is another memory which left behind an equally deep and painful influence upon my childish heart.

Memory-drawing and drawing from a model were my favourite subjects and I always had good reports for them. Another pupil whose name followed mine in the alphabet was also good at drawing, and was competing with me in the last drawing lesson for the class report classification which would depend upon the marks we should receive for the drawings to be completed that day. For this he needed to get a *good* and I a *very good*. When a few days later we received our reports, it was turned exactly the other way about, I had *good* and he *very good*. This was an obvious mistake and consequently I went to the teacher about it.

"Of course," said he, "that is certainly my mistake, but in spite of that I cannot give you a new report on account of such a trifle!"

Cast down and embittered I went home. "That was that—on account of such a trifle!" I thought and wept bitterly.

That was the last time that I cried—later I bit my lips.

During my last year at school I suffered much from our then Director, who had political aspirations. This man used to tyrannise not only over the pupils, but the teachers also. An example: At the end of a drawing lesson a comrade of mine was kind enough to take my water-colour things to clean, because I was very busy. He met with an accident while doing this because some of the green paint ran out upon the floor. He did not notice what he had done and the drops remained there.

That afternoon the above-mentioned Director took a class in this same room, noticed the spots and came into our class.

"Who has spilt green paint on the floor?"

No one answered. The Director became irritable.

"Who has been using green paint?"

Several held up their hands; but I considered that

the matter had nothing to do with me and held my tongue.

My friend, who had cleared up my paint-box, was also silent. Then somebody else told the Director that I had been working with green paint. Immediately all the Director's anger was loosed upon me. I glanced at my friend and saw that he had turned pale.

"Confess that it was you!" thundered the Director.

"No!" I said, between clenched teeth. I got a box on the ears. The Director repeated his question and also the box on the ears when I did not answer. At that moment I could have killed him, I hated him so much. And yet it would have only required a more gentle enquiry on the part of the Director for me to have given him a quiet explanation.

A. O.

CHAPTER VIII

COMRADESHIP

(*a*) I WANT TO SIT NEXT TO FRITZ (f. aged 36)

I HAD no fear of school. I went there gladly enough. But that was already laughed out of me on my first day. I took that very hard and suffered on account of it quite considerably.

I had a rather shy nature. My mother sent me to school on that first day with Fritz from next door, who was the same age as I. He was a wide-awake, bright boy, and was not afraid to speak to anybody. My mother told him to be my sponsor. I then took Fritz by the hand and we trotted off happily.

We lived in a village in Oberland at that time. At the school where we had to go there was a teacher who was rather elderly. She divided her class into two parts. She put the boys in a row along the wall and the girls sat in front of the window. A wide pathway separated the two sexes. I was taken away from Fritz. The teacher herself had separated our little hands, which had been clasped so tightly. I began to cry then. The teacher had to ask me for a long time, before I finally managed to sob out: "I want to sit next to Fritz!"

All the children laughed aloud and the teacher too. But afterwards she let me sit right in the middle among the boys, beside my playmate. I was comforted. But I dared not look up because I still felt frightened of the laughing faces of the others. Fritz helped me through faithfully. He put my few school things in order under the form, wiped my slate clean and quickly wrote me a line of i's, because I worked very slowly. After some time I became troubled with a physical need. But I dared not say anything. Fritz noticed it. He went up to the desk at once and told the teacher quietly. She scolded mockingly: "Yes, but Annie must ask herself if she wants to go outside. Otherwise she will have to wait."

I did not dare to ask now, naturally, because I noticed how they were all looking at me, smiling and giggling. I suffered a little while longer, and then suddenly it ran damp and warm down my little sock on to the floor. Fritz turned red. But he whispered quickly: "It doesn't matter, Annie; we will wipe it up after school." At last it was mid-day. I remained sitting in my place until all the others had gone. Fritz made a great business of packing up his and my school things. Finally the teacher went too. We were alone. Quickly we wiped up the wet patch with the blackboard cloth as well as we could. But soon afterwards the girl from the upper school came with her broom to sweep the class-room. She immediately saw what had happened. "Ugh!" she scolded. "She's done something on the floor—ugh! ugh!"

I began to cry once more. Fritz took me quickly by the hand and went home with me. "*Meiteler, Meiteler*," resounded after us from a window. But he took no notice.

When we got home my mother grumbled about the school teacher.

The next day I did not want to go to school again. I was so very terrified of being laughed at. But I was obliged to go. Fritz gave me some good advice. "You can go down to the lake and look for pretty little stones and make little pools in the sand. It will soon be mid-day then, and I will come and fetch you. I will say at school that you are ill. They will not know anything about it at home," he explained with the utmost certainty. I obeyed him. We did this for a few days, and then we were found out. I had to go to school again and was at once greeted with ridicule. Then I became obstinate, as the teacher expressed it.

That same spring my father was obliged to move. We went to a large town which was also in Oberland. When we arrived the pupils were having a long holiday while the school buildings were undergoing reconstruction. But then at last came the first day that I was so afraid of, and the many new faces. I went with my elder sister as far as the school-house. There were three rooms where the juniors were taught. My sister told me to wait before one of these doors until the teacher should come. She herself had to go one floor higher. I waited with a fearful heart. From time to time school-children came up, looked me over and asked me questions. I gave them no answer. Then a quite big girl came along and said: "You mustn't wait here. In there is a cross teacher. Go outside that door. That is a very nice one."

I went to wait at the other door. I now felt rather more cheerful. It was going to be a *dear teacher* who would come soon! All at once she came, and spoke so kindly and took my hand. Then everything seemed quite easy and happy once more. In my lessons I was much more backward than the others. The teacher, however, said that it did not matter; I should soon catch up. She had a great deal of patience with me, and was never angry and nobody laughed at me. Everything went so well. Already in my second year I brought home a good report.

In my third year I went on to a school-master. He was a cheerful soul. He gave us a lot of fun and often went for excursions with us. In his class I was most responsive and continued to be a good pupil. In my fourth school-year there was also a man teacher. He liked the girls very much who wore pretty hair-ribbons. He would constantly pull at them and joke about them. I wore my hair in a tight plait, and because I always lost my hair-ribbons, my mother tied it with a shoe-lace. That used to stay on well. Once when I was bending my head down, the teacher held up my plait and said: "But this isn't a hair-ribbon; it's a shoe-lace!"

The whole class laughed at his joke. But I did badly with my lessons from that very day of this speech, and was such a bad scholar that by the spring my parents were doubtful about sending me on to the secondary school as they had planned.

In this secondary school, where I went a year afterwards, the boys and girls were separated. That did not suit me because I always did better when I was with boys. Also there were only school-mistresses there. I had to learn a good many new subjects. The teacher was very reserved in the school. Everything gave evidence of the fact that it was a superior school. In the German class we always had to say to the teacher before we asked her for anything. "Please, Fräulein, would you be so kind?"

I could never get this sentence out quickly enough and was often scolded on this account. For this reason I used to ask questions very seldom. The consequence was that I could not follow the lesson at all well and became confused and absent-minded. I found French very hard too. Our teacher practically always spoke French to us. I did not understand a word and gave very silly answers. That made the others laugh. Therefore I left off talking. Once she dictated a German sentence to us that we had to write down in French. We had to ask about the words that we did not know. I asked, therefore, and was told: "But, Anna, one does not ask about such an easy word." I then began to puzzle over this word and forgot to write any more. Out of my wondering came a drawing, a man with a long beard. That was my drawing speciality, as a matter of fact. Suddenly the teacher came up to me, seized my exercise-book and looked at me very, very angrily. That was the first moment I realised what I had drawn, or that I had drawn anything. I had not meant anything wrong by it. I was called into the teacher's room during the break. There lay my exercise-book open upon the table. All the teachers were present. The class teacher made a long speech of reproach. That was cheating, she said of me, and if I went on like that I should end up in a reformatory. I then had to apologise. I could not do it. I could not get the words out of my mouth. I was not in the least sorry about it. And what she had said about cheating and the reformatory I did not understand in the least. I therefore received a very bad mark of censure in my report.

However my mother comforted me. "We shall be moving away from here quite soon. Then you will be going to another school. There it will be much better for you than here. That was true. This was a secondary school near Berne. Boys and girls were taught together there again and we had young, enthusiastic teachers. I loved this school. I got over all my shyness. I was never laughed at. I became a good and later on one of the best scholars there. I was sorry when the two lovely years had passed. But the reformatory will continue to wait for me in vain.

H. F.

(b) EGOISM IS ENCOURAGED (m. aged 35)

Place: a town on the Rhine. A secondary school bearing the name of our most renowned Swiss pedagogue whose bust was exhibited in the hall, the pedagogue surrounded by a group of children! In my time this school was dominated by the most severe thrashing discipline that one can imagine. We had at least a dozen teachers who were well known for their own specialities, such as a hefty box on the ears, caning and other activities. Whoever happened to be the victim would look forward to it for several hours beforehand with a general feeling of tension. The gymnastic class especially, which should have given us physical strength and an opportunity for relaxation for our minds, was transformed by every gymnastic teacher into hours of idiotic military drill, full of discipline and violence. Besides these we had, however, a good number of very quiet and understanding teachers whose good offices were not made any easier by the first-mentioned power-merchants! The writer of this report did not have to suffer directly from this state of affairs, because he had very little to do with them. I can therefore write without prejudice, but practically all the pupils suffered visibly from these brutalities. Friends of mine who are teachers themselves tell me that such a thrashing discipline is no longer possible. However, for us pupils these frequent corporal punishments expressed a signal failure of the school's aims.

How did our school behave, considered in the light of the community spirit? The strong were set to compete against the weak (in the gymnastic classes), and the intelligent scholars against those who were not so highly gifted. It was never suggested that a talented pupil with a capacity for getting through his work more easily should help one who was weaker than himself during or after school-hours. Each of us worked consistently for his own good! Among the foremost scholars there was always a standing race for the title of *first* in the class. Consequently the rest came off badly. The egoistic component of our instincts naturally suffered no diminution through this method, but rather was increased and encouraged! The writer had to learn for the first time after his school-days were over to subordinate his own ego tendencies to the good of the community. The year immediately after we left school first brought us a group of several boys who were fond of work and activity, happy hours spent together happily in free and yet serious work by ourselves, as well as a vivid sense of enjoyment in which games and excursions played their part, and this took place under the guidance of a teacher from Basle.

H. R.

(c) HE WOULD BE A PREFECT NO MORE (m. aged 30)

It was a cold, clear winter's day in Schaffhausen in the year 1918. A lively conversation was taking place in the class-room, conversation that always goes on when young boys are together and the teacher is absent. In any case his representative was taking charge in his place. He was a prefect appointed to undertake the duty of seeing that silence and discipline were maintained. This is what the teacher said, but in actuality he had to carry out the work of a spy. However, the boys did not seem to take his task very seriously. When toboggan parties, skating and snowball fights are the subject of conversation it is easy enough to forget one's office and one's duty. And the prefect discussed the prospects with his comrades, making suggestions for the next half-holiday. Youthful happiness and enjoyment gleamed from the eyes of this group of young schoolfellows. In sparkling, overflowing excitement one of them threw his text-book into the air. Hurrah for winter time! Happy time!

Suddenly the teacher came into the room. Suddenly all was silent as the grave. The obedience of the dead appeared. Gone was the merry mood. The pupils sat bent over their work, apparently deeply absorbed in their study. The teacher said nothing, yet his sinister glance took in everything forebodingly. He cast a brief glance at the sheet of paper that lay on the table in front of the prefect. Even on this was no usual list of offenders.

The blank paper grinned at the teacher with the whiteness of innocence.

Roughly he dragged the recalcitrant prefect from his seat and pulled him to his desk. From its interior he took the cane, which he would frequently set dancing over the backs and hands of his scholars if he felt it necessary to give special emphasis to his views. He now started to beat the boy. Not in haste or rashly; no, like an automaton, with regularity and precision. Each blow was followed by a short pause to take breath. Each stroke left in its wake a red weal on the boy's slender hand which became obviously swollen. But the boy did not cry. He silently suppressed the pain. An uncertain feeling constricted his throat. In his mind, however, raged turmoil, resentment. His heart-beat raced, his pulse fluttered. The teacher feasted his eyes on the torment of his pupil with a cynical smile and he went on hitting him. Eight times he repeated the same play-acting, eight times the teacher's cane whistled down on this child's hand.

Raging anger seized the teacher on account of this defiant fellow, who would not utter a sound. The veins on his forehead stood out, forming thick cords; his face became as red as glowing coals. The two stood there together like champions in an arena, the man and the boy. Their eyes searched each other's hearts. No word was exchanged. An oppressive silence lay over the room. And from the wall the gently smiling Father Pestalozzi looked down upon the scene. The silence became uncanny. Would this cruel game never come to an end?

"You have done me a bitter injustice!" cried the boy's eyes. He gazed at the teacher with an infinitely terrified glance and with a look of revenge which gave expression to his helpless anger. The cynical smile vanished from the teacher's face. He turned pale and looked away.

It had only been for a few moments that these two had faced one another. But, nevertheless, it signified a turning-point in the boy's thoughts and feelings for life. He could not grasp the horror of the situation, that he had been punished so brutally because he would not give away to the teacher any of his comrades, with whom he lived day after day and with whom he spent his free time. From that time forward an insuperable rift stood between the teacher and himself. The teacher had lost the boy's confidence. For the boy he was no leader, no longer an adviser, but an enemy.

Many years have passed since this incident occurred. But the picture always remains before the boy's eyes, and shows him that might is greater than right. It continually accompanies him on his life's path. He was prefect no more. He had refused this part of Judas from the first.

E. L.

(d) FRIENDSHIPS WERE STRICTLY FORBIDDEN
(f. aged 22)

I have attended three different institutions that were conducted by nuns. Each of these institutions had different methods of education. I went to the School of St. Agnes, in X, as a little girl six years old. I went as a day pupil, but spent almost the whole day at school during my first year there. That troubled me the most; hour after hour intellect spoke with intellect and never one heart with another. There was no one there in whom one could confide all the little troubles and worries that school-life so frequently provides. The table and chair of the teacher were so high that she could only mount up to them herself with the help of a footstool. This presented me with a problem on my first day at school: "Doesn't it mean that as the table and chair of the teacher are so high we must understand that she is unapproachable to us?" Although I discovered later on that the height of her desk was necessary to keep good supervision over the length of that school-room, I continued to feel its remoteness.

The Head-teacher explained in our lessons on polite behaviour: "One must never show what one feels. One should always remain equally cheerful. One should keep what one suffers to oneself; it does not concern anyone else." According to this viewpoint school friendships were not regarded with favour. None of us school-children were allowed to make friends with a pupil belonging to another class; we were never allowed to talk in the breaks, we were only allowed to play and to learn. At mealtimes also conversation was strictly forbidden, as well as in the corridors and in the classrooms and bedrooms. In this way we lived side by side like the little wheels in some large piece of clockwork. From time to time, shy attempts at friendships, confidential conversations, were received by the teachers with chilly politeness and an attitude of reserve. Not to be understood, to be without a friend, without work that one enjoyed, and in addition this severe silence and harsh discipline were the sorrows of our first eight school-years.

According to the opinion of our Head-teacher I had then to be transplanted into fresh soil. My parents chose as my next school the Institute of T., near B. The period which I spent there as a boarder, of eighteen months, was a dreadful time for me. Think of it, over three hundred pupils and only one plan of education for all of them! The Head of the school was anxiously careful not *to win* the confidence of her pupils but *to compel it*. "I am your mother for the time being, therefore you must have confidence in me." Because of this we were not allowed to tell our parents if we were ill or if we were having any difficulties in school; if we did so our letters used to be confiscated.

The pupils were required to be distant with one another. Friendship was strictly forbidden; even a simple pressure of the hand was severely punished "as leading to sensuality." The teachers took no trouble to study the characters of their pupils, but would explain: "We are not to blame if they (the girls) do not express our ideal pupil. We train with this end in view, and regard one type as our ideal; the children must follow it." I could not follow it, neither could a large number of others, and for this reason suffered doubly. Although corporal punishment was not allowed, there were some brutal mistresses before whom we literally trembled. One of these, Sister M., used to make her long cane whistle over her desk or round our heads until we asked her pardon for something that we had not done. (Sometimes we had not the least suspicion what we were supposed to have done.) Suffering in body and mind I returned to my parents after one and a half years. Even my return home was made more difficult from the side of the teacher, and it was constantly put off. They tried to persuade me to come back for Easter—it was then March. "If not, you need not come back at all," the Head said as she bade me farewell. Neither did I return. At the beginning of October I became a pupil at the Villa R. in L. There we lived in quite another atmosphere, but we had almost too much freedom.

Here they had nothing against the making of friendships; in fact, they used to encourage them. When, for example, two of the pupils had had a little quarrel, they would say to them before the whole class, "Now kiss one another and make it up!" Also this method was supposed to be efficacious in the case of deep-rooted enmity, but it would often tend to increase the hatred still more. Many of the pupils were friendly with the teachers and they gave each other unlimited confidence. Here and there this would lead to difficulties between the pupils. If, however, a teacher saw that a fellow-pupil had a greater influence over a protégée than she had herself, she would explain that God required the sacrifice of this friendship. How many spiritual battles were occasioned by this means I cannot describe, although I often found myself in the position of the sacrificed friend.

M. D.

(*e*) THE BATTLE OF ALL AGAINST ALL (m. aged 30)

I was a student at the University and as such am not a very long way from my school-days, which were spent in Z. My general inclinations did not attract me to the University by any means, because my distaste for school began upon my first day and ended upon that when I celebrated my exit from the Gymnasium.

When your questionnaire was first published, I talked it over with my colleagues, who thought much as I did about schools, and we came to the conclusion that the reasons must have been the same for many of us.

But in spite of this we found it very difficult to throw any light on the matter, and I can only make a few suggestions in this article.

Many of the causes of the following facts must, however, be allowed to lapse because they come into existence rather differently and are not connected with the schools themselves as closely as they are related to a widespread feeling of unhappiness. For example, one says, "Yes, the seriousness of life begins with the first day of school, and the difference between our experiences there and our first care-free years of childhood that are passed in play is hard to adjust ourselves to." But then, why should the sorrow caused by the seriousness of life last as long as our education and leave off when we start our business life, when life becomes still more serious?

One also says that the child does not realise why he should learn this and that. Yet that does not play any part in the first year of school-life, because there is hardly any pupil in an elementary school who is so stupid as not to be able to grasp why he should have to learn to read, write and do arithmetic. One only begins to doubt later whether a knowledge of the government of ancient Carthage is of any particular use to us for our equipment in life.

Contrary to the opinion which is so often expressed, I think that the teacher should keep himself away from his pupils more. Many teachers, and especially those who mean well, give themselves a great deal of trouble to develop the individuality of their pupils by entering into a strongly personal relationship with them. By reason of his age, his education and his borrowed authority, he is practically always a stronger personality than the scholar. The pupil must feel this influence, even when exercised in the best sense, as domination. He is not accustomed to the teacher nor related to him, as to his parents, so that this new influence of a strange, strong personality must unconsciously disturb the pupil.

In any case I particularly remember that in our class at the Gymnasium the teachers who were the most popular made the material of their teaching interesting, because they obviously brought their personality into a certain relationship to their subject, but never into relationship with us. They occupied a neutral position regarding our individuality, and they behaved quite impersonally and like policemen when the effects of our individuality went too far, that is, if we injured the interests of the teachers or the school itself with our noise or any other foolishness.

COMRADESHIP

These teachers' classes were an absolute mental recreation. In them we unconsciously learned the rule that everyone is free as long as he does not unjustly molest the interests of others.

Usually a school-master will adhere to this hypothesis more closely than a school-mistress. From the first to the third class we had a woman teacher and afterwards a man. Although the first far exceeded the last in knowledge, I found the change to the reserved and dry teacher quite pleasant. It was like coming out of a drawing-room that was alternately too hot and draughty into a sensibly ventilated work-room.

I remember that now and again this school-mistress would read stories to us. It would sometimes happen that the class, for some reason, would be unruly, would not pay attention or made a noise. Then the teacher would suddenly shut up her book with a bang, go and sit at her desk, prop her chin on her hand and dictate arithmetic exercises to us in a hard, metallic voice. This typically feminine scene was even then terribly unpleasant to me. The whole class expressed their thoughts on the subject thus: "We have to do sums because she is angry."

We were angry too, and forgot that it should have been as follows: "Because we made a noise we have to do sums."

By means of a too keen investigation of the personality of the pupils, suspicions of partiality will naturally be aroused, and one knows how extremely sensitive children are to this kind of thing.

Playing thus with the minds of their pupils is a common failing of young teachers and, as we have already said, they are often quite well-meaning.

Old teachers have another fault that has nothing to do with that which we have already named but which is equally unpleasant.

They forget the true aim of education, and that of the unconscious mind. It becomes a sort of sham fight, where the teacher has to try to catch the pupil out in some mistake and the pupil's job is to escape. There are some teachers who actually go out hunting for mistakes; they put leading questions; they mark down inattentive scholars, in order to be able suddenly to hurl an unexpected question triumphantly at their heads. If the pupil is feeling strong this game becomes a joke. I myself have often pretended to be asleep while I was, however, following the lesson with the greatest attention. If the teacher shouted a question at me in the hope of having caught a victim, then I would whip out the right answer like a dagger, so that he would be obliged to draw back again disappointed.

If one was weak in any subject, however, one had the feeling every morning of being a hare who hears the approaching chase.

The teacher should give far more attention to the positive side of the pupil. The most important dynamic of school-life should be not the occasion when a pupil is caught, but that when he is successful in some way. Otherwise the pupil makes it his habit for life always to feel restless and discontented if nothing particular is happening.

A third cause of school troubles lies not in the teachers but in the pupils themselves. They would be able to get through life far more easily if there were more comradeship in the schools. Everyone who has done military service knows what that means. Unfortunately the tendency for it often develops but late, perhaps in the upper classes of the Gymnasium. Most of the pupils in the preparatory schools are terribly cruel to one another and cause one another more suffering than all the bad teachers in the world put together.

They are not far removed from wild beasts. A feeling

for the value of mutual help, for suffering or protecting the weak is a product of experience in individual persons and of civilisation in the race.

Here the parents will have to play their part. But the school must take a share also without being afraid to do so, to destroy the essential principle of convention. There are some teachers, naturally, who prefer it when their pupils devour one another instead of loosing their hostility upon their teachers.

The teachers, however, should be neither the enemies nor the overpowering friends of the students, but well-intentioned, true fellow-workers.

F. P.

(f) FRIENDS MUST BE SEPARATED (m.)

I remember the following incident from my school-days. A new teacher said practically these words to us at the opening of the school-year: "I do not know you. I do not know which of you get on well together. But if I should find that two especially good friends are sitting together, I shall notice it soon enough and separate them!"

Would it not be better for the schools to consider it their duty to encourage every friendship and to realise this tendency in the children, so that they may help to strengthen it?

(g) DIVIDE ET IMPERA (m. aged 30)

Although more than twenty years have passed since the commencement of my school-life, my recollections of my past school-days still include some that are very strong, very permanent, and at the same time some that are most unpleasant. In spite of the many happy hours which, naturally, school-life also brought me, the undertone remains grey. Even to-day the mere thought that I have escaped from this institution for ever makes me very happy, and I feel with the self-same intensity the truth of this rhyme, which we made at the end of our matriculation examination and carried around publicly:

> "Six and a half years of torment
> Gone for ever, to our content!"

My chief worry was the lack of companionship. I suffered the most from this, as did many of my school-mates. At the time itself, however, I did not realise it and I only became conscious of it many years later, after I had left school. My memories of our companionship that we did experience in common, nevertheless, remain among my most beautiful, and I believe them to be also some of the most important that I have carried away from the school. But I have neither the school itself nor the teacher to thank for them—it always seems to me almost a miracle that such friendship was possible in spite of school and teacher. It would seem that even in the lowest class the slightest attempt on the part of the pupils to make friends or to plan some project together is regarded as dangerous rebellion and is punished accordingly.

From time to time we would take part in some common quarrel or a little rough horse-play, which at that time was extremely popular among the scholars in some of the different parts of the town of Z. And why should the schools have tried to suppress it? It is, in point of fact, a trick that is easier and more familiar than that which is carried out later on during military service, to keep a class of some thirty pupils within bounds by making it impossible for them to get into contact with one another as individuals. But then each pupil is thrown back upon his own resources and remains the weaker for it.

In this way, too, each will be turned into an informer

against the others and become the betrayer of his comrades. The teacher, however, rewards him with a good report and increases the false ambition of the pupil. Characteristics that would be of the greatest value later on are not developed. It so happens that each pupil suspects a kind of enemy in the others and hides as such from them in order to be first. A typical example of this is the pupil who always keeps his excellently carried out homework hidden and only produces it at the very last moment in the class, so that his neighbour will not be able to copy it. These best scholars are always the worst comrades, and for this reason, nevertheless: good tools for the teachers to use against the other pupils. At the present time perhaps these conditions may have improved because the pupils have opportunities to take part in common athletic sports.

H. K.

CHAPTER IX

PROVISIONAL LIFE

(*a*) WITH ONE'S WATCH IN ONE'S HAND (m. aged 33)

"THE sparrow is the street-urchin among the birds." The teacher wrote this sentence on the blackboard. He would then repeat it. Afterwards the second half of the sentence was rubbed out.

"The sparrow is . . ."; then came the second half-sentence. In this way we used to prepare our school essays.

A stuffed sparrow stood on the teacher's desk.

I have written down the sentence word for word as the teacher gave it to us because I always had a good memory. For this reason I used to get a 6 for the essays.

And yet, in spite of this, I used not to grasp in the least the meaning of what I wrote. It never occurred to me that the sparrow in the class-room was the same bird as the friendly little fellow one saw in the street. The sparrow, that I had watched ever since I was two years old, was as familiar to me as father and mother and the railway. The sparrow had been deeply impressed upon my mind because my first experience of death was connected with it. I had once found one dead under a tree.

It was obvious to my mind that nothing that I had learned to know in my everyday life could be in any way connected with school. "The hare," about which something was written in our reading-books, was quite another animal from that which I once saw leaping about during a walk. "The rabbit" had nothing at all to do with a real rabbit that I knew so well. Here again, inconceivable as it may sound, I had no idea that the same animals could be meant. For me it was absolutely self-evident; one was real life, the other was the school. They were two entirely different worlds that had nothing to do with one another.

It never crossed my mind to criticise this attitude; I took it as a matter of course. But by degrees I began to suffer from the antithesis between these two worlds.

Principally at the Gymnasium. Compelled thereto by duty, I translated Caesar and Ovid, learned the names of the Roman Emperors and the generals by heart; tormented myself with chemical formulae that I did not understand and wrote essays upon such subjects as *Familiarity Breeds Contempt* and *The Significance of Fire for Mankind*.

But all these things had nothing really in common with real life and real interests. Real life consisted for me of only that small amount of free time we were allowed and in my phantasies of the future. From my second year at the Gymnasium I sat for nearly five and a half years with my watch in my hand and waited for the release from the enchantment; or this watch lay under the form, and I counted every single hour that brought my aim nearer: Freedom; I counted the hours as a criminal who had been condemned to seven years' penal servitude might count the hours of his sentence.

In course of time this waiting became so unbearable to me that I sank into a kind of lethargy and did not want to undertake any fresh activity. My whole mind and ideas were concentrated upon the future.

When at last the moment of deliverance approached we gave our joy full expression in all manner of verses, which we wrote up upon placards and drove about the town on a wagon.

"Herr Rektor, ich habe Dir die Hand gegeben;
Gottlob, der Abschied war fürs Leben!"

or aimed at one of our teachers:

> "Der Abschied tut bekanntlich weh,
> Doch öfters nur auf eine Seite.
> Du, Frosch, Du bleibst in Sumpf, juhee,
> Wir aber ziehen in die Weite!"

Then came the University, and with it a great disappointment. I had passed so many years in passivity that I was no longer able to begin to unpack this life now that at last it lay before me.

I now began an unfortunate period of self-deception; I shifted my aim a few years farther off until after the State examination. "Then," I said to myself, "real life will begin; then at last this make-believe existence will come to an end." But after the State examination it was not very much better than before. Somehow life always seemed to slip between my fingers. I had lost my direct contact with it through the long sitting still on the school form and it needed several more years of professional activity to restore it. It needed, before anything else, the experience of my first real strong love before the fetters were broken and I was able to break through that phase which had become a habit of mine since I was in the third class of the preparatory school.

To-day I think of my school-days as an endlessly long anxiety dream. I have the feeling that I was buried alive then.

This world of make-believe in which the schools have their existence seems to me to be their greatest evil. They rob people of their direct contact with life and weaken them to their very bones.

Dr. F. T.

(b) NO GREATER AIM THAN TO GROW TALL
(f. aged 30)

At last it came, my long-expected first day at school, and with it the beginning of a school-life which during the first two years especially brought me so much bitter disappointment and heartache.

At first it fulfilled my expectations to the utmost. Everything seemed interesting to me, beautiful and good; the sunny room with the brightly coloured pictures, the large numbers of school-fellows, and as the focus of our attention, the raised desk of the teacher himself. I gazed at this man with shy reverence, who had already played the part of a kind, omniscient overlord in my little heart for a long time. I now wanted nothing so much as to put my game with my dolls into reality and play at being the good, clever pupil.

I had plenty of opportunity for this. Writing upon a slate especially gave me a great deal of pleasure. With the utmost enthusiasm I scratched up and down with my slate-pencil, up and down. I soon noticed that it went a good deal better if I used my left hand. When the teacher came round to see what I was doing, I rejoiced in silence because I believed that I was making particularly beautiful strokes, since I began making them with my left hand. His ruler swished down on my fingers, and he scolded me in a sharp voice for writing with my left hand. The slate-pencil fell from my fingers and, with an astonishment that I have never felt again, I must have stared at the man, who then gave my hair a sharp pull.

The world fell from under my feet. The teacher had beaten me when I was being so industrious! Crying, I crept under the form, where, abandoned by all to defiance, I mourned over my vanished fairy world with loud, unending, resounding sobs, and felt heart-brokenly sorry for myself. This strange behaviour must have aroused in Mr. B. the impression that I was a most peculiar, self-willed child, who would have to be treated very strictly in the future.

He certainly did not forget his determination concerning his strict treatment of me in the time to come, so that I scarcely dared to answer a question for fear of getting some punishment. And yet the others got on so well. Trudy and Annie, for example, were never scolded. At last something happened that was especially bad, which was taken with much malicious joy to my father's office for his signature.

Another little occurrence robbed me of the remnants of my self-confidence.

One morning on my way to school I had the misfortune to trip over my umbrella and to fall flat on the newly mended road, whereby I got my hands and face covered with scratches. Freshly washed and with a new frock on, and a piece of sticking-plaster over my grazed nose, my mother started me off again half an hour later. I entered the class-room with a beating heart. The teacher greeted me with a laugh that cut me to the heart. To draw attention to my accident he put me on his desk and told the whole class to take a good look at a child who comes in late with a scratched nose. I did not mind so much about this mockery, and yet children can be terribly cruel.

From this day on I hated the school. With my rather delicate constitution I easily caught all the usual children's diseases. Formerly being ill, with the sickly invalid foods like rice and gruel, not to mention the endless lying in bed, was a real torture, but now I welcomed every indisposition with secret satisfaction because it made it possible for me to stay away from the hated school with all its troubles.

These constant breaks hindered my progress very much, naturally, so that I could only have kept up with the others with the greatest industry. But this was missing entirely from my character, and every suggestion, every punishment, however small, I encountered with endless tears. I became an artist in the use of tears and sobs.

An object of anger to the teacher and one of contempt with the children, I vegetated there for two years with no higher aim before my eyes than to grow up as quickly as possible so that I should be able to turn my back upon the school for ever.

If I look back upon that time it is now quite inexplicable that I did not have to stay on for another year under these circumstances. Probably Mr. B. would have found it a punishment for himself also to have to go on seeing this cry-baby amongst his pupils.

I gained very, very little knowledge in the passage of these two years, but a feeling of inferiority and suspicion had taken their place in my over-sensitive soul, that never allowed me to enjoy any happiness either in the school or out of it.

The new teacher, an elderly, dignified gentleman, now treated us all with the same consideration and, if it were necessary, with the same severity. The ruler came down, if possible, still more sharply on our fingers, but the punishments happened less frequently, and must have awakened in all of us the feeling that they had been really earned and had not been merely the result of persecution. They would be accepted as the necessary consequences of naughtiness of some kind. Mockery and malicious joy played no part in the new régime.

Once more I found my balance slowly, very slowly, in this atmosphere. My tears did not flow so quickly and because there only laziness, and not ignorance, was punished, I began of necessity to give up my passive behaviour during the lessons and to follow them with interest. I did not welcome illness as I had done in the past and stayed well practically the whole year.

Consequently I became stronger in body and mind, my work became better and by degrees I became a normal pupil, whom the school did not exactly love, although it no longer hated me. Even if I was deficient in happiness and terribly shy, I had a keen sense of justice and equality.

I loved the school because it gave me an opportunity to come in contact with fellow-scholars every day. I loved them because they enabled me to feel happy with others for the first time in my life; I loved them also for themselves; if only the necessity of learning had not come into the bargain!

There was no lack of school troubles here also, but as a rule I considered them to be due to my own altogether too arrogant character.

It was only some few years after I had left school that learning became a necessity and a joy to me.

H. S.

(c) INACTIVE DAY-DREAMING (f. aged 40)

From what did I suffer the most at school? I still know perfectly well what it was. Many years have passed and one easily and willingly forgets all the trifles which, although they are scarcely appreciable, are more capable of poisoning one's life than more important experiences.

To-day, to my own astonishment, I am no longer tormented by school dreams. I have no longer in my dreams to run and race through an icy winter landscape so as not to get to school too late as I used to only a few years ago. I no longer suffer during nights of anxiety from a nameless fear of trying to recall lessons which I had not learned properly. I no longer tremble on account of the beatings which did not descend upon me but upon my school-fellows most cruelly.

And yet.... How do I know whether the anxiety which still lashes me secretly even at the present is not a fruit of my school-days? Whether a certain indecision and inefficiency in my character, inactive day-dreaming, for instance, which sometimes keeps me for days and hours from getting to work successfully upon some definite and concentrated work, did not have its source in the school?

But what then? Must the school take over the responsibility for everything which happens afterwards? Even for the laziness of a grown-up person who cannot pull herself together? What are the causes of this? Perhaps in the

Boredom

This was the worst affliction from which I suffered.

Let us take this for an example: forty to fifty children sit imprisoned in an evil-smelling room! Someone is reading some set piece from a reading-book. The more advanced have already read it at home and know what it is about. The others, nevertheless, and by far the greater number, cannot read yet. Many of them stumble over every word and others come to a full-stop twice during each sentence and the teacher corrects them. That will go on perhaps for half an hour.

During this half-hour the child who can read sits there absolutely idle. It has nothing to think about, nothing to work at, has no occasion whatsoever to collect its thoughts unless the teacher suddenly flips it on the head with his cane and says: "You there, go on reading! What! you have not been paying attention again? . . . Stay in after school and write out fifty times: 'In school we must pay attention.'" But in spite of this the child does not pay attention, cannot do it, in point of fact, when there is nothing to pay attention to nor to grasp.

It is then, when the childish thoughts are unoccupied, when they, instead of being concentrated upon a certain point, become aimless and hopelessly scattered and rendered valueless, that their healthy vivacity and activity will be condemned by compulsion to an inner idleness, to laziness and to killing time.

Outside—the other side of the prison walls, let us say —life is calling; the rain is falling, the sun shines, birds sing, a neighbouring blacksmith is hammering, the forest is green and red. But inside, in the class-room, boredom reigns, and death.

But people will argue that under these circumstances the child learns self-control. Self-control? It learns rather a lack of it, to be without any aim in life and to be bored. Are there any worse people in the world than those who are bored?

The School Form

And apart from this what instrument of torture is more conducive to the oppression of intellectual movement than being confined to a school form? The feet scrape along the dusty floor and those who let them scrape get a slap! The little knees press against a hard wooden plank at every movement, on which lie also the books and the school satchel. Their backs are tortured through a too straight angle; in front of their bodies presses the desk, which is often so close that they are almost suffocated—the whole situation provides a terrible prison against which the small human beings revolt in helpless anger and from which they cannot escape except when they get off it and quickly stretch their cramped bodies in the narrow gangway between the forms which naturally brings down an imposition at once or at very least a stern reproof from the teacher.

No; these are not the most important dark places of our school-days which I describe here, no brutal, far-reaching difficulties of education! Only trifles. But still a child's life may be ruined. How easily can these years which were made for so much happy life and joyous experiences be made oppressive and a torment!

Only trifles—experts may condemn our schools on account of more important faults.

E. Th.

(d) SCHOOL UNDER A CLOUD (m. aged 25)

When I turned my back upon my school four years ago I did my best to shake off all the troubles and memories of that time which was now past at the same moment and with a sigh of relief entered upon my *real life*.

Although I was always one of the first pupils at school, and therefore had not actual cause for anxiety on account of the work that was required of me, I was still secretly filled with a sort of fear which I prefer to call *school-fear*. The exact definition of this school-fear you yourselves have already given in your questionnaire. It arose from "the general and essential inadequacies of which every observer must be aware." Even the dull school-room smells of this school-fear—a mixture of dried-up ink and that of freshly varnished forms. Once I had entered school a constant shadow lay upon my spirit which only lightened a little during the intervals. Then there was always the teacher, who every three years was changed for another, with a different manner and a different method; and finally one was always persecuted by the goad of education, which narrowed one's freedom and provided one with knowledge of every description. Sometimes this would be carried out with severity and sometimes with kindness, but in any case I knew well that the teacher always had the advantage over me. I was always opposed to any encroachment upon my liberty, wherever it might come from. In some subjects which interested me particularly I longed for more knowledge, in others the burden of the time-table lay doubly strong upon me, and thoughts about the free life to be found in the forests and on the mountains became trebly enticing.

All my comrades felt the same way about these things as I did. Perhaps here and there one would feel a particular dislike for one of his teachers, one might be especially afraid of the cane, but the fundamental fear—school-fear, that is to say—began and ended with the limitation of our freedom. The thousand other inadequacies affected each pupil in a different way.

E. H.

CHAPTER X

PARTIALITY

(*a*) THE HIRELING (m. aged 39)

I WILL lay a wager that by far the greater number of answers to your questionnaire will be sent in by your readers, male and female, who belong to the towns, who require a higher standard of education, and therefore learn to know the dark side of the problems of child education in a relatively more painful fashion.

If you should direct your question to some isolated country boy or some child of the proletariat, you would not be so likely to hear complaints about the schools as such. Just for the simple reason that the life in the schools would be still more refined and humane than that to be met with in the home. A child who has at home a violent, thrashing drunkard for his father and a degraded person for his mother, gets accustomed to feeling and hearing things in comparison with which an occasional beating from his teacher, scoldings or being put to stand in the corner will make but little impression upon him in the light of worry or *rows*, but which may seem to him to represent conditions that in comparison resemble paradise.

The first three years of my school-life were happy ones. After that I became a hired boy, and as such my whole childhood became without any ray of comfort. For nearly six years I attended a school in a large town near Lucerne, at Amte Sursee. As I had been brought up in the Reformed Church, I was now obliged to embrace the Catholic religion instead of my original faith.

The school work seemed to me to be recreation intervals, and the tasks which were set before me were no trouble. Because the work in the house of my peasants was so hard and difficult to understand for anyone of my age, the class-room always struck me as a perfect paradise, where one might sit still and not be disturbed by the scoldings and blows of my foster-father.

The thing that I suffered from most in my paradise was that I was not regarded as upon the same footing as the rest, nor was I treated as they were, but as a *hireling*. And that particularly from the side of the teaching staff. One woman teacher, into whose class I first went, was always kind, motherly and just to me. But the others would prefer to punish me only and without any reason for things which another of the pupils had done, or because the father of the offender was either some town official, on the school council, or also, and more generally, just some rather substantial peasant.

The injustice of the teachers, their habit of blinking at the rights of the case, was that which troubled me at first and caused me to become in course of time still more obstinate and embittered. I indeed found at times some comfort and sunshine from my first teacher, but in spite of this my character suffered. And what could I think of my teachers when I saw how they always wrote on my monthly report after the reasons for their complaints: "Many thrashings and bad marks!"—even when the thrashings had not been deserved. The beatings in themselves left me cold, since they were so much more gentle and less dangerous than those I received from my peasant in exchange for these bad reports, but the *injustice* of them, that a poor wretch of a hired lad should be treated as though he were a creature without feelings or mind, without any right to understanding or kindness, I shall never, never forgive on the part of those people.

I had as great a respect for the calling of a teacher as for any other. In later life I have got to know some who who were excellent and blameless persons. And I have such a high opinion of the vocation of a teacher that

I often say to myself that only the most worthy, the most serious and just people should be allowed to join this profession. According to my own conviction half of the teaching profession have missed their vocation because they are not brave enough to protect neglected children, those who are poor or without parents, against the domination of the offspring of town or village authorities. That, however, is a peculiarity of human nature—to flatter those who are on top and let the underdogs feel their power—and it is as prevalent among the factory owners as among the master-masons. But a teacher should not do so. Love, understanding, a pair of eyes from which kindness and sympathy beam, as well in the home as at school, that is what makes childhood so beautiful and later life so much the more easy. Heart and mind! We have indeed a brilliant example of this combination in that man who devoted himself to providing this kind of childhood. Pestalozzi! But it is so difficult for others to imitate him!

K. R.

(b) THE FINAL JUDGMENT (f. aged 34)

If the following lines concerning the diagnosis of the disease of education can be useful I shall rejoice to have contributed my mite to a most important problem.

In the elementary school I was a good pupil without any troubles. That I did not come first I had my handwriting to thank, because that was a trouble to me throughout my whole school-life.

Therefore when the time came for me to go on to another girls' school, I believed that I should run through it equally easily. But I had reckoned without taking account of the teacher.

She was anxious to add to the prestige of her school. My childish self-sufficiency brought me into her disfavour.

The fight between a teacher and a pupil, however, is unequal! Everyone can despise a really unjust teacher from the bottom of his heart who sets to work more or less to destroy an inconvenient pupil. I say "more or less." In my case many of my school-years were wrecked in this way. My teacher revenged herself upon me because she was unable to make me take an interest in any of the special subjects. Not that she could find anything bad to say about me, but she seemed to doubt whether I could do continued good work, or she would express the opinion that she did not find me earnest enough when I was working at a serious subject. I can hardly say how much I suffered from this bad influence. Only through the most persistent effort of will was I able at that time to regain my old confidence in the teachers who were responsible for the special subjects and it produced the most unspeakable bitterness in my heart by the unequal struggle. How frequently had I to watch how indifferent strivers after exaggerated praise were made much of whilst I had to put up with the heaviest reproaches for the smallest omissions!

Later on, when these unpleasant years were a thing of the past, I noticed that, time and again, when one teacher was telling another new one about the standard of my work, she would be surprised to hear how far advanced I was. Certainly these were but shadows which passed quickly and could not darken my spirits for more than a few days at a time. I am now fully conscious to-day that I did not derive the full benefit from my bad years, and very, very easily fell into a habit of superficial work, so that I often think about the silent, doubt-tormented struggle which I had to endure at that time.

I could have wished for nothing better than to have been able to love and to respect my teacher. Yet there was always this horrible rift between us.

Day after day I hoped to see some tendency to justice

PARTIALITY

in my teacher. She never understood my silent plea. The dignity of her profession had unfortunately made her too self-confident, so that once her judgment had been made it appeared to exclude all further doubts.

It seemed to me to be quite unreasonable to make up one's mind conclusively about any young person just at the period of her greatest development. The teacher then can no longer think of the pupil without prejudice. Once children have been ranked among the group of the good pupils they may often remain for a long time in that category where the teacher has put them with a very indifferent output of work, whilst other gifted pupils who failed to make a good impression at the start can only win their true valuation after a terrible struggle.

R. E.

(c) A ZEPPELIN FLEW PAST; THE CLASS WAS DOING ARITHMETIC (f. aged 43)

My little daughter was full of excitement when she changed from the third- to the fourth-year class. But she passed on to another teacher and experienced many bitter disappointments during the few years which followed.

Once she explained in a roundabout way that she was not going to school any more! The extremely great injustice of the teachers, caused principally by the mood in which they happened to be at the moment, which influenced their behaviour and treatment of the class, aroused my child so much that she was never able to overcome her hatred against teachers for the rest of her life and she made up her mind, in consequence, never to greet these teachers in the street. She carried out her plan and I was not able to get her to change her mind about it. Why will people not make an old teacher resign before it is actually his time to do so if his delicate health causes him always to be irritable in his class? Dare they not do so, or cannot it be done? Is it the outcome of economy on the part of the pension committee? Is it the result of lack of courage or fear, which undermines everyone's better judgment?

When the great Zeppelin *America* flew over the country during school-hours, all the school-children ought to have been let out into the playground to look at her; but my child was obliged by her teacher to stay in the class-room and go on with their arithmetic lesson. I have never seen a more complete disgust felt on account of any teacher. The child came home with tears of resentment streaming down her face.

Once I went past the playground during one of the intervals. When I was still a long way off I saw my little daughter waiting for me right at the end of the yard, standing with a school-fellow. When I saw the tears in her eyes and asked the reason, I heard that she had been made to stand in a corner without knowing why, and she always suffered severely under these continual acts of injustice. And her friend said to me: "Yes, the teacher is often quite horrid to her."

One day I asked my little boy, who, three years younger than his sister, still had the *good fortune* to be going to the same school, for his opinions on the matter. He gave them to me as follows: "If we see in the morning that his eyebrows are drawn down, then we know directly what is the matter, and that we shall have to look out; but when his eyebrows are in their right place, then he is in a good temper." Further: "We know from the start in the morning whether the teacher is in a bad temper, and then we know what it will be like all day." Or: "When we have been making corrections and have to take them up to the desk to show them, I always go up as quickly as I can, so that I get there one of the

PARTIALITY

first when the teacher is still in a good temper, and if there are a lot of them there already, he gets angry and then he will flick off somebody's exercise-book from the table with his finger, so that it flies up into the air and finishes up in a corner of the room. If the President of the School Council is there he is the nicest possible teacher, and when no visitor is there he is as angry as usual." The best sign which will show how my boy *loves* his school were the tears that he shed when I went to call him the first morning after the summer holidays. Does that not speak volumes?

I always try not to make too much of the complaints that I hear; the children will also have to come up against a good many unpleasant things in their later life to which they will have to adjust themselves. In addition to this we have no opportunity of sending them to any other school. We have only one class of each school-year in our school. Yes, Dr. Schohaus, I could write you a whole book upon this one question! There are apparently no very great faults on the part of the teachers, but are not these daily recurring frictions and torments, this constant condition of irritation on the part of the teacher towards his pupils, an equal amount of poison for them, and reasons enough to get any teacher dismissed? And when I have given mine, which are not so bad, then comes immediately my daughter's answer, "Only wait until we get to the sixth class; it is much worse there, so that one can't stand it any longer!"

E. W.

(d) THE PREJUDICE AGAINST GIRLS (f. aged 35)

The greatest injustice of all, about the existence of which most men have apparently no idea because it has never happened to them, is that as a girl one is treated in the school as an inferior being, who is allowed to run with the rest, so to say, because she just happens to be there; and yet we live in an age when people can no longer quite deny that a woman has a soul. In the Engadine, for instance, there is absolutely no possibility for girls to compete against the boys, and if a girl should be exceptionally ambitious it will be a perpetual burden for her. My first trouble in this direction goes back as far as the beginning of the century, when ski-running was introduced. Immediately ski-races were held; skis were given out to the children . . . but of course only to the boys. That girls could also take pleasure in this exercise and that it would be good for them seemed to occur to nobody; we were simply overlooked and certainly not because of any ill-will, but just because no one took the least interest in us. I wanted to do it so much, too, that I was given a pair of skis for a Christmas present because I simply could not understand why I should be excluded from this pleasure. Could I help it that I wasn't a boy? But the hardest of all was not that one could not take part in the ski-running competitions, but that we had to look on to see the boys winning all the lovely prizes, and just had to watch them do so! Not that we were any the less capable of taking part, but because no one had taken the trouble to test out our ability. At that time I realised that we had not only to fight for success but also for the right to compete. And this realisation persecuted me throughout my whole school-life, and I have always striven against it.

Consequently the boys, at least in their first year at school, had two free afternoons while we, from the first, only had one, and on the other had a handwork lesson from an old spinster when one had to learn to make quite unusable stockings and equally useless chemises all cut to a pattern. Later I went on to another, better-natured teacher who was not so keen on this idiotic programme and let us make more useful things.

At that time this lesson was my favourite during the whole week, because then one had plenty of competition and one could really feel oneself to be successful. That was because there were no boys there to be given the preference, simply because it was considered an established fact that a girl could not work as well as they could.

In the eighth and ninth classes we had a very good teacher who was considered to be quite impartial, and who did not give the preference to the rich children rather than to the poor ones, which would often happen. (It is easy for me to say this because it is not founded upon any feeling of resentment upon my part, since I myself often obtained an advantage in this way.) But his contempt for girls was exaggerated, although he was probably not conscious of it. He was most stingy with free time. If he were obliged to attend a conference or a funeral, we were compelled to go to school all the same. It was horrid for us girls then because he would always set one or two boys to watch us as prefects. Anyone who chattered would have her name put up on the blackboard. We girls knew, however, what was in store for us and we were very quiet. Occasionally we would want to know something about our work and would ask our neighbour. But even then, up would go the name on the board! And the boys? They ran around the room, wrestled, shouted and chattered, and the prefect joined in too. Naturally a boy's name was never put up on the blackboard. Once I tried to defend myself; but it did not come off. I was answered by the words: "But one knows that you girls must have talked." There was no justice for us!

The eighth class had been given a prize of 80 francs annually by a wealthy Englishman for the best two scholars, a boy and a girl. At that time there were four girls in the class. I was expecting to win this prize with a fair amount of certainty because, although there were two other girls as good as I was in most subjects, I excelled them in drawing and singing. Still I did not want to divide the prize with them. The teacher, however, did not see the necessity of making any choice between the girls, and the prize was split into four parts, in spite of the fact that two of the girls had a considerably lower standard of work. Also this same teacher abolished the physics class for the girls about a year after I left the school because they were too stupid, although he had once gone as far as to rank me amongst the boys in this subject by giving me a 1. Once, nevertheless, he was obliged to give expression to his opinion of my superiority, namely, when he once found me giving a hefty thrashing to a school-fellow who had purposely spoilt some of my work. He shouted at me with resentment: "But, Lucy, you are a lot more troublesome than the boys!" He meant it for a reproach. But I was happy. At last, at last, I had won some recognition!

How long shall we have to put up with the fact that people allow their daughters, who are as much their children as their sons, to be actually brought up to have such feeling of inferiority? Must not girls always get from this sort of treatment an idea of the despotism of their fathers (and this is prevalent enough too) and the injustice of the schools? And will not girls in this way have all their interest in intellectual work buried, so that it will never be able to attain its full development, whilst others are forced into an unhealthy masculinity? It is possible that a great many of these handicaps never come into consciousness, or that they are accepted as something that is perfectly natural. Still a great many girls might be rescued from this mouldering condition and in my opinion it would be quite worth while to do so.

L. F.

PARTIALITY

(e) I SUFFERED FROM THE PREFERENCE SHOWN ME
(f. aged 29)

My school-days ended twelve years ago. I went to school in a tiny village. There were six classes of boys and girls in a comparatively small room. My entire school-life was a torment. I have no happy memories at all. I believe that many of my bad character-traits may be traced back to this time of my life. In my little village, which was so delightful, I was the only so-called gentleman's child among all the peasant children. My father was a wealthy man for those parts, and president of the school. Nothing in that village could have been decided without his advice.

From the first day that I went to school I occupied a special position there. I wore prettier clothes, I had white bread for my tea, and the old teacher talked a little French to me on the first day. All this was enough to single me out from the other children. They did not want to play with me, nor to include me among their intimate friends. They always regarded me with a certain amount of jealousy. Unfortunately my mother had taught me to read and write. In this way I was different from them once again. When the school was inspected my ability was always praised. In this first year I had no idea how lonely I was. I lived only in a semi-conscious state under this dull oppression.

The teacher would often have to give funeral orations. He would lock us pupils into the school-house for an hour or two while he went to attend them. So that everything would go smoothly during his absence he would set one of the oldest and best scholars at the blackboard with chalk and a ruler. The names of all those who chattered would be written down. One day, when I was a pupil in the second class, I was put to keep the others in order. A general grumbling ensued.

It was most uncomfortable for me. I had also been given instructions to do some mental arithmetic for a time with the class. At first all was quiet. Then we started this senseless mental arithmetic. I had already written up eight names in my stiff, childish handwriting. At each fresh name the little group clenched their fists and threatened to hit and bite me. When I told them to say their six-times table, a rebellious pupil shouted, "Six times six is thirty-six, you deserve to be put in a fix." All at once a wonderful sense of superiority overcame me. As my first deed I rubbed out all the names that were up on the blackboard and went back to my own place. I incited my class-mates to all manner of mischief. We covered the door-handles with paint, and spat wet blotting-paper in the shape of tiny balls on to the white-washed wall. At last our games came to an end. There was a glorious muddle in the room. At this magnificent, but unfortunate moment, the teacher came back. Just then I happened to be standing before the blackboard and had written *Ape*, but was able to rub it out in a second. The teacher took his cane—God knows how we all hated this piece of stick!—and raged around striking everyone within reach. Who had been talking?

Without exception all the other twenty-eight pupils were beaten. I, however, the twenty-ninth, was allowed to go back to my place with a speech of praise. I can still remember perfectly how painful this whole situation was and how I would much rather have spat at the teacher. In getting back to my place one of the boys hit at me on the sly and another put out his leg. All at once I realised my privileged position. I ran back to the teacher and told him that I had been to blame for the disturbance. But my honourable sense of justice was immediately repressed. The teacher had noticed that the boys had hit me when I was going back to my place and believed my truthfulness to have been caused by my fear of the boys. On the top of all the rest the class was kept in for an hour, but not me, naturally.

Once later, when I had been chattering my next-door neighbour was punished. I considered that to be cruel and unjust. I would often pray to God in my childish anxiety that He would allow the teacher to punish me just for once. As, however, God, to whom I had been taught to pray, did not listen to me, I tried another plan.

In the third class I had a doll. She could close her eyes and had beautiful long hair. She was certainly one of my most treasured childish possessions. I carried this doll into a dark corner of the barn and hung around her sweets, tinsel, coloured ribbons and apples. Every day I added something fresh. Before this doll I would then prostrate myself and sobbed and prayed, strangely enough always in silly school German. But all in vain!

I suffered from further injustice because I always had good reports. I was commissioned to hang a comforter round the neck of a pencil-sucker. I received little sweets in front of all the children. Every day the teacher sent me home with a message for my father, given with a most ingratiating smile.

In our fourth year we were given religion lessons. I set all my hopes upon our pastor. He would surely be just in the true sense of the Saviour. He would never see the gentleman's child in me. Our pastor was kind to all of us. But he was still kinder to me than to the rest. This became particularly emphatic if he had been invited to dinner with us that week. Then I could never say anything wrong. As the pupils complained and I also never learned anything by heart, the pastor had to arrange it so that I always had only the first verse of a hymn to say after him. As a matter of fact, I never did learn the second verse of any single one. In this way my sense of duty was suppressed.

I spent most of the day out of doors because it was

always easy enough to cheat over the school-exercises, whenever that was possible at all. In a short time I became one of the worst pupils. From this time onwards I became the object of my class-mates' anger. They began to persecute me. They were so skilful in tormenting me that in a short time I had lost all my healthy self-confidence entirely. I could not work independently at anything. I was particularly backward in arithmetic. I used to beg my neighbours to tell me how to do my sums in whispers. For a piece of white bread John would read my composition through and correct it. For one of my beautiful, wide hair-ribbons, the girls would do my sums for me. Then I was obliged to tell lies at home; once I had lost my hair-ribbon, once I said that it had been snatched from me on purpose by one of the boys.

My small capital was soon exhausted. I then slipped small articles out of the house in order to be able to go on paying for my help. If ever I had to go up to the blackboard to do a sum I was so terrified that my whole thinking capacity would give out, and would listen almost unconscious with fear for the whispers of my allies.

I said a word that I had not understood properly they would all laugh. Then I would lose my head so completely that I would fail to hear the hints that the teacher gave me and tell myself: "It is all in vain, all in vain, all in vain." I remember that I would spend the whole afternoon, especially when we were doing arithmetic, with my hands clasped, praying silently: "Please, God, don't let me have to go up to the blackboard! Please, God, I won't steal any more if I don't have to go to the board this time! Oh, God, dear God, I will put my yearly fair money into the Missionary-box if I don't have to go to the blackboard!" But still from time to time I had to go to it. Then as a happy release I got the idea of making myself ill so that I could lie in bed and have no more sums to do and not have to go to school. I found out a particularly clever way of tying my arm under me at night so that it was quite swollen by the morning. In this way I deceived both my mother and the doctor. At last I deceived myself too, because without tying it up I used to get pain in it and it would become quite swollen.

There was not very much left of my personality that remained healthy. I began to excel myself in lies and gave myself up to phantasies. I enjoyed telling myself quite long stories. I developed the most perfect technique in stealing from our little village shop. The first time I sent the proprietress down to the cellar because she kept her petroleum down there. While she was down there I took money out of the till. Beautiful round coins. The next day I would divide my little fortune among my allies. Finally I was so efficient in stealing that I was able to pay for the love and the help of my classmates with good, round sums.

When I was in the fifth class I robbed my teacher, because I took a franc out of his desk. Now, I thought, I shall be punished. The teacher would discover what I had done; I could tell my mother and ask for forgiveness and start a new life. A new life seemed to me to be so beautiful and so much to be desired! I was weary of my bad conscience. Contrite and suffering from spiritual pain I went up to the teacher's desk during the interval. He smiled and took the franc that I offered him, putting it into his waistcoat pocket, tickled me under the chin, and said without any severity: "I have been invited by your father to go to supper this evening; I won't say anything about it to your parents. But don't do it any more in the future."

That, then, was all he had to say to me about it! My conscience had no boundary-stones! Consequently I went on during my sixth year as dishonestly as in the rest.

I had a dear, understanding teacher in my secondary

school. He did his best to get to know each of his pupils. He at once discovered my crooked ways. He must also have noticed at the same time that I suffered from a terrible feeling of inferiority. He gave me very, very simple lessons that I was able to do by myself. My friends at the elementary school had not gone on to the secondary school. Therefore I was absolutely cut off from my previous sources of help. The teacher would ask me easy questions and then say coaxingly each time: "See, you know what it is, you must have just a little more confidence!" Once, even, he said: "Good gracious, that girl has quite a good head on her shoulders!" I worked well and industriously, but I was aware of all my lost years. I continued to be backward in arithmetic and in any subject where I had to think things out for myself. I gave up my habit of stealing gradually. But I went on lying and making phantasies for a good many years after that. Often did I wish that I could get into an entirely new environment so that I need not keep my ball of lies rolling any longer. From now on my reports were very bad. My father, who was clever at everything, just shrugged his shoulders and said every time: "Good, you are a girl, and therefore can't help it. There are some intelligent people and some who are not." My mother hid my bad marks from my brothers and sisters. And it was naturally taken for granted that I was stupid. I could never gather enough courage to overcome my inferiority feeling. I still get a feeling of indisposition even to-day when I get among my relations. If I ever express an opinion, or say that such and such has interested me, that I have read this or that book, worked through it, understood and loved it, my father and brothers begin to smile! One can see that behind their smiling faces they think: "Yes, by jove, it is quite touching that you take so much trouble over things of that sort!"

I cannot ever expand in the circle of my relatives. Certainly I should have gone under entirely if I had not been able to get away into a totally different environment.

I shall bring up my three boys to have plenty of sound self-confidence. They shall experience the best that school can give them, and before anything else, have the possibility of turning to their mother with perfect confidence.

E. D.

(*f*) A RASCAL AND A GOOD-FOR-NOTHING (f. aged 30)

How far the influence of the school extends we can only compute, because we still as adults think about our teachers with affection who extended to us love and understanding, and hate with a burning hatred those who were unjust to us.

Injustice is the most acute of all childish sufferings. Here are shoals whence hatred and curses, sorrow and bitter tears are born. Gentle, tender childish hearts here learn to thirst for revenge.

I can say little about my own school-days. That was owing to the circumstances in which I lived, and the fact that I was the child of respected parents. Everyone closed their eyes to my failings. Still, that did not prevent my coming up against the injustice suffered by poorer children who were no less good than I, who felt it just as deeply and who often disliked me in consequence.

And whence comes the source of this large amount of sorrow which is to be found in our school-days? The chief cause is certainly the teaching staff. Look at the teachers in our elementary school! If they could but realise how responsible is their office! But they stroll along to their schools exactly like town officials to their offices, with just as little enthusiasm and an equal amount of boredom. And yet they do not have to work with the same dead material as these others, but with the hearts of children, pure, soft, deeply sensitive children's souls.

At the training colleges they have to pass examinations in all the subjects they will be expected to teach and their selection is largely influenced by political considerations. At the same time they may be coarse, sadistic people, often afflicted with moral defects. No cock crows on this account, however. Once they have passed the examination for their certificate they can go on just as they please.

Who is going to bring them to account if it should please them to ride rough-shod over a few children, or to torture them with biting scorn if they do not know something? And how many of them are there who will say to a child who is not very clever: "Yes, there is nothing to be done with you, you are much too stupid"? How many will be ruined with such words as these, and how much valuable material will be lost in this way is dreadful to contemplate!

Should this sermon come to the eyes of a teacher he may indeed say: "Yes, it is easier to condemn than to be a teacher oneself." Certainly! But the writer is a teacher and has experienced for herself how much can be got from children who have been pushed on one side as lazy and worthless. I should like to give you a few examples.

As a nineteen-year-old student from Berne, I was sent to my first post as temporary teacher in a remote co-educational school in Emmental which had fifty-six children, ranging from the smallest infants to strong, well-grown boys. I entered upon my first position with the greatest alarm. At the start the president of the school commission called my attention to the fact that there was a boy in the ninth class with whom the teacher had been able to do nothing. He was a rascal and a good-for-nothing, whom they wanted to send on to a reformatory later. If he were tiresome with me in any way I was to report him at once. It was right; the boy sat at the very back of the row, with a bad-tempered, glum face. I treated him just the same as the rest, or rather, if ever I found an opportunity to praise him, I would say something like this: "See, Fritz, that is really beautiful writing. Take a little more trouble and then it will soon come quite right."

And who would believe it? The next Monday Fritz came to me after school with his reading-book; he had learned two pages of *Tell* by heart, and wanted me to hear him say it. God knows how this previously lazy and stupid pupil had managed to learn so much entirely of his own accord! And as I listened to him with astonishment and pleasure, how his eyes had shone and how happy he had looked!

The time came round for the other teacher to return. Fritz was not quite so happy about that. He came to school downcast. I had a talk with him and asked him what was the matter. Then he burst out with his trouble: "Teacher, can't you stay here? If the teacher comes back the same story will begin all over again." I comforted him by saying that now he was so good and industrious his teacher would be very pleased with him. But his face did not get any brighter. "No, teacher, look here! The teacher doesn't believe me any more. I am the good-for-nothing of the class!"

Reader, you can see what results the unconsidered words of a teacher may have. A bad, tiresome good-for-nothing can be produced out of a good, kind boy. Fritz promised me at least to make an attempt to win the teacher's friendship and before I left I talked to the teacher himself about the boy. From that time on all went well. And afterwards many a disconnected but dear little letter arrived for me from Fritz, who was so happy that everything was going on so much better at school for him.

With this example I should like to prove how easy it often is to approach the child's heart. One has only to take the child seriously and to try to look at his best side. With teachers as a rule the scientific aspect of things should be a secondary consideration. The first should be his own personality and his character. For this reason everyone should think twice before he stretches out his hand to gain this profession and should not allow himself to be influenced by the idea of salary or holidays if he does not possess a real love for children and for people, if he cannot see his way to sympathise with them in their joys and in their sorrows.

M. M.

(g) THE SCAPEGOAT (f. aged 31)

Although I left school nearly fifteen years ago I can still only look back upon it with fear. This means that from the first four years, during my primary school-days, I can remember nothing except that at first I had a kind woman-teacher for two years, and for the next two a man in whom I can still find my ideal of a teacher, and for whom as a child I had a devoted veneration. But after these four carefree years in the elementary school came the secondary school and then my troubles began.

My teacher had told me when I first went there that I was the third best scholar in the class, and if I were to continue so, I should become one of the best pupils in the whole school, but I must not talk quite so much and I must pay rather more attention. Now at that time my parents were blessed with more children than wealth and so I obtained a so-called scholarship, that meant that I had not to pay for school-fees nor for books; I was allowed to borrow the latter.

At the end of the first lesson the school-mistress told another fellow-pupil and myself to come to her in the interval, at which I heard that another girl whispered to her neighbour behind me: "Oh, they are going to have their books for nothing; they are so poor!" Immediately I had the feeling that this was a terrible disgrace, and did not dare to look to the right nor left, because I felt that the whole class was staring at me and was taking notice of the fact that I was not able to pay for my books.

The teacher gave us both a little lecture, quite harmless on the whole, that we must work hard, and learn nicely, and then gave us the necessary books. I took a great deal of trouble with my work, but it was not much use. I was always obliged to keep in mind this thought that I was receiving a sort of charity in this school. Here and there also one of the teachers would also let me feel that I had a scholarship, and the fact that most of the girls were more prettily dressed than I did not help to raise my self-esteem.

But still the first two years were tolerable in comparison with those which were to come. I had made up my mind to work twice as hard with my new teacher, so that she would have no reason to despise me on account of my *scholarship*. But she had scarcely made her first appearance and taken some stock of us than she called out to me: "You, there, at the back with the cheeky face, what is your name?"

At first I did not realise that she meant me, because no one had ever told me before that I had a cheeky face, and therefore just glanced at the teacher a moment and remained quietly in my place. Then she came right up to me, shook me and shouted with the whole force of her lungs, quite red in the face: "You obstinate girl, can't you answer me?" I was as if paralysed and could not say a single word. I forget what happened next.

I only remember that from this time onwards, until I left school, I used to cry every morning before I started off for school, and that my ability decreased in spite of all the trouble I took over my work, until I was one of the worst pupils.

Also I was now the recognised scapegoat of the class. Every time that there was any trouble or any mischief was done, and I did not immediately own up to having been the perpetrator, I was made to atone for it. I was often kept in and was given a great many impositions without knowing why. If I tried to defend myself, the teacher would say to me in a honeyed voice I should be grateful that she took so much trouble to train me to become a useful person, because I was a completely worthless girl and, above all, I should learn to be modest because I had a scholarship. In course of time I did not dare to try to defend myself any more, and my parents warned me not to attempt to stand up for myself as long as I was there.

I have become acquainted with a great number of people whose lives were embittered by some hysterical, nervous or complex-ridden teacher, merely because something connected with them *"got on her nerves."*

In such a case one should try to arrange for the child to be removed at once into another class. But it is naturally bad when it is always necessary for a teacher to have one pupil of this kind. In that case the teacher herself should be transferred and given her *congé*. There are quite enough school-mistresses who have a true vocation for their calling and yet cannot get a position for years on end.

Th. R.

CHAPTER XI

THE FIGHT AGAINST DEFIANCE

(a) WITH A SMILING FACE (m. aged 33)

I DID not have a *bad* teacher while I was in the first to third classes of the elementary school. Yet it did not seem to me to be quite right that he should break rulers over the children's heads and throw school equipment out of the window into the playground when he was angry, all the same. But it never occurred to me to criticise him, even in my secret thoughts at that time.

This spirit of criticism arose first when I was in the fourth to the sixth classes, because I was older then. Neither was this a *bad* teacher. He, too, made use of the ruler daily. Yet he did not have any very strong influence upon me until I noticed how prejudiced he was. The poorer children were his whipping-boys and I had to accept this fact.

When I noticed this I began to hate the teacher, although I was not one of these poor children.

I now began to promote disturbances from time to time. If I then got punished with the ruler I took the greatest pride not to move a muscle of my face. The teacher wanted to make us all cry, whatever happened. In course of time I was able to offer him a smiling face, however much pain I might be suffering.

I reduced many of the professors in the middle school to distraction later on with my smiling face.

In the Gymnasium, however, my attitude of defiance grew to gigantic proportions. It would be always the same things that provoked my resentment: injustice directed towards the weaker pupils and lack of respect for personality. We had, particularly, a member of the teaching staff who from a pedagogic point of view was an unique specimen of his kind. Our Latin master, a little, bad-tempered dwarf of a man, was already in such a condition of mental confusion that he could not distinguish scholars from one another whom he had already had for several years.

Another example: our Director, a writer, at one time wanted to institute self-government among the pupils. That sounded well and was a beautiful gesture. In actuality, however, the self-government consisted of nothing but this—that the pupils were given certain police duties to carry out which formerly had fallen to the lot of the teachers, namely, to open the windows during the intervals and conduct the class out of doors in fine weather.

For this reason some of the pupils were opposed to the introduction of this self-government. A great gathering of the scholars took place at the instance of the Director in which the introduction of the system was discussed. The Director gave a speech in which he recommended it, and at the end of it he put the following resolution to the vote: "Therefore, those who are in favour of this self-government, the progressive boys, the up-to-date ones, go and stand on the right; and those who are against it, the retrogressives, stand over on the other side."

With about twenty more companions I belonged to the few retrogressives. Things of that kind, and I could tell of hundreds of others, embittered me a great deal. I now became, as they used to say among the teachers, *a disturbing element*.

My only fear was that one day my opinions about the teachers might escape from my control, and that I should be betrayed into some action which might lead to my expulsion. I suffered from the obsession that I must suddenly stand up and give one of the professors a box on the ear, and therefore would sit for hours together with both hands clenched round the edge of the form.

The larger number of the pupils in every class in that Gymnasium were of much the same mind, but we were generally able to hide what we thought. When we made class excursions, which were usually forbidden without the permission of the Director, we would make effigies of the teachers and dance round them in a sort of Indian war-dance before we burned them. We thought of ourselves as slaves and fought against our slave-owners with the same weapons with which the slaves themselves fought: with passive resistance and with deception. Usually it would be the innocent that suffered most—the temporary teachers who were usually there but for a short time, upon whom we unloaded the whole of our pent-up hatred, especially because we did not fear them so much.

One evening I was going for a walk along a path in the forest when suddenly I met our class-master. He said to me: "And so you are taking a walk?"

These few silly words touched me so much that the tears sprang into my eyes.

In the fifth class at the Gymnasium we had a temporary teacher for a fortnight, who for some reason treated us very well. He left us to go to Paris. Upon the platform the whole class was assembled; we had bought him a huge basket of flowers and another containing eatables. They cost 45 francs. As the train steamed out of the station one might have experienced the remarkable spectacle of eighteen young boys down whose cheeks the tears were streaming fast.

What a little did it need to break through our attitude of defiance! We had been treated to punishments, with being kept in, with warnings, with every possible policeman's trick. If anything happened, the Director came round as detective, questioned everybody, and suggested that we should turn informers against our comrades. But, during my whole time spent at the Gymnasium, it never happened either to me nor to any of my school-friends that a teacher had ever said a single encouraging word in private with one of us.

Not one of them ever had a chat with us, nor asked one of us to go for a walk with him, nor made an enquiry about any psychological troubles that we might have, never, in the six and a half years, not once.

The teaching staff had but the one conception of their duties—to provide knowledge in all its various departments and to maintain discipline with more or less rigorous methods.

And this is the state of affairs in a cantonal Gymnasium just a hundred years after Pestalozzi.

Dr. E. B.

(*b*) THE TEACHER WANTED ME NEITHER BOILED NOR ROASTED

"Mrs. Miller, your Emil got slapped four times in school to-day." My mother was given this news when I had been to school for exactly one week.

"Now what can my gentle little Emil have been doing that he should have been so much punished?" she thought, and wanted me to tell her all about it at once.

"Oh!" I said, "it was so very boring that I yawned out loud, and then everyone laughed. That was why the teacher gave me four slaps on my hands."

I did not think much more about it, but then the painter's little girl, Fanny, did the same a few days later, and the teacher rapped her over the knuckles with her little cane. That made me angry, and I am still annoyed to think that I should have been more punished than she for the same thing. And it was this partiality on the part of some of the teachers that caused me the greatest suffering. The teacher did not want me either boiled or roasted, and I often suffered for the misdeeds of others. It was worst of all in the fifth class. There we experienced just the opposite from love. There was scarcely a day when the teacher's hazel-twig did not dance upon my back. He could not give me the so-called strokes upon the hands because I would never hold them out to him. Learning was no great trouble to me and I was always one of the best pupils, and it often seemed that it only annoyed the teacher when he had to announce that mine was the best essay.

One day my neighbour in the class whispered to me, and, although I had not answered one word, the teacher's voice bellowed that Emil would be kept in for an hour because of talking.

This obvious injustice made me furious and I immediately packed up my writing materials, because I thought that if I was to be kept in on George's account, I would not go on writing then! Then the fight began! The teacher came along with "Cousin Hazel," as we called his hazel-switch, and commanded me to get out my exercise-book so that I could go on with my writing. I did so. "Write!" he ordered. I did not write. "Write!" he shouted, and gave me one stroke across the back. I still did not begin to write.

When he had repeated his commands and blows several times I threw my book down on the floor, upon which the blows fell as thick and fast on my back as though I was a mealsack without any feelings. The teacher continued to scream: "Pick your book up!"

Suddenly I seethed with resentment, looked the teacher straight between the eyes and shouted as loud as I could: "Even if you should kill me I won't do as you tell me!"

After that he pulled me off the form by my hair, shook me hither and thither, and threw me back on the bench. But I remained victorious.

In the following interval my school-fellows wanted to make a pyramid, and one of them tried to climb up on to my back. But, naturally enough, I could not let that happen, because after the thrashing I had got, it was not unlike a junction railway station. Looking up at the window of our class-room, I saw that our teacher was watching us. "All right! Come on!" I shouted, and one of them immediately climbed up on my back, so that everything went green and blue before my eyes. But I would never let that man up there at the window know that it was hurting me, although it was many nights before I was able to go to sleep lying on my back.

The next day our teacher was taken ill and until nearly the end of the school-year we had another teacher. This one, like the others whom we had during the two following years, had very few opportunities to grumble at us, and never again did I get any more corporal punishment. But they were all just and not prejudiced.

E. B.

CHAPTER XII

CORPORAL PUNISHMENT

(a) THE DUMMY-SUCKER (m. aged 28)

WE boys never called Karl Krummacher for choice by his right name. We called him the *Dummy-sucker*. That was an established fact and nothing could alter it. Yes, indeed, this nickname seemed to be obvious to Krummacher himself too, for he never showed the least resentment about it. In this way the *Dummy-sucker* was far too good-natured.

It happened on the first day at school. The forenoon was not yet over when my right-hand neighbour, Straubart, whispered something in my ear. He had seen Krummacher in the *summerhouse*, as we called our lavatory, crouched up in the corner all alone. And what did I think he was sucking in his mouth? Actually, a real dummy! Straubart, naturally, could not keep this wonderful piece of news to himself, but spread it around among all the boys of the village. Krummacher's dummy wandered about from one boy's rough hand to another, and thence to that of the teacher and finished up at last in the rubbish-pail, whence Krummacher himself pulled it out once more, amid the mocking laughter of the rest of us.

From then on Dummy-sucker became his nickname. When he ambled slowly through the village, his hands buried deeply in his trouser-pockets, the street urchins would shout it after him, and the little stream that ran beside the road whispered it in echo later on. A dummy-sucker, a weakling, a sneak; all that and more insulting things as well did Krummacher appear in the eyes of both the pupils and the teacher. He looked the part to perfection. His short, crooked legs, his little frail body, the rusty red hair that straggled over his face, all contributed to give him a miserable appearance. The Dummy-sucker was always the last if we boys ran out to play. No party wanted to have him to make up one of their circle because he was the most clumsy, the stupidest of our whole troop of young bandits. And woe betide him if Straubart or Long Sepp set his small, piercing eyes on him or seized him in his great, hard fists. He would then scream aloud and afterwards whimper like some poor, whipped dog, that does not know why this destiny of affliction should have descended on him. Krummacher must often have suffered from doubts concerning the goodness and beauty of the world with his meagre wits, especially when Straubart and Long Sepp, the lanky son of a fat widow, set about him roughly. And behind these two came all the rest of the thirty-odd noisy, remorseless ruffians which the dried-up old school-master never attempted to keep within bounds in any way. Yes, indeed, this old teacher—had he the least idea of all the troubles and torments that the Dummy-sucker had to endure day after day? We were the boring moths and the consuming worms that fretted and wore away his spirit, so that he himself soon believed in the hard fate that the village terrors decreed for him, poor boy!

An icy cold winter morning broke over the village.

Our severe school-master swung his hazel-twig, Liesel, wandered along the form and inspected the fingers of the boys entrusted to him. His hands twitched, his brows were drawn down into a frown, and his glance alighted on the Dummy-sucker, and his eyes pierced his soul like two arrows. He went towards him like a flash. The Dummy-sucker, however, just went on staring in silence at a little hole in the wood. He was helpless against his wrath. Could he have told him that there was not a drop of water to be found in the old gypsy hut where he lived, that everything was frozen hard, that his mother had not waked up that morning and that his father, crying wildly, had rushed off to find the doctor, and that he had had nothing at all to eat that morning? His lips did not move.

When the teacher's cane came down upon his blue chilblains his face was distorted ready to cry, and puckers that might have melted anyone's heart wrinkled up his little freckled face. His hot tears ran in little rivulets down his pale cheeks.

At the back of the class-room, Long Sepp made a contemptuous grimace.

The next morning the village boys whispered and talked eagerly together; the Dummy-sucker's mother was dead. For a few days all their mockery disappeared. Even the teacher treated him more kindly. He must have seen that his eyes were ready to brim over with tears. And now and again if he could not guess what a letter was, or if a line of a piece of poetry had got under the ice, so that he could not drag it out into his memory, then he closed his eyes and his face wrinkled up into little folds and puckers.

I know now that the Dummy-sucker was a little weak-minded. But he could not help that. Why should he have to pay the penalty for the sins of some ancestor, some reprobate drunkard? And how bitter was the cup that was held out to him every day!

"You are a fool, and will have to remain one. You will never be able to do anything right." Oh, it used to cut deep into the Dummy-sucker's poor heart if the teacher said that to him.

He went on his way of sorrows throughout his whole eight years of school. Nothing was changed except that he waxed in stature and knowledge; he remained a useless individual, abandoned to his fate by teacher and comrades. His strength was hardly equal to the journey along the martyr's path that took him every day through the village to the school.

Yet once a soft light broke over his face like a faint ray of sunshine. Krummacher helped me to look after the cows during one long summer holiday. When the time came to an end, my father pressed four large coins into his thin hand. He clutched the pieces of money convulsively. When I saw how delighted he was with his first earned reward, I gave him two of my yellow rabbits. A happy feeling crept into his soft heart—perhaps after all he was of some use, perhaps some day there would be something he could do in the world.

Four years afterwards I went across the frontier and suddenly came across Krummacher. He had become a mole-catcher in a large village. He understood that better than anybody else. Happily he strode over the fields and uplands. And his money-bag was not so empty either. His face lighted up when I shook him by the hand. He had become a happy man and his intelligence was quite equal to the job of catching moles. He had three things that he could call his own—a little wife, a healthy baby and a nice little house. I thought involuntarily of the thin little boy, of the dummy-sucker, about the hard words of the teacher, "Krummacher, we shall never be able to make anything of you," as this tall, bronzed fellow stood in front of me.

O. B.

(b) THE CONSEQUENCES OF CORPORAL PUNISHMENT
(m. aged 33)

School exerted such an injurious effect upon my life that it extensively influenced my subsequent physical and mental development, so that now, at the beginning of my thirties, I have had to undertake treatment for severe nervous disturbances. In the course of this it has been discovered that the small amount of corporal punishment and canings which came my way—they were not much in themselves, it is true, although now it is recognised that they are a frequent cause of nervousness—caused me to suffer from a great deal of fear and anxiety, and increased and favoured my nervous disposition in such a fashion that they finally caused a terrible nervous breakdown. Such deeply implanted injuries in body and mind are difficult to cure and take a long time. All corporal punishment should be most heartily condemned, because the consequences of the canings can contribute to the sadistic-masochistic tendencies of the child which I dare not describe here.

N. N.

(c) CANES AND HAZEL-TWIGS (m. aged 43)

I suffered most from the fear of canings when I was at school and I can scarcely think that I can be the only one who has done so. It must be easy to understand that when I saw anyone dragged from the form and up to the desk, whether he was defiant or frightened, whether he put out his hand tremblingly or reluctantly, I was filled with horror which I do not find diminished in any way if I should think about it to-day. Yet I myself was never caned. From this one might reach a false conclusion, that at least one of the aims of caning had been achieved, that of intimidation. But that was not so. This much one soon realised, that the one who received the caning was seldom the one who deserved it; chance played a very large part in the sharing out of these events. Many of the boys took the punishment as a thing of little consequence; their hands seemed to be insensitive to it. They were more fitted for the blows than those soft, sensitively tender boys' hands that might be compared to the leaves of that mimosa, which is sometimes called the Sensitive Plant.

To hit these with a cane or a hazel-twig is a crime for which I shall never forgive the schools of the past. Neither for corporal punishment before the whole class. Although I was never laid across the teacher's knees, I still blush with shame when I think of it. Others almost enjoyed it. They made grimaces at the time and felt important in such a position. There are some people, however, in whose disposition lies a tendency to accept such humiliations as an irreparable disgrace.

I have never found that well-deserved limitation of freedom, being kept in or an imposition had any bad effect. When the guilt was atoned for in this way even the memory of the punishment itself was wiped away.

H. S.

(d) I WILL DRIVE THE MIDGES AWAY! (m. aged 45)

In the elementary school I was reckoned as the first in my class, which was not particularly difficult to accomplish, seeing that there were only ten pupils in it. In the secondary school this was not quite so simple to bring about, because of the presence of a school-fellow who was cleverer than I. But in spite of this I liked the school better because of the stimulus provided by the teacher.

Our teacher in the elementary school had six classes to teach in the same room: obviously a difficult task, and a great burden for him to carry. At the same time he undertook several other kinds of work and was a capable journalist. He wrote a large number of poems and stories, some of them humorous and others serious that were founded upon his pupils. As a writer he ought to have been more just to the psychology of the children whom he had to instruct, but the opposite was nearer the truth. His capacity as author seemed to estrange

CORPORAL PUNISHMENT

him from reality rather than make him more intimate with it, because in his connection with us children he would only begin to take rather more interest in us when the yearly examinations were approaching. The means which he employed to incite us to harder work, and his chief method of education, was to thrash us.

If a pupil was not prompt in giving him the right answer to any question put to him he took up his position in front of the form where the child sat, and snorted at him: "Hurry up! Hurry up!" If now fear hindered the boy from giving an immediate or correct reply, he would strike left and right with a box on the ear, or his heavy and hard fist, protected by his signet-ring, would hammer the *blockhead*, or the *idiot*, until the teacher himself got tired. The timidity and inefficiency of the little scholars he would call *obstinacy*. They always aroused especial anger in him. "I will teach you! I will drive the midges away!" he would shout, and a handful of torn-out hair would show how energetic his educational methods were.

What sort of memories will such an unhappy child, who may have grown up in the domestic misery of a hard-drinking family, carry with him through life of the school, that might have been a friendly refuge, and of the teacher, who could have been a silent protector to him?

Although I constantly enjoyed the favour of my respected teacher, and whilst I got through my six years at the elementary school with a box on the ear or two and a few canings—once because during a game of hide-and-seek in the interval, I jumped out of the window on to the back of the teacher, who was at that moment coming up out of the cellar, so that he fell down and his bottle of wine fell in the brook; again, because in company with my school-fellows I decorated the long, freshly washed sandstone wall of the garden belonging to one of the richest villa-owners in the place with a coat of green juice squeezed from soft walnut husks, and two days before a church concert to be given by the Ladies' Choir, made finger-prints over the newly prepared hectograph wax for the copies of the songs that were being anxiously expected—I thus suffered as much as the rest under the perpetual anxiety of receiving serious corporal punishment, from which I was only freed when I was transferred to the secondary school.

Our teacher there well deserved the name of a kind-hearted fellow. Corporal punishment was not altogether unknown even here, but it was never only an expression of the teacher's bad temper, merely a means to an end to refresh our respect for authority which appeared to have become somewhat weak.

Also the tone of the mutual relationship between teachers and pupils had a more pleasant ring about it; it was human and not military, and the instruction that we had was not simple drilling, but true education.

E. H.

(e) THE CANING MANIA (m. aged 30)

While I was at my elementary school I suffered constantly from their thrashing technique. Each year one went on to the next class and to a new teacher. And all of them used to distribute canings. These were my great handicap. That most of us behaved as we should was the result of our fear of the cane. I considered such a punishment terrible, and actually I never had one myself. The very small results that were achieved by this caning mania I could notice by watching my comrades, who, after a few moments' pain, felt anything but respect for the teacher.

Now that I am myself a school-master I take care that my pupils never feel these punishments from which I suffered so much in the past. I have kept to this determination during my seven years of office as a teacher. Many times it rested in my hands whether this easily carried out punishment should be made use of; but each time my school-days arose before my eyes, and, delivered from the temptation, I put the ruler down again. Since then I have been glad that I have overcome the caning mania. I punish disobedience with other positive methods whereby the boys can gain some kind of mental improvement from their written impositions. *W. H.*

(*f*) THE MONKEY-CAGE (m. aged 31)

In the most northern part of a German-Swiss canton a town lies on the banks of a clear, blue river where I spent my boyhood.

Our teacher, whom we will call Hartmeier, was a very intelligent man, but of a most peculiar stature, and not much taller than we fifth-class boys. A large body, rather stouter than usual, swayed upon his short pair of legs, and his thick neck carried his relatively large head, the prominent features of which were light, watery eyes and an untidy beard. His clothing was also untidy, unbrushed and dirty, his hat was shapeless, battered and greasy. That was the model that stood before us for two long years.

Now this teacher was a thrashing pedagogue, as it says in the book, and yet I ascribe chiefly to his smallness of mind and his lack of consideration the fact that he only believed it to be possible to win the respect of his pupils through beating them. When one left the third class with its kind teacher to go on to one's two years with Hartmeier, one could be sure of having the sympathy of one's school-fellows of every age, from the youngest to the eldest. The younger ones looked forward with anxiety and fear to the time when, two or three years later, they would be delivered into the hands of this teacher, whilst those who were older sympathised with their successors now that they had gone through that hard time. Therefore they could not refrain, and we in our time also knew no better, from describing the Hartmeierish school methods as crudely as possible, so that I entered upon my first day in his class full of fearful expectations of what was going to happen to me there.

Hartmeier seemed full of significance from the very first minute. I still remember well how he stood to the left of the door when we came into his class-room doing the goose-step on this first morning, to take stock of this new flock of sheep, probably dividing the mangy ones from the healthy at first glance. Suddenly the boy in front of me got a resounding box on the ear, I had the next and two more behind me were treated in the same way. Thus were we immediately hall-marked before the whole class. Why did I get my ears boxed? At the time itself, as well as later, I have almost broken my head trying to think, but I have never been able to work out the reason.

At the end of the first morning's work we four victims got together. Round us gathered a large group of children who had that morning also made their first acquaintance with the yard-measure of the teacher, his favourite instrument. We separated with the firm conviction that the teacher could not endure us, and we well knew from the experiences of that first day what the following six hundred would bring us. In course of time we got so accustomed to his methods that a day with rather less caning seemed like a day with a smaller ration of bread. We became fairly hardened to this corporal punishment. What did hurt us, however, was the fact that it was only a few of us who got treated like this, and the rest of the class derived an entertainment from it which they would not readily have forgone. Children whose fathers were upon good terms with the teacher, or who came to school better dressed than we, seldom got any rough handling from him.

The monkey-cage was the girls' chief punishment. This is what Hartmeier called his writing-desk, but naturally only when he wasn't sitting in it himself. If he should catch a girl doing something that she shouldn't, she would be sent to sit in the monkey-cage. Two or three were generally up there. There were some days when Hartmeier did practically nothing else but ordering girls to go into the monkey-cage and fetching them down again, and thrashing the boys. The monkey-cage was generally reserved for the best pupils; the rest got a caning.

The usual daily programme was generally carried out upon these lines. First the corrected exercise-books would be given round. These would often amount to some hundred or more. They would be carried round to the teacher's house in the evening by the *best pupils*, and fetched again in the morning. What sort of work they contained was generally taken little notice of; he would only pay attention to the writing. Mine was never good. Mistakes would be marked in red ink. Anyone who failed to get marked as *good* or *tidy* might expect some sort of punishment, which was often already written down in the exercise-book. When the good pupils arrived with the books, they would be besieged by the outcasts, who wanted to discover, out of dull curiosity, what they had to expect. That often happened in the street.

Once I found an entry that ran more or less like this: "Filthy. Just wait, you messer, you filthy swine, wait until to-morrow. I will teach you to write better in future. You get yourself in the mood for a breeches-tanning." Unfortunately I threw this exercise-book away about five years ago after having kept it faithfully for some fifteen years. The thrashing that followed made me faint and vomit. A medical examination discovered my back garnished with red-and-blue weals which exceeded anything that I had experienced previously from the famous yard-stick. Because after this episode my parents finally remonstrated, and the old head-teacher, Mr. R., took some interest in my case, my treatment greatly improved. Unfortunately, however, this only happened during the last term.

Now I will return to our daily programme. The handing round of the exercise-books and the consequent canings usually took about an hour. There was quite a fair amount of good writing to be found in them on the whole. But after four to sixteen strokes across the fingers (I would often have this number), it is scarcely to be wondered at that one could not write particularly well. We sat six in a row, yet the hazel-switch, which the teacher cut for himself, was still much longer than that. If one of these six were not writing well enough and he saw the teacher's switch poised he would bend down as far as he could over his desk. His five desk companions naturally bent down too, and offered the teacher six expectant backs. Therefore instead of the one getting the full brunt of the cane, all six would generally have a taste of it. Six flies at a blow! At 10.30 we would generally have a short interval. Then he would sit behind the monkey-cage, the lid of the desk leaning against his forehead, and he would eat his lunch—sausage, bread and so on. That would happen every day, but only because some poor soul had provided something for it. But it was only later that my friend Jacob confessed to me once that his grandmother now and again would thrust some dainty into his hands, saying, "Jacob dear, take that to Mr. Hartmeier so that he will be kind to you for a week or two!" So it was not so bad for *dear Jacob*, and then, too, he wrote very well.

Friend Gysi, for the same reason—bad handwriting—twice carried home a head with a hole in it.

A further punishment was to be made to sit beside Murbach, who smelt nasty, some of the *better pupils* averred. There were one or two such poor devils, but unfortunately I cannot remember their names now. I myself sat for a whole term as a punishment next to a wretched girl who had a rash on her face and who had perpetually red eyes. Our teacher was never ashamed of holding up to shame the poverty and physical defects of the children, and to lower them in the estimation of the whole class. He himself, as I have already mentioned, was also no Adonis, and was not blessed with the gifts of this world.

At this time I was in such a state that by night I would see ghosts and robbers wherever I went or stood. All these ghosts resembled Hartmeier, only they were a great deal larger. My parents had often to come to my bed at night, where I lay bathed in perspiration, persecuted by these delusions. And in the morning before I went to school it would often happen that I fell down in a faint for fear of what should occur during the day.

Subsequently Hartmeier became head-teacher (!) and took over the seventh and eighth classes. Once, so I was told, he was himself thrashed by his eighth-class pupils when he was going to dole out thrashings amongst them, so that he was obliged to stay in bed for several days. I hope that this information was correct, and I am only thoroughly sorry that I was not there at the time.

O. F.

(g) TWENTY HAZEL-SWITCHES (m. aged 32)

"Oh, look! You have got white hair already at your temples!" Yes, it is a pity, but that is my souvenir of the elementary school, and I am often obliged to give this answer to the astonished enquirer. A nice souvenir, to get a crop of white hair on one's temples, isn't it?

It is just twenty years ago now since I had to leave a little village on the upper right-hand bank of the Lake of Zurich and be transferred from my old fifth class to a new sixth class in a larger one in the same district, on account of my parents moving house.

After this change of school that I have just mentioned it soon became apparent in the first few days that I was far behind the other pupils in class-work, and therefore became the victim of the bad-tempered teacher on this account, particularly during the arithmetic class. They were terrible hours and weeks for me, and ploughed deep wounds into my tender childish heart, as well as wiping out all my respect for my teacher, so that I was actually delighted when we received the news of his sudden death on the mountains. Although I was a really obedient and industrious pupil, I was treated in a most sadistic fashion by my teacher, and it would often happen that I would be the object of his outbursts of anger during the entire arithmetic lesson. One must also mention that he had his special victim in each subject.

I still remember even to-day, as though it might have been only last week, the torture which was provided for me by the geometry lessons, when his wrath would descend upon all the boys. The girls were spared from it. This lesson used to take place on Thursday morning from 7 to 8 o'clock; and if he could not condense his attack of rage, he would extend the lesson for as long as he liked. At the beginning of the geometry lesson he would show us a bundle of freshly cut hazel-twigs, about twenty of them, all of which would be broken to pieces upon the backs or hands of the terrified boys. He would try to compel our attention by these wild demonstrations instead of making use of simple teaching material.

We always had a heavy burden of tasks to carry out over Sunday. In consideration of the events that have been described above, which awaited the non-fulfilment of these duties, wounds that can never be obliterated engraved themselves deeply in my unconscious mind, so that I can still feel to this day some traces of old inhibitions.

H. Z.

(*h*) THE DISGRACE OF BEING THRASHED IN THE PRESENCE OF GIRLS (m. aged 36)

Elementary and Secondary Schools

I attended both schools in Zurich. These years of my school-life as a boy were particularly unpleasant to me because boys and girls were together. I cannot say how painful I found it. I lived in a constant state of anxiety lest I should say or do something stupid which would bring me before the attention of the whole class. This anxiety state continued until I had been at the cantonal school for some few years. When I was there my mother would also complain to the teacher about all my naughtiness at home, so that he was, so to say, asked from my home to punish me upon all occasions. Therefore no smallest opportunity was ever missed of bestowing corporal punishment upon me. And because these punishments were carried out in front of the whole class, the shame of it, particularly because of the presence of the girls, was far worse and more painful than the punishment itself. I consider that it is absolute madness to dole out a box on the ear or a caning. Such a method seems to me to be evidence of the poor quality of the teacher as an educator. My teacher in the secondary school would give us a certain number of strokes for every wrong figure in the answer to a sum, for words that were written wrongly, and so on.

Cantonal School, attended from 1909 *to* 1913

I really breathed quite freely once again when I read in the regulations of this school that corporal punishment had been abolished. And I was overjoyed that the instruction would take place without girls being present. But all that glitters is not gold. What I had already noticed in the previous years, and what was still to be observed plainly enough here too, was the so-called *partiality* of the professors. Some of them considered nothing but whether a boy had a wealthy father. One teacher particularly stays in my memory on account of this. Still in his same room, he continues to tutor pupils, who wish to have private lessons at 10 francs an hour, during which he still smokes his cigar or busies himself in some such way. These private pupils were, and are, very popular and he would carry on with them until their matriculation. Woe betide the poor devils who could not afford the luxury of this expensive private tuition; they might be sure that they would not be given any more peace in the class. During the regular class teaching the master would go round to his favourites encouraging them, helping them over difficult places, etc. Because I was shy by nature, which had been increased by my former thrashing educational system, and because all class instruction set me off into a state of excitement, a good word now and then would have helped me a great deal. Just to be told that one had understood a mathematical problem correctly, for example, would give one courage to go on and work it out. But never once during all the four and a half years had anyone come to me and said: "Yes, that's right, now finish it!" That mathematics became a subject that I loathed is scarcely to be wondered. The class still meets each month, and that man is present too who still estimates them in the same way as he used to do, because of their old valuation in his eyes as well as from what he considers to be their importance at the present, if they are drawing high salaries as engineers, etc., or have become wealthy factory owners.

L. R.

(*i*) THRASHING WITHOUT END (m. aged 45)

The young school-mistress with whom I passed the first two years of my school-life seems to live in my memory still as having been particularly lovable. When I went up into the third class there was a complete change. The one there, with whom I had to spend the next two years, gained from her pupils the bad name of *hypocrite*. She was exceptionally tall and had an unusual appearance for a woman. She had actually two faces, one for the street and the examinations, and the other for the classroom. Without knowing why, I aroused her constant disapproval.

I may mention two occurrences, both from this two years' experience of troubles.

It was a close, thundery summer's day, the sky was a grey-black and the air terribly oppressive as before some calamity. At last the storm came, the clouds burst, split into shreds by shattering lightning. The girls started to cry. I was fascinated by this display of natural phenomena and stared out of the window across the landscape. The teacher may have told me to pay attention, but I did not hear, all sounds being obliterated. The twigs that had been broken off by the hail fell to the ground, then there was a shrill cry, and from the top of the tree a yellow bird fell dead upon the ground. I only came to myself when the teacher dragged me from the form up to her desk. She took a ruler out of it, and hit me angrily across the head with it so that it broke in the middle. I looked up at the giantess. In her hand she still held the short end. She was red as fire. She threw away the stump, took up another ruler and hit me over the skull as though she would like to split it in two. Once more it broke in half. In a furious voice she ordered me back to my place. I felt a ridge as thick as a pencil under my hair and thought of the dead bird.

A forgotten rule of the school forbade the children to visit slaughter-houses. But because I happened to live near one I used to spend some time every day in front of the bars of the window, perhaps to hear a great, mad bull shot, perhaps to shed a few tears over a dying calf. One evening a school-fellow accompanied me there; I knew that an enormous beast was to be slaughtered that night. Some girls who saw us go split to the teacher. Without any questions being asked I received a punishment, but my comrade was overlooked. In my resentment I said: "S. was there too." He lied about it and I had first one and then another box on the ear. Now I understood what was the matter. But there was nothing to be done about it; I was kept in. The following morning S. brought a note from his very short-sighted mother to say that her boy "never lied." Therefore I was thrashed and as a liar was sent to stand before the door. Neither before nor after that occasion have I ever cried over many and brutal corporal punishments. But then I howled before the door, so that the whole school was disturbed by it. The teacher could not do anything about it. She called the attendant, an old trickster and a timeserver. She commanded him to put me in the lock-up. This old wretch took me into custody gladly enough as a rascal, and dragged me, a nine-year-old boy, down to the cellar by the hair, where I wandered about in the darkness among filth that had not been cleared away until I finally found a bench at the end of the room.

When I was eleven I attended classes for preparation for our first Communion, given by our assistant pastor, a young, intelligent man of more than usual vivacity.

CORPORAL PUNISHMENT

Having been brought up very strictly at home, I was a model of behaviour in this class. But because there were many rough lads and urchins in the class the instruction became a test of anyone's patience. But was it really necessary to make use of a walking-stick made of blackthorn? For the hundredth time the question was repeated, "What did the priest distribute at the Communion?" My neighbour was too dull to be able to give an answer to this question. I found this quite ridiculous and whispered: "Well, surely not a bit of apple?" There was a roar of derisive laughter. The pastor brayed "Nonsense!" struck me, in spite of his holiness, a blow on each hand so that I might easily count the knobs of the blackthorn. I ground my teeth together. My *friend* tittered and grinned broadly until the pastor turned to him and asked him the reason. Then the Judas in him awoke and he repeated what I had said. This pastor of thirty took me up from the form like a curl-paper and thrashed me in front of the altar-piece, half-mad, with his stick. He must have injured one of the sinews behind one knee. For months I had a swelling of extravasated blood and could only limp about at home with the greatest difficulty. To-day I can think a little more gently about the man, but it would fill me with horror if I were to know that my own boy was going to be delivered into the arms of such an excitable soul-seeker.

W. M.

(*j*) THE DANCING NIGGER (m.)

When I was moved up into the class where we boys and girls had to learn fractions and decimal fractions, and in common to go through this hard labour, we got on very slowly, for this reason: our teacher would often be seized with a nervous irritability which was announced to us by this statement: "In any case I shall have to let the *nigger* dance once more." He would then go to his desk, lift up the lid and take out a lithe black cane that he had baptized with the name of Nigger for short. He would begin either at the back row or the front one and let the Nigger dance along our backs—naturally the boys only—and in this way divided the fractions, because it was far more difficult then to add them together or to distinguish them one from another. He made use of the same method in other subjects as well. This teacher was instinctively more considerate of the weaker sex. He had a smaller, yellow cane that he used for them.

I am of the opinion that this method is not to be recommended. Because of it I, as well as my school-fellows, have suffered very little from home-sickness for the school; that which we felt after our short holidays was something quite different. Another great evil may also be that the child is made far too much afraid of the teacher. We also treated our pastor with so much veneration, respect and reverence that we were scarcely able to give him an answer to any question, so that usually, even the most familiar hymns would be repeated to him with much fear and stammering. It is necessary to free the child from his sense of oppression, but this cannot be accomplished with a *Nigger,* nor yet with a *Chinaman.*

A. Sch.

CHAPTER XIII

MOCKERY, CONTEMPT AND SARCASM

(a) "WHAT! YOU WANT TO COMPEL YOUR TEACHER?"
(m. aged 36)

As I am only noticing now more and more, I suffered very much from the teacher's mockery, and this happened particularly in the Middle School, when I was between sixteen and twenty, when a contributory factor may well have been that I was extraordinarily late in developing at puberty. A few episodes still remain clear in my memory.

I can still see the mathematics master running round the class-room in order to escape from my sight. "There is B. looking at me; he wants to see whether he has given the right answer. I must run away. . . ." This was a great spectacle which caused much joy on the part of the class, while B. became still more uncertain and shy.

I exerted myself to the utmost in the German lessons so that I might get on as quickly as possible. For composition we had to write about the pictures which hung in the corridor, such as the Self-portrait of Leonardo da Vinci. In all simplicity I wrote what I thought about it, and that was not flattering. The teacher was exceedingly critical about the lack of understanding shown by this particular pupil, whose name, however, he had not noticed at the time, and then during the lesson he was anxious to know who it might be. I remained quite silent, because his sharp criticism had humiliated me. He took out all the exercise-books and found that this essay happened to be mine. Then I watched the catastrophe coming nearer with a beating heart, scared to death that I was going to be exposed before the whole class.

If I now come to think of it, it would seem that my worst torments had been suffered during the singing class, and then because one might have to sing something alone. I always had an inhibition about that. Once, nevertheless, I screwed up my courage to get out a few bars. That was before I went to the Middle School. They did not come quite in the right order, however. Perhaps there were a few that I had left out. But with a little good will and with the help of a few words, one could guess quite well what had been meant. This attempt, nevertheless, came in for extreme mockery from the teacher. After that I never dared sing in the class again. I was never again able to squeeze out a single note, and was at last dispensed with from the class, because after being a martyr for a long time I had broken down and howled in front of the singing master!

Another episode that belongs to the subject of school justice, and so well shows the teacher's lack of understanding:

An arithmetic test paper. Hurry and fear. I always wrote abominably, and particularly under circumstances such as these. Result: the work was not corrected and I was marked as though the solutions of the problems had not been correct. After that I was kept in for two hours. Then something awoke in me and I declared that I would not be punished twice over, both by bad marks and detention, and demanded that my work should be corrected. The teacher looked at me hard and declared that I was shameless or something of the sort. I could leave the class; he would ask me no more questions. I remained sitting in my place. As a demonstration the others sitting around me were asked questions in a pointed manner. I stayed away from school for the rest of the day and got my father to write a note to the Director of the school, who was supposed to be a terrible tyrant, and before whom I trembled. I was sent for to go to see him in order to explain what had happened, and began in this way: "I wanted to compel Professor O. . . ." to correct my work. I would have continued, but was not allowed to get so far. "What! you wanted to *compel* your teacher . . ." shouted the Director, and almost went for me physically, so that I drew back and very nearly fainted from fear. The tempest took its course in a terrible manner, and only abated when I found time to begin to cry in a miserable fashion. Then his voice became more and more gentle. He advised me to carry out my detention and then to come back to him to discuss the question of my marks. However, I did not go back to him again. Yet in his speech at the end of term he referred to it again before the whole school under the heading, *Corruption of Morals*. This had now extended so far that one pupil had tried to intimidate his teacher. . . ! This, to be said in connection with the most timid rabbit in the first class at the Gymnasium, that he had been so impudent as to wish to compel his teacher, was too much. Now I am forced to laugh over the short-sightedness of the remark.

My recollections belonging to my third and fourth years at school are hardly worth recording. I remember a thrashing which was given to a school-fellow, and cannot think of it without some kind of unpleasant feeling coming back into my mind in connection with it. I find there is always a thought that remains at the back of the memory how one teacher came in to our class-master and both started to discuss the splendid cane that belonged to our teacher, which had a steel tip. They made the cane whistle through the air, and I can still see the cruel expression on the face of my then teacher when he was balancing this cane.

I liked my teacher in the fifth class of the elementary school most, and have forgiven him the occasional box on the ear that he used to give me from time to time on account of my bad handwriting. But because the son of a government official came off with a series of resounding whacks over the head for being the chief offender in some stupid piece of mischief, and his companion in crime, the boy of a horse-breaker, was terribly thrashed with a piece of rubber hose-pipe, I was awfully worried about it and it served to destroy to a large extent the ideal I had formed of that teacher.

The secondary school where I went was divided into three sections at first. The sections A and B had their nature study and geography with a tyrant who was always somewhat ill, and section C was given the same subjects by a young and very human master. I still remember how envious we were of this C class, and felt a kind of malicious joy when they were obliged to join us with our tyrant, and how disappointed because he was more polite with these older pupils and we were left to bear the brunt of the shocks of the whole first class alone. I never counted how many times I got a box on the ear. Twice, however, I was badly hurt by a caning. Once I escaped by crawling under the form. Another time, when I was up at the blackboard, I was able to draw in my body so that only my knickers suffered, but that made the good man so angry that we had a regular set-to, in which my main concern was to try to keep as much clothing as possible between the cane and myself. I got off from that encounter with the loss of a tooth. Then, because a couple of *better boys* came next me on the form, that is, boys of better family, I was the last of his series of whipping-boys. This partial treatment worried me more than the loss of my tooth.

On the whole this teacher usually was refreshingly impartial in his thrashings. The son of the government official to whom I have referred before was the cause of considerable alarm where I was concerned at that time. He sat in the last row but one, and would always bring the right flowers with him to nature-study classes. He brought large bunches of them, tied up tightly. But I still remember well how he too trembled with fear if the teacher came to see what he had and he was not able to untie the string round the flowers. Then he also would get a resounding box on the ear. The school provided him with a great deal of trouble, too. How much he would have liked to have got a job on the railway and how industriously he would have worked then! But he was the son of a government official and had to do something better than that for his living. He became a most pathetic figure because there was always too much expected of him, and yet no one gave him any help to achieve it.

F. B.

(b) A SPEECH DEFECT (m. aged 47)

In the elementary school I was considered one of the best pupils, and my speech was never objected to there. Then I went to the Gymnasium at Z. "You have a potato in your mouth!" was one of the first things my German master said to me. Derisive laughter followed on the part of my school-fellows, and a deep wound to my pride. My little defect in speech was never attended to, but neglected, and therefore it became worse.

Had the teacher taken the trouble to distinguish what was natural to me and what had been acquired, and had called attention to my peculiarities of diction in a more kindly way, perhaps to have given me tête-à-tête lessons in speaking correctly and in reading, much could have been done. But anyone who has once been made a laughing-stock of innocently before others remains permanently a victim of the defect.

E. B.

(c) THE STATIONS OF SORROW (m. aged 38)

I am furious when I think about my school-days. I have no wish to have back a single hour of them. We boys were thrashed half to death in the classes between the fourth and the sixth, especially the poorer ones. If, for instance, we had learned a poem by heart, and one boy got stuck for a moment, he was sent to a "station." The class-room was divided up into stations. I often got sent to thirty or more stations, and consequently received thirty or more strokes with a table-lath.

If I were beaten before my school-fellows I would not let a single word cross my lips. I went to my station and received the corresponding strokes. In spite of terrible pain I did not move a muscle of my face. I gazed at the teacher straight in the eyes with a deadly contempt.

While some of us were beaten, which would happen often enough, dead silence reigned in the room. Every face was pale, all those who were not the victims held their breath, no one moved a finger. Then in order to bring back life into these petrified boys the teacher would make us presents of pens. If one of the boys who had been punished was bleeding he would also get one. Not infrequently he would give us a Bible lesson or one on Bible history afterwards.

We had certain words that carried with them their special punishments. He would say *Arzt* (doctor) is not written with *tz*. Anyone who puts *tz* will get a thrashing. If in our writing we came to a word like this, we would look fearfully at one another. I would then write down *tz*, and others would do so likewise.

Upon the first page of every exercise-book he would inscribe the sentence: "Not quickly, but correctly and beautifully." This motto had the effect of a red rag on a bull with me. Should we happen to make a smudge on this first page, then woe betide us! Once a blot fell on his motto in my book and I was thoroughly well thrashed for that.

Th. W.

(*d*) "NOT YOU, TOO, FREDERICK!" (m. aged 30)

When I read your questionnaire a teacher in my elementary school arose before me with ecclesiastically pathetic gestures. I can still see him standing before the class and hear him saying after a question that no one could answer: "Not you, too, Frederick! not you, too!" with prophetic accents which belied the truth of the undercurrent of mockery in his words.

I still feel I am standing in full sight of the whole class; my entire mental capital, carefully accumulated and guarded with industry and goodness, would now be exposed. What else could I do but cry? But exactly in this way our despot achieved his aim. He wanted to make us cry. (Crying was considered to be the sign of spiritual repentance.) He knew that I was a frightened child, lived in fear of punishment, and, nevertheless, he would increase my feeling of inferiority through making me stand there before the class and make me an object of his affected mockery, by which means he easily achieved his goal.

To-day I can do nothing less than consider such an unpedagogic method of treatment was a deliberate attempt to suppress my independent tendency. I was an intelligent pupil, which he felt to be a threat to his pose of overlord, and at the same time he wished to add the necessary *little bit more* to his own high dignity. It is unbelievable with what unhappiness I used to get up in the morning during these years of my school-life and make my way to school, how often I would take refuge in illness, only to be able to escape from these often-repeated provocations, and how much self-confidence I sacrificed through this unreasonable method of treatment.

At school I suffered the most from my fears.

R. K.

(e) I WAS RIDICULED BECAUSE OF MY WAY OF SPEAKING (m.)

I have attended six different schools in four towns, during thirteen years I have been in sixteen classes and have been in the hands of forty different teachers. But in spite of this I have now become a teacher myself, although I have more disagreeable memories of these forty teachers than I have pleasant ones, and can recollect each one of them.

I was obliged to change my school-town four times and each time was held up to derision by my fellow-pupils because of my different way of speaking, ridiculed by them and teased about it. Because of this I suffered much more than from other more material things; for instance, because each different canton had its own time-table and a different method of teaching. In a very short time there was nothing about my work which would show that I had not long belonged to the class, with the exception of my writing, if it had not been for my speech. But on account of that I came in for enough rough-handling and sly digs. And not one of the teachers ever took me under his protection in a comradely sort of way; no, to my grief, I was known in Schaffhausen by one of the teachers not by my name, but very contemptuously as "that boy from Basle," or the "Berne chap."

Most of all I suffered from that type of teacher who always considers his own subject to be the most important thing in the world. I had to put up with being called *camel* and *pachyderm* from one drawing-master, which only made me stubborn and did not assist in my development otherwise. In the second class of the secondary school in Zurich I was put to sing alto. I was expected to be able to do this, which was quite a new thing for me, immediately, but it did not come off. Because of this the teacher, who had had a University education, and is now the editor of a paper, loaded me with insults. From this tactless behaviour I suffered extremely during my eighth year at school, and could think of no way out of my difficulty. I consulted the school doctor about it, who gave me a certificate of some kind which immediately freed me from the necessity of having to attend the singing class.

I also suffered from those teachers who would simply never ask one a question if one held up one's hand, but with the cruelty of a cat always went back to torment the same victim over and over again.

My relations with the French master were most painful; this man was suspicious of everything and in the tiniest trifles could always think that there was something aimed at him, and that it was my fault. He seemed always to think that people wished to injure him in some way.

My lessons with this man were miserable and caused me great trouble, because in the eyes of my parents and other grown-up people he seemed a *big-wig*, although he played but an insignificant part in the school. Another example of this kind of difficulty might be seen from this incident. A teacher at Zurich, in the secondary school there, would go and sit at his desk and read us extracts from the Berne history-lesson course, which was not quite the same as those which were in our lesson-books. He would yawn and then read a little more to us until one was almost asleep, then he would suddenly ask someone a question, get annoyed and hit out at the first person he could reach and then go on reading until the bell rang.

A. E.

EPILOGUE

EPILOGUE

EDUCATION is necessarily always full of problems. It should adjust itself to Life. But the outward manifestations of life are subject to constant change, and therefore constant alterations must take place both in the internal and external organisation of the schools.

Education to-day is particularly problematical. The contrasts which are to be found in its spirit, its aims and its organisation that can never be entirely overcome, relative to the conditions and requirements of the time, have never been more striking than they are at present. Because of this we have all the more reason occasionally to consider the fundamental elements of education and its mission for the future relative to these demands.

Regarded as a whole our schools are not bad, but they could be much, much better. It is easy to see the progress that has been made during the last few decades, and we rejoice over the fact that new ideas and forces are extensively in operation. But we must look upon this work of re-creation as being only in its infancy. The reforms so far have concerned the external organisation of the schools too exclusively. It is an established fact, for instance, that *educational method* has advanced enormously since the days of Pestalozzi, and we should grant this our full recognition. But one frequently encounters the danger of overestimating the significance of systems of education. Naturally, also, the improved reading and text-books, better equipment, work-shops and kitchens, laboratories, epidiascopes and school cinemas provide important stimuli, which we should recognise with gratitude. Our own age, in respect of technical and organisation facilities, is without comparison. Therefore the essentials of education have developed also in a satisfactory manner as far as they may be organised from the external point of view, as far as it is possible to establish a method of systematic thought.

But let us imagine that Pestalozzi should come and hold a review. Would we not be obliged to feel rather small under his critical eyes, in spite of all our achievements? The internal progress has not really kept step with the external perfecting of *the organisation of education*. We still suffer so much from a great lack of those values for which Pestalozzi's teaching and life bore passionate witness; from lack of pedagogic understanding, from lack of the spirit of goodness, understanding, devotion, brotherliness. In this spirit is contained the whole of educational requirements, and yet Pestalozzi seems to have been the only one who arrived at its truth. He must smile rather sadly over the superstition which is so prevalent to-day concerning the value of reforms in organisation. He would warn us about having a too naïve confidence such as may be seen when new methods, founded upon the old ones, are regarded as representing decided progress.

Every nation has, in course of time, the kind of education it deserves. The blessings and curses of the schools reflect the virtues and crimes of the whole generation. The school is finally nothing but the channel in which flows the spirit of the times and in which its own characteristics may be recognised. Behind the system of education stand all our intelligence and our lack of intelligence, which will compel the teacher to take one course or the other. When the children suffer the teachers also suffer because of the same causes.

The children have nothing more to suffer from the inadequacies of their teachers than from the mistakes of adults in general where they are concerned. School troubles merely represent a special aspect of them. Most of the mistakes and blunders, for instance, which darken school-life, overshadow family and professional life

EPILOGUE

also, even when the manifestations may be different on account of varied conditions. The several aspects of life are closely connected; the educational spirit of our schools will not be elevated until our entire generation obtains a more understanding, happy and self-sacrificing attitude towards youth.

Therefore we must forgo the temptation of trying to make one profession or even single persons responsible for the troubles to which we have been calling attention. We are all of us guilty on account of these evils, teachers as well as the lay population.

We are to blame that such one-sided interest is given to external progress, to technical success and that of organisation in our epoch.

We are to blame for the indifference, the lack of consciousness of responsibility and lack of understanding with which many parents regard the failings of their children.

We are to blame for our fear of taxation, the lack of a readiness to show a spirit of self-sacrifice especially where the schools are concerned, for lack of the insight that the most satisfactory capital investment for our children is the most suitable education for them. Relative to this we must believe that a generation which has grown up by means of a vital and happy school-life will develop so much more energy which will subsequently be available as an economic resource.

To blame also are the authorities who put stones in the way of teachers who are eager for reform, and who defend as inviolable former methods of education.

Those are also to blame who would like to make politicians of the teachers, and who see party-men in them rather than pedagogues.

We teachers are also to blame because we are always getting weary; because we do not hold to our demands for an educational ideal with sufficient tenacity; because we allow ourselves to be swamped by resistances and often become resigned or indifferent to the most burning educational questions. We are particularly to blame for subscribing to the self-deception that since so many school reforms have taken place during the last century we can now afford to rest on our laurels.

For more than a century Switzerland has represented in Europe the spirit of educational ideas and progress. But she will have to exert herself, however, if she wishes to keep this position in the future, or it will slip away from her, without anyone being aware of it at the time, perhaps. Some of our neighbours are already far ahead of us because of the character, impetus and suitability of their new work in connection with education.

We teachers are not alone entirely answerable for the schools, yet we must accept the largest share of responsibility, since we stand in the most direct relationship to them as their essential organ. Therefore it is most reasonable that we should always begin by directing educational criticism upon ourselves.

* * *

The old schools were, according to their fundamental nature, organisations for the supervision and protection of youth and for the provision of skill and knowledge. Their problems, therefore, were mainly those of the technique of instruction, besides that of maintaining external discipline, so that by these means the great organised task of educating their children was solved to the satisfaction of all classes of the population.

The schools of the future have a more comprehensive mission to fulfil. They should be centres which furnish a many-sided, happy child-life and intensive education for communal existence. Economic and other social factors show that the training to be obtained at home increasingly sacrifices reality. The standard of the requirements of education therefore must be considerably extended. The school where only instruction was to be had must give place to a school which will provide general training, and in connection with this wide pedagogic ideal, the school must also not only be a work-shop but a club-house for the children, too.

We should rejoice to live in an age which demands more from us teachers than the qualities necessary for an industrious official instructor! Let us rejoice to be the pioneers of the schools of the future, where everything possible will be done lovingly to confirm young people in all their impulses for life and development and to provide for them a free, happy and a strong existence.

"Die bedeutsamsten Ereignisse in der Geschichte sind doch immer die Verwirklichungen von Dingen, die man für unmöglich gehalten hatte. Es ist vergeblich, dem Fortschritt des Genies Grenzen setzen zu wollen; aber es ist noch aussichtsloser, die Auswirkungen des Wohlwollens zu begrenzen." (Pestalozzi, in *Mutter und Kind*.)[1]

BURIER-SUR-VEVEY,
  VAUD, SWITZERLAND

April 18, 1932

---

[1] "The most significant experiences in history are indeed always to be found when things we have deemed impossible come to pass. It is vain to try to set limitations to the progress of genius; but it is still of less purpose to confine the effects of kindness." (Pestalozzi, *Mother and Child*.)—Trans.

INDEX

Ability, 27, 28, 29, 33, 35, 46, 50, 55, 56, 57, 67, 81, 82, 128, 139, 144, 162, 163, 170, 211, 220, 221, 225, 235, 280, 283
Acceptance, 46
Accident, 183, 222
Achievement, 34, 44, 46, 47, 49, 56, 71, 77, 92, 94, 134, 334
Acquaintanceship, 139
Acquisition, 84
Activity, 18, 33, 46, 47, 48, 67, 98, 149, 263
Adjustment, 44
Admiration, 86
Adolescent boys, 88, 100, 226, 228
  girls, 76, 88
Adult or adults, 29, 33, 88, 104, 105, 112, 115, 118, 142, 186, 206
Advancement, 93
Advantages, 84, 99
Advice, 222, 283
Affects, 109
Affection, 37, 46, 91, 102, 216, 222, 229, 230, 289
  lack of, 104
Affliction, 31, 35, 269, 302
Aim, 42, 43, 116, 138, 173, 231, 249, 258, 267, 270
Algebra, 155, 170, 220, 238
Ambition, 35, 83, 85, 94, 127, 138, 166, 180, 261
Anaemia, 138
Anger, 108, 109, 178, 184, 211, 241, 243, 251, 267, 270, 295, 214
"Animal, My Favourite," 186
Animals, 39, 108, 183, 262
Annoyance, 108
Anxiety, 17, 42, 45, 83, 85, 138, 160, 189, 194, 201, 231, 234, 264, 268, 271, 305, 309, 315
  dreams, 31, 50, 156, 166, 219, 264
Apparatus, 49
Apprentices, 87, 103
Argument, 19, 20, 115, 165
Arithmetic, 50, 65, 95, 124, 126, 128, 129, 146, 153, 154, 161, 177, 194, 219, 256, 257, 284, 286, 288, 314, 322

Army, 25, 26
Arrogance, 30, 119
Art, 59
Artist, 42, 266
Artistry, 98
Assistance, 90
Assurance, 43
Astonishment, 125, 167, 265, 268, 291
Athletics, 143, 241
Atmosphere, 33, 49, 70, 71, 87, 98, 172, 177, 216, 229, 254
Atonement, 107, 225
Attainment, 56, 57, 67
Attention, 26, 35, 38, 41, 47, 56, 61, 87, 108, 119, 135, 142, 155, 157, 159, 162, 166, 195, 196, 222, 238, 241, 257, 269, 290, 311, 314, 325, 335
Attitude, 44, 59, 75, 79, 81, 97, 98, 105, 115, 118, 179, 212, 229, 231, 263
Audacity, 42
Austrians, 60
Authorities, 79, 83, 84, 94, 103, 130, 135, 158, 160, 170, 275, 335
  educational and school, 43, 49, 62, 83, 124
Authority, 28, 43, 45, 62, 72, 74, 78, 80, 104, 105, 115, 116, 198, 200, 308
Autocracy, 28, 37
Automatonism, 42
Average, 27
Aversion, 31, 134
Avocation, 30, 37

Bad, 58
Backward, 136, 246
Balance, 35, 48, 267
Barrier, 172, 238
Basle, 142, 143, 199, 214, 215, 250, 328
Bavaria, 157
Beard, 131
Beating, see also Corporal Punishment, 87, 108, 274
Beautiful, 58
Beauty, 57, 100
Bees, 54, 60

Behaviour, 17, 29, 41, 44, 49, 60, 62, 72, 73, 74, 77, 78, 80, 101, 102, 108, 114, 119, 128, 131, 163, 165, 227, 236, 252, 265, 277, 329
Belief, 29, 56, 74, 100, 103, 114, 174
Benefit, 28, 29, 40, 65
Berne, 174, 216, 248, 328
Birth-rate, 26
Blackboard, 155, 176, 177, 186, 189, 204, 219, 220, 262, 281, 283, 284, 286, 325
Blacksmith, 270
Blame, 179, 184, 202, 222, 284, 335
Blessings, 31, 334
Books, 292, 293, 299, 326, 327
Boredom, 34, 46, 70, 83, 88, 144, 145, 188, 189, 210, 270, 290
Botany, 145
Box on the ear, 113, 117, 124, 156, 178, 196, 224, 243, 248, 296, 307, 310, 318, 323, 325
Boy, 246, 278, 284, 290, 304, 319
Boyhood, 223, 224, 319
Boys, 46, 47, 76, 87, 88, 131, 190, 192, 200, 202, 208, 248, 249, 251, 280, 281, 289, 305, 310, 314, 326
Brain, 47, 138, 159
Bridge, 91
Brother or brothers, 80, 184, 188, 196, 224, 288
Burden, 26, 27, 32, 119, 149, 209, 225, 271, 280, 315
Bureaucracy, 25

Cantons, 41, 69, 84, 192
Capacities, 56, 57, 67
Carpentry, 47
Causes, 33, 37, 44, 87, 100, 209, 334
Certainty, 88, 282
Certificates, 55, 166, 216, 290, 329
Chance, 88
Change or changes, 89, 333
Character or characters, 20, 32, 35, 45, 70, 74, 76, 81, 102, 103, 141, 179, 211, 232, 236, 266, 292
Character-construction, 75
Character-formation, 166
Characteristics, 72, 74, 261, 283, 334
Chattering, 61
Cheating, 144, 152, 153, 286
Cheerfulness, 33
Chemistry, 161, 171, 172

Child or children, 7, 16, 19, 27, 30, 31, 32, 33, 34, 35, 37, 39, 40, 41, 42, 43, 45, 46, 48, 50, 55, 56, 57, 60, 61, 65, 68, 69, 70, 71, 72, 75, 76, 77, 78, 79, 82, 86, 90, 92, 93, 94, 98, 100, 101, 103, 104, 106, 109, 111, 112, 115, 119, 128, 129, 132, 138, 141, 142, 143, 144, 155, 157, 171, 184, 188, 191, 195, 197, 200, 206, 207, 208, 209, 213, 224, 232, 238, 248, 256, 257, 258, 259, 269, 273, 277, 279, 281, 283, 289, 290, 292, 306, 307, 310, 322, 334, 335, 337
average, 50
backward, 165
cheeky, 124, 125, *et seq.*
mentally defective, 56
model, 32
nervous, 160, 185
normal, 32, 56, 132
pre-school, 46, 91
Childhood, 16, 33, 34, 40, 86, 90, 91, 99, 101, 116, 154, 164, 186, 222, 224, 228, 232, 239, 255, 273, 275
China, 215
Church, 148
Citizens, 174, 233
Civilisation or culture, 17, 18, 26, 36, 49, 51, 54, 59, 60, 95, 158, 161, 259
Class or classes, 41, 45, 49, 63, 69, 71, 102, 105, 124, 125, 126, 129, 130, 131, 138, 146, 155, 167, 179, 190, 211, 215, 217, 221, 227, 242, 247, 250, 257, 260, 278, 281, 291, 293, 299, 313, 319, 322, 326
Class-master, 297
Class-mates, 80, 229, 284, 287
Class-room, 28, 29, 39, 42, 44, 73, 86, 91, 112, 117, 130, 142, 177, 189, 193, 194, 197, 201, 223, 245, 262, 270, 274, 300, 310
Class-spirit, 72, 73, 92
Classics, 28
College or University, 150, 155, 264, 329
training for teachers, 84, 85, 86, 87, 88, 89, 127, 133, 157, 166, 172, 179, 290
Comfort, 25, 32, 76, 85, 273, 274
Communion Service, 318, 319
Community, 29, 90, 95, 111, 249

INDEX

Community life, 92, 95, 336
Companions or company, 34, 125, 137, 150, 193, 224, 260, 296, 312
Comparison, 52, 111
Compensation, 30, 44, 55
Competition, 94, 95
Complaints, 17, 35, 51, 142, 172, 222, 273, 279
Complexes, 81, 227
Compositions or essays, 48, 50, 85, 87, 95, 124, 139, 140, 152, 185, 200, 221, 262, 263, 299, 321
Compulsion, 31, 32, 33, 44, 46, 135, 136, 171, 178
Comrades, 166, 200, 231, 235, 241, 261, 272, 298, 304, 308, 318
Comradeship, 36, 45, 61, 77, 90, 91, 96, 98, 152, 192
Concentration, 171
Conception, 39
Conclusions, 107, 109
Conditions, 33, 35, 77, 104, 166, 178, 232, 234, 261, 273, 282, 333, 335
Condolence, 31, 131
Conduct, 61
Confederates, 60
Confidence, 32, 104, 112, 118, 136, 137, 139, 141, 156, 237, 240, 253, 255, 276, 289
Confirmation, 223
  candidates, 225
Conflict, 72, 73, 75, 97, 109, 141, 144, 210, 233, 235, 236, 238
Confusion, 37, 112, 296
Congratulations, 31
Connection, 68
Conscience, 62, 63, 72, 75, 98, 106, 287
Conscientiousness, 51
Consciousness, 72, 115
Consequences, 55, 104, 128, 138, 195, 237
Consideration, 39, 84, 103, 184, 239
Consolation, 76
Construction, *see* Organisation
Contact, 67, 69, 83, 91, 94, 116, 179, 186, 228, 260, 264, 268
Contemplation, 26
Contemporaries, 68, 90, 163
Contempt, 112, 117, 119, 267, 281
Continuity, 100
Contradiction, 117
Controversy, 18

Convention, 259
Conviction, 41, 44, 63, 140, 143, 201, 275
Cooking, 47
Co-operation, 36, 45, 47, 90, 95, 115, 224, 230, 237
Copying or cribbing, 92
Cornerstone, 27, 49, 95
Correction, 62, 114
Country, 49, 192
Courage, 32, 34, 50, 56, 79, 80, 105, 106, 133, 156, 193, 218, 225, 227, 237, 316
Courtesy, 77
Cowardice, 72
Cramming, 153, 159
Cravings, 39
Credits, 209
Crime, 201, 206, 225, 306, 334
Criterion, 33, 34
Criticism, 15, 18, 43, 60, 79, 179, 229, 295, 321, 336
Cruelty, 111, 119
Cry, 126, 317, 323, 327
Cry-baby, 267
Crying, 265
Curiosity, 16, 311
Curriculum, 42, 47, 53, 58, 160, 171
Custom, 187

Daemons, 25, 26, 46
Danger, 21, 28, 54, 69, 72, 79, 100, 105, 109, 110, 119, 131
Daughter, 164, 278, 279, 282
Day, 31, 139
Day-dreaming, 70, 268
Death, 154, 262, 270, 314
Deceit, 93
Deception, 152
Decision, 89, 97, 99
Deductions, 48
Defence, 105
  mechanism, 104
Defiance, 34, 104, 105, 218, 294, 297
Deficiencies, 15
Degradation, 107, 118
Deliberation, 32, 36
Deliverance, 154
Delusion, 55, 313
Demands, 27, 31, 40, 42, 65, 72, 74, 209, 333, 335
Dependence, 35

Depositions, 119
Desire, 86
Desk, 93, 245, 251, 253, 262, 266, 270, 278, 287, 305, 312, 317
Despotism, 80, 282
Destiny, 21, 32, 190
Destruction, 36, 276
Determination, 46, 309
Development, 32, 33, 34, 39, 40, 46, 47, 49, 50, 58, 60, 68, 75, 81, 83, 85, 88, 91, 96, 99, 100, 108, 110, 118, 139, 148, 211, 228, 229, 235, 236, 238, 277, 282, 304, 329, 337
  child, 136
  future, 35, 304
  general, 27
  psychological, 81
Devotion, 86, 169, 221, 232, 334
Dexterity, 48
Diagnosis, 16, 25, 275
Differences, 165, 213
Difficulties, 33, 35, 36, 37, 74, 76, 210, 227, 254, 255, 270, 329
Dignity, 79, 80, 277, 327
Disappointment, 131, 140, 258, 264, 265, 277
Disapproval, 134, 167
Discipline, 27, 36, 39, 40, 41, 42, 44, 45, 80, 114, 116, 118, 119, 200, 249, 250, 253, 298, 336
Discomfort, 16, 33, 46
Discovery, 34, 102, 173, 174
Discrepancy, 69, 71
Discrimination, 59, 72
Discussion, 18, 82, 222
Diseases, 101
  professional, 28, 30, 275
Disgrace, 111, 129, 190, 293, 306
Disgust, 34, 278
Disillusionment, 101, 135
Disobedience, 44, 61, 138, 309
Displacement, 110
Disproportion, 67, 68, 109
Distance, 116
Distortion or distortions, 33, 79
Documents, 17, 18, 76
Doll, 285
Domination, 86, 104
Door, 126, 127
Doubts, 76, 276, 302
Drawing, 47, 66, 95, 167, 242, 247

Dreams, 135, 166, 167, 217, 219
  anxiety, 31, 50, 156, 166, 219, 264
Drill, 129, 230, 249
Dullness, 34
"Dummy-sucker," 301
Dunce, 126
Duties or Duty, 26, 98, 127, 179, 180, 197, 214, 237, 250, 285, 298, 315

Ear, 130
Economy, 278
Education, 17, 26, 32, 34, 36, 41, 51, 52, 56, 57, 59, 60, 67, 68, 70, 72, 81, 89, 91, 94, 95, 102, 111, 115, 116, 118, 119, 134, 149, 150, 158, 173, 192, 204, 220, 228, 230, 232, 256, 270, 308, 333, 335, 336, 337
  dark places of, 17, 270
  evils of, 16
  general, 36, 52, 60
  methods, 30, 49, 71, 77, 95, 252, 307, 333
  spirit of, 18, 19, 333
Educationists, 20, 47
Effects, 110, 134
Effort or efforts, 33, 39, 56, 96
Ego, 107, 178
  instinct, 40
  tendencies, 249
Emotions, 58, 90, 94, 103, 109, 144, 228, 229
Encounter, 31
Encouragement, 28, 76, 158, 239, 259, 298
Endurance, 60
Enemy, 252, 259, 261
Energy, 28, 42, 51, 56, 73, 82, 95, 96, 106, 116
"Engineer," 192
England, 143, 144
English, 152
Englishman, 281
Enquiry, 103, 226
Enthusiasm, 49, 62, 69, 70, 180, 239, 289
Environment, 52, 59, 68, 131, 159, 225, 233, 288, 289
Envy, 61, 93
Errors, 115
Escape, 258, 321
Essays, *see* Compositions

INDEX 343

Esteem, *see* Self-esteem
Evils, 17, 20, 36, 75, 98, 101, 105, 264, 320
Exaggeration, 32, 79
Examinations, 55, 88, 147, 148, 153, 162, 167, 185, 209, 222, 290, 307, 312, 317
    fear, 166
    matriculation, 192, 193, 208, 209, 260, 316
Examiners, 158, 167
Example, 119, 127, 134, 240, 261, 290, 292
Exceptions, 202
Excitement, 139, 250, 277, 316
Excursions, 49, 204, 206, 221, 246, 250, 297
Existence, 32, 40, 44, 85, 99, 100, 264, 279, 337
Expectations, 37, 77, 99, 188
Expeditions, 71
Expenditure, 65, 67, 70, 82, 116
Experience or experiences, 17, 18, 19, 29, 45, 48, 77, 83, 90, 104, 107, 132, 167, 196, 197, 213, 222, 232, 269
Experiment, 47, 95, 172
Explanation, 44, 83, 164, 225, 227, 237, 238, 243
Expression, 34, 108, 139, 207
Eyes, 34, 86, 96, 109, 110, 126, 149, 156, 158, 176, 210, 224, 225, 250, 267, 289, 303, 316, 334

Face, 138, 131, 317,
Factors, 76, 85, 87, 92, 106, 336
Facts, 50
Failings, 38, 101
Failure, 55, 56, 92
Faith, 40, 41, 76, 115
Familiarity, 78
Family, 91, 190, 192, 196, 241, 324, 334
Fate, 188, 302, 303
Father or fathers, 46, 86, 98, 104, 130, 132, 138, 141, 154, 156, 161, 190, 217, 224, 226, 240, 246, 262, 273, 274, 282, 283, 285, 287, 288, 304, 310, 322
Faults, 61, 102, 106, 107, 139, 257, 271, 279, 329
Faust, 97

Fear, 42, 43, 50, 55, 106, 111, 126, 138, 154, 155, 158, 166, 183, 187, 188, 201, 202, 206, 208, 223, 225, 244, 268, 271, 272, 285, 286, 292, 296, 305, 310, 313, 320, 322, 323, 325, 328
Feelings, 48, 110, 112, 201, 218, 274
Fetishism, 37, 42
Fixation, 87, 97, 98
Flexibility 26, 37, 42
Fluency, 59, 67
Food, 33
Form, 93, 125, 135, 143, 234, 270, 271, 297, 305
Freedom or liberty, 26, 42, 43, 55, 58, 60, 71, 72, 77, 79, 98, 107, 131, 132, 135, 136, 170, 207, 236, 254, 271, 272, 306
French, 170, 202, 215, 216, 247, 283, 329
Fresh air, 33, 143
Friends, 116, 131, 132, 141, 150, 185, 206, 219, 225, 243, 249, 259, 319
Friendships, 80, 90, 91, 199, 239, 253, 254, 260, 291
Fruit, 16
Functions, 57, 75, 82, 90, 111
Future, 81, 97, 157, 263, 265, 336

Gain, 84, 85, 236
Game or games, 87, 143, 187, 251, 265, 284
Gardening, 47
Generation, 168, 236, 334, 335
    coming, 16
    older, 58
Genius, 74
Geography, 48, 66, 211, 212, 215, 324
Geometry, 155, 159, 220
German, 130, 179, 185, 201, 216, 221, 247, 285, 321, 325
Germany, 95, 144
Gesture or gestures, 79, 327
Gifts, *see* Talents
Girls, 46, 47, 76, 86, 87, 88, 112, 126, 128, 131, 141, 200, 244, 248, 279, 280, 281, 282, 288, 294, 315, 316, 317
Glöckel, 174
Goal, 42
God, 204, 285, 286
Goethe, 97, 153
Good, 58

Good fellowship, 36
Goodness, 40, 42, 60, 74, 76, 81, 82, 232
Government, 25
Grammar, 48, 215
Gratification, 34, 47, 76, 102, 111, 119
Greek, 28, 197, 198, 209
Grievances, 18, 19
Grimace, 124, 305
Growth, 83, 111
Grumbling, 70, 283
Guidance, 67, 73
Guides, 116, 213, 224, 229
Guilt, 75, 105, 106, 207, 225, 234, 235, 237, 306
Gymnasium, 144, 146, 147, 255, 256, 258, 263, 295, 297, 298, 322, 325
Gymnastics, 66, 153, 168

Häberlin, Paul, 80
Habits, 20, 48, 88, 91, 110, 129, 227, 231
Hair, 246, 299, 302, 307, 313, 318
Hair-ribbons, 246, 286
Handicrafts, 66, 95
Hands, 48, 93, 105, 124, 127, 132, 155, 176, 189, 195, 205, 227, 244, 251, 297, 298, 302, 305
Happiness, 21, 25, 26, 32, 35, 40, 50, 76, 81, 82, 90, 93, 95, 96, 99, 106, 135, 143, 144, 153, 250, 267, 268
Hardships, 32, 35, 50, 56, 157, 211
Hare, 262
Hatred, 112, 145, 184, 218, 277, 289, 297
Head, 188, 247, 269, 288, 309, 313, 317
Headache, 177
Health, 143
Heart, 32, 127, 130, 144, 206, 208, 240, 252, 275, 289, 290, 302, 314, 321
Hedin, Sven, 215
Help, 95, 116, 151, 259, 288
Hesse, Hermann, 212
Hints, 93, 218, 286
History, 48, 50, 59, 66, 124, 146, 168, 201
Hobby, 135
Holidays, 85, 98, 99, 128, 140, 143, 217, 279, 304
Home, 51, 68, 115, 129, 131, 132, 137, 141, 143, 151, 178, 186, 201, 206, 236, 238, 241, 245, 269, 273, 275, 313, 315, 319, 336

Home-training, 37
Home-work, 65, 127, 143, 147, 152, 154, 158, 169, 187, 214, 221, 261
Honest, 103
Honesty, 7, 144, 156
Honey, 54
Hope, 98
Horror, 173, 239, 319
Hostility, 16, 72, 74, 259
House, 25
Human being, 38, 45, 88, 107, 111, 116, 189, 197
Humanity, 57, 75, 78, 81, 205, 224, 229, 232
Humiliation, 218, 223, 306
Humour, 40, 119
  false good-, 16
  lack of, 27
  sense of, 42, 45, 70, 80
Hypocrisy, 61
Hypocrite, 116, 129, 317

Ideal or ideals, 15, 27, 44, 49, 53, 55, 59, 86, 111, 116, 182
Ideas, 47, 48, 80, 81, 103, 112, 116, 182, 239, 263, 279, 286, 333, 336
  confusion of, 25
Identification, 86
Idleness, 116, 270
Ignorance, 135, 267
Illness, 67, 97, 98, 267, 286, 327
Imagination, 46
Immaturity, 27, 116, 118
Immobility, 40
Impartiality, 30, 109
Importance, 28, 51, 81, 83, 84, 91, 134, 317
Impression, 60, 78, 94, 127, 137, 141, 188, 205, 277
Improvement, 19, 68, 103, 106, 115
Impulses, 43, 63, 86, 108, 109, 111, 163, 337
Inadequacy or inadequacies, 15, 21, 37, 38, 82, 210, 272, 334
Inclination, 90
Independence, 59
Indictment, 32
Indifference, 34, 335
Indignation, 62, 103, 131
Individual, 25, 72, 77, 93, 95, 96
Individuality, 31, 36, 48, 60, 73, 256

Industry, 60, 128, 134, 174, 202, 208, 221, 266, 327
Infallibility, 79
Inferiority, 43, 55, 75, 105, 169, 212, 267, 282, 288
Influence, 33, 60, 81, 91, 103, 105, 227, 229, 241, 255, 256, 276, 295
Information, 16, 19, 27, 86, 164, 167, 180
Inhibitions, 51, 71, 91, 109, 148, 315
Injury, 111, 118, 223, 305
Injustice, 92, 101, 102, 190, 210, 227, 251, 274, 277, 279, 285, 289, 294, 299
Innocence, 111, 157, 251
Inquisition, 94
Inspector, 34, 125, 170, 207
Inspiration, 215
Instincts, 39, 79, 119, 225, 249
  asocial, 94, 111
Institution or institutions, 33, 192, 231, 239, 240, 252, 260
Instruction, 33, 39, 47, 52, 58, 67, 71, 76, 90, 131, 142, 146, 185, 210, 219, 225, 239, 240, 284, 336, 337
Instrument, 270
Insubordination, 87
Insult, 138, 221, 329
Intellect, 119, 144, 152, 160
Intellectualism, 51, 52, 54, 149
Intelligence, 36, 211, 307
Interest, 28, 44, 46, 50, 57, 62, 76, 81, 82, 92, 95, 100, 135, 159, 181, 198, 215, 216, 229, 237, 263, 282, 335
Interference, 102
Interruptions, 41
Intimidation, 106, 107, 116, 305
Introduction, 153
Investigation, 15, 38, 51, 68, 226, 257
Irony, 92, 117
Irritability, 44, 108, 278, 319
Isolation, 90, 93, 235

Jealousy, 283
Jest, 117, 118, 226
Joy or joys, 32, 34, 56, 90, 128, 135, 185, 205, 263, 266, 268, 292, 324
Judgment, 51, 67, 72, 81, 88, 94, 277, 278
Justice, 101, 163, 207, 276, 322

Keller, Gottfried, 148

Kindness, 164, 195, 271, 274
Kiss, 154
Kissing, 108
Kitchens, 46, 333
Knowledge, 28, 34, 36, 48, 51, 52, 53, 58, 59, 60, 62, 67, 71, 75, 82, 89, 116, 147, 160, 171, 173, 175, 193, 200, 204, 209, 213, 220, 226, 230, 235, 257, 267, 271, 298, 303, 336

Labours, 42, 201, 319
Language, 48, 168, 197, 201, 228
Latin, 28, 209, 296
Laugh, 128
Laughter, 119, 125, 183, 192, 145, 301, 319, 325
Lawlessness, 42
Laziness, 16, 42, 72, 97, 98, 113, 267, 269, 270
Leaders, 30, 133
Leadership, 78, 90
Learning, 36, 47, 86, 128, 174, 214, 299
Lectures, 223, 293
Leonardo da Vinci, 321
Lessons, 93, 131, 157, 214, 216, 218, 241, 246, 253, 268, 281, 293, 325, 329
  Bible, 326
Liberty, *see* Freedom
Lies or untruthfulness, 61, 62, 288
Life, 21, 25, 26, 27, 29, 32, 34, 40, 43, 44, 48, 58, 59, 61, 63, 81, 84, 87, 90, 94, 96, 99, 110, 128, 132, 140, 144, 145, 148, 159, 168, 172, 180, 189, 232, 238, 234, 256, 258, 263, 270, 287, 304, 333, 337
  joys of, 32
  provisional, 97
  social, 86
Life-work, 48
Limitations, 40, 74, 136, 231, 306
Limits, 39
Literature, German, 66
Logarithm, 202
Loneliness, 98
Looking, 110, 111
Love, 47, 51, 76, 104, 105, 166, 200, 218, 226, 229, 264, 275, 276, 289
  of achievement, 34
  of learning, 138

Lovely, 283
Lucerne, 273

Machines, 26
Make-believe, 264
Malice, 41
Man, 63, 188, 265, 300, 304, 309
Mankind, 26, 55, 230
Manners, 63, 188, 265, 300, 304, 309
Mark-books, 61, 138
Marks, 55, 61, 93, 94, 192, 322, 323
    bad, 35, 92, 144, 175, 274, 288
    good, 35, 61, 92, 175
Masculinity, 282
Masochism, 109, 110
Mass-production, 69, 73
Mastery, 94, 106
Material, 46, 111, 181, 208, 290, 299, 314
Mathematics, 146, 155, 157, 168, 201, 220, 316, 321
Maturity, 29, 30, 81, 99
Meaning, 99, 100
Member, 90
Memories or memory, 16, 34, 36, 47, 51, 87, 93, 132, 167, 168, 180, 186, 197, 199, 244, 271, 283, 307, 317, 328
Men, 26, 84, 100, 133
Mentally Defective, 73, 197
Mercy, 138
Merits, 117
Metabolism, 53, 145
Methods, 26, 30, 47, 68, 78, 96, 107, 109, 114, 134, 252, 254, 310, 320, 328, 335
Mind or minds, 32, 34, 36, 108, 111, 131, 132, 160, 166, 198, 213, 254, 257, 258, 263, 275, 278, 309
    conscious, 86
    unconscious, 31, 234, 315
Mis-education, 59, 63
Misfortunes, 95, 110, 125, 171
Mistake or mistakes, 37, 92, 100, 101, 102, 104, 112, 185, 187, 195, 202, 219, 242, 258, 311, 334
Misunderstanding, 48, 139
Mockery, 117, 118, 119, 149, 217, 219, 266, 267, 303, 321, 322, 327
Modesty, lack of, 61
Moloch, 25
Morality, 60

Moral Code, 108
Mother or mothers, 46, 124, 128, 129, 144, 206, 226, 245, 248, 262, 273, 282, 287, 288, 289, 298, 303, 315, 318
Motives, 85, 87, 109, 118
Moustache, 131
Movement, 40, 41, 216, 270
Mutiny, 131

Name, 127, 129, 135, 173, 176, 281, 293
Nation, 25
Nature, 49, 54, 74, 106, 135, 138, 172, 198, 211, 235, 237, 336
    human, 58, 75, 240
    love of, 145
Nature-study, 46, 66, 95, 228, 324, 325
Naughtiness, 41, 61, 104, 267, 315
Necessity, 32, 39, 41, 83, 95, 213, 268
Needs, 35, 37, 39, 70, 83, 115, 244
Neglect, 92, 222
Nervous breakdown, 219
Nervous disturbance, 305
Nervous tension, 35
Night, 126, 128, 134, 152, 303
Nose-bleeding, 196
Nourishment, 110, 111, 173
Numbers, 41

Obedience, 60, 250
Object, 33, 95
Obligation, 93
Obsession, 296
Observation, 47, 49, 54
Observer, 271
Occupations, 100
Offences, 112
Omission, 147
One-sidedness, 50, 54, 55
Opinion or opinions, 15, 33, 34, 39, 47, 51, 59, 61, 106, 115, 140, 144, 166, 175, 179, 182, 209, 216, 231, 233, 253, 274, 276, 282, 288, 296, 320
    public, 43
Opponents, 17, 109, 231
Opportunities, 34, 39, 77, 91, 96, 99, 119, 139, 238, 249, 261, 265, 268, 279
Opposition, 40, 49, 74, 179, 231

INDEX

Oppression, 32, 53, 80, 83, 98, 116, 171, 198, 199, 209, 251, 270, 320
Order, 39, 63
Organisation, 29, 31, 39, 57, 75, 83, 92, 95, 117, 252, 333, 335
Originality, 60, 73, 74
Outcast, 73, 128, 194, 223, 239
Outlet, 41
Overconscientiousness, 44
Overestimation, 35, 43, 52
Oversensitiveness, 37

Pain, 108, 109, 110, 111, 131, 154, 176, 251, 295, 308
Palestrina, 200
Pallor, 138
Parents, 49, 102, 103, 134, 137, 138, 140, 141, 154, 184, 185, 191, 200, 225, 226, 252, 259, 275, 287, 289, 292, 294, 314, 316, 329, 335
Paris, 297
Partiality or prejudice, 19, 92, 88, 101, 102, 233, 249, 257, 273, 277, 298, 316
Passivity, 40, 46, 264
Pastor, 223, 224, 225, 227, 285, 318, 319, 320
Patience, 105, 131, 160, 166, 177, 240, 241
Pattern, 72
Peace, 61, 63
Peculiarities, 35, 139, 161, 275
Peculiarity, 16
Pedagogues, 41, 47, 160, 162, 207, 248
Pedantry, 41, 44, 70, 139
People, 25
Perfection, 79, 175
Persecution, 218, 267
Perseverance, 40, 168
Personality, 39, 45, 54, 60, 63, 70, 72, 82, 98, 107, 213, 215, 256, 292, 294
Persons, 18, 110
Pessimists, 114
Pestalozzi, 21, 34, 39, 47, 51, 55, 100, 140, 174, 222, 231, 232, 251, 275, 298, 333, 334, 337
Phantasies, 46, 54, 57, 61, 99, 113, 139, 140, 190, 225, 287, 288
Phenomenon, 92, 109, 317
Philosophy, 59, 63
Pictures, 198

Pioneer, 49, 182
Plants, 145, 149
Play, 128, 231, 253
Play-instruction, 33
Pleasure, 33, 34, 35, 107, 110, 111, 112, 119, 132, 139, 171, 184, 214, 225, 229, 265, 291
  masochistic, 109, 110
  sadistic, 110, 111
Poem, 63, 129, 306, 326
Politeness, 77
Population, 26, 34, 67, 83, 153, 335, 336
Position, 40, 43, 82
  social, 85
Possessions, 25
Possibilities, 76
Power, 25, 42, 43, 49, 58, 74, 80, 86, 87, 93, 103, 105, 119, 197, 198, 209, 275
Practice, 111, 182
Praise, 35, 276
Precosity, 60
Preference, 88, 92, 102, 280
Prejudice, *see* Partiality
Preparation, 85, 100, 201
Pressure, 42
Presumption, 116
Priest, 40
Principle, 41
Privilege, 39, 214
Problem, 15, 17, 18, 29, 30, 35, 41, 44, 50, 59, 83, 115, 174, 220, 234, 252, 273, 333, 336
Process, 141, 233
Profession, 18, 20, 25, 30, 81, 84, 114, 116, 133, 275, 292
  choice of, 84, 86, 87, 88, 99, 181
Prognosis, 74, 96
Programme, 39, 231, 280, 311, 312
Progress, 56, 68, 71, 80, 115, 127, 240, 333, 335
Project method, 57
Prophets, 32
Proportion, sense of, 42, 70
Protection, 25, 336
Protests, 157
Psychological problems, 97
  troubles, 298
Psychologist, 133, 224, 228
Psychology, 109, 111, 175, 186, 203, 306

Psychology, crowd or group, 72
Puberty, 74, 75, 76, 153, 234, 321
Public, 25, 110, 117
Publicity, 17, 20, 157, 212, 232
Punctuality, 136
Punishment, 87, 106, 107, 127, 132, 138, 143, 156, 158, 189, 190, 191, 195, 207, 266, 267, 297, 300, 309, 311, 313, 318
    corporal, 105, 107, 108, 109, 110, 111, 112, 117, 154, 175, 184, 207, 238, 249, 254, 305, 306, 308, 310, 315, 316
Pupils, 34, 35, 39, 47, 61, 71, 73, 75, 77, 78, 92, 94, 102, 103, 106, 110, 118, 119, 132, 136, 137, 140, 141, 143, 145, 166, 168, 169, 171, 174, 178, 182, 190, 192, 202, 204, 207, 212, 217, 222, 238, 239, 249, 250, 253, 258, 260, 261, 274, 277, 279, 281, 283, 284, 288, 295, 297, 302, 306, 308, 309, 311, 314, 316, 325, 326
Purse, 132

Qualification, pedagogic, 37, 87
Qualities, 88, 113, 337
Quarrel, 254, 260
Quest, 35
Question, 35, 37, 41, 48, 68, 83, 87, 151, 157, 191, 200, 205, 207, 208, 210, 229, 234, 246, 273, 279, 288, 318, 320, 322, 329, 336
Questionnaire, 15, 16, 17, 18, 19, 76, 166, 168, 202, 220, 222, 228, 255, 271, 273, 327
Quixotism, 28

Rabbit, 262, 304
Radicals, 41
Reactions, 35, 61, 72, 76
Read, 256, 283
Reading, 65, 68
Readjustment, 16, 75
Realisation, 80, 83, 92, 94
Reality, 19, 44, 52, 53, 81, 182, 307, 336
Reason, 42, 55, 77, 87, 109, 113, 132, 195, 203, 217
Reasonableness, 40, 255
Reassurance, 35
Reform, 16, 36, 49, 69, 71, 83, 87, 96, 111, 214, 334, 335, 336
Regression, 229

Regulations, 83
Relations, 85, 289
Relationships, 30, 65, 76, 78, 79, 80, 102, 104, 109, 111, 142, 179, 336
Release, 93, 111, 142, 179, 336
Religion, 58, 229, 285
Remarks, 180
Remorse, 107
Renunciation, 95, 107
Repetition, 92
Reports, 15, 17, 18, 34, 92, 93, 94, 102, 128, 130, 138, 167, 169, 192, 226, 238, 242, 246, 274, 288
Representatives, 18, 29
Reproaches, 134, 142, 227, 239, 248
Reputation, 127
Requirements, 39, 41, 57, 67, 100, 112, 116, 136, 222, 235, 333, 337
Research, 38, 95
Resentment, 112, 128, 207, 282, 294
Resignation, 34, 56
Resistance, 105, 336
Respect, 39, 43, 47, 51, 80, 163, 174, 184, 195
Responsibility, 16, 28, 33, 72, 91, 182, 237, 269, 289, 335, 336
Results, 65, 67, 71, 85, 110, 201, 202, 203, 227, 308
Retribution, 108
Revenge, 78, 109, 118, 190, 251, 277
Reverence, 50, 78, 240, 320
Revolt, 32
Reward, 82, 164, 304
Rhyme, 260
Rhythm, 32, 70
Right, 58
Rights, 41, 100, 106
Rigidity, 37, 42
Rivalry, 93, 96
Romance, 33
Ruler, 267, 283, 295, 309, 317, 318
Rules, 40, 43, 155, 159, 162, 202, 257

Sacrifice, 17, 70, 157, 336
Sadism or sadistic tendency, 290, 305
Sand-heap, 46
Sarcasm, 117, 321
Satchel, 36, 128, 140, 270
Satire, 79, 118, 137
Satisfaction, 108, 208
Scapegoat, 127, 156, 292, 294, 321
Scene, 109

INDEX

Scepticism, 29
Scholars, 36, 55, 127, 135, 150
Scholarship, 292, 293, 294
School-age, 37
School authorities, 49
School-boy, 27, 31
School-days, 16, 19, 31, 35, 48, 50, 76, 82, 91, 98, 99, 130, 140, 145, 148, 197, 198, 201, 202, 209, 210, 213, 216, 220, 236, 242, 255, 259, 283, 289, 326
School-girl, 31
School-learning, 51, 92, 101, 143, 183, 186
School-life, 37, 55, 70, 71, 223, 256, 264, 280, 315, 327, 334
School-work, 67, 69
School-masters, *see* Teachers
School-masterishness, 27, 29, 30, 83, 210
Schools, 15, 16, 17, 26, 27, 29, 31, 34, 36, 37, 39, 40, 44, 46, 49, 53, 56, 61, 65, 67, 70, 71, 72, 82, 95, 101, 126, 130, 134, 143, 144, 148, 162, 171, 172, 173, 175, 191, 200, 208, 212, 213, 226, 231, 234, 238, 255, 258, 259, 302, 303, 304, 328, 333, 336
  Central, 154, 155, 157, 159, 195
  Elementary, 29, 57, 70, 71, 124, 164, 172, 191, 214, 231, 275, 288, 289, 295, 306, 308, 314, 323, 325
  ideal, 34, 337
  inadequacies of, 15
  Middle, 73, 74, 94, 158, 220, 294, 321, 322
  modern or new type of, 20, 46, 99
  of the future, 14, 336
  Secondary, 70, 151, 169, 172, 177, 187, 190, 192, 197, 214, 247, 288, 292, 308, 315, 324
Schweizer-Spiegel, 15, 17, 19, 165, 228
Science or scientific subjects, 150, 159, 172
Scorn, 118, 290
Secrets, 75
Selection, 87, 88, 89
Self-abuse, 226
Self-assertion, 80, 91
Self-assurance, 74
Self-complacency, 35

Self-confidence, 35, 43, 51, 56, 72, 74, 75, 106, 116, 193, 237, 240, 266, 277
Self-control, 39, 60, 103, 229, 270
Self-deception, 51, 264, 336
Self-denial, 33
Self-discipline, 37, 102
Self-esteem, 56, 118, 119, 293
Self-experiment, 48
Self-government, 296
Selfishness, 95
Self-knowledge, 163
Self-sacrifice, 91, 335
Self-seeking, 93
Sensitiveness, 32
Sentimentality, 33
Severity, 42, 44, 70, 80, 104, 136, 137, 195, 267, 271
Services, 82, 95
Sexual difficulties, 110, 234
  enlightenment, 222, 226, 227, 237, 238
  instinct, 236
  offence, 223
  pleasure, 109
Shadow, 31
Shame, 34, 111, 119, 129, 225, 306, 315
Shaw, G. Bernard, 94
Shrove Tuesday, 215
Shy or shyness, 128, 137, 244, 268
Silence, 39, 41, 63, 142, 138, 250, 251, 326
Singing, 66, 168, 175, 322
Sister or sisters, 80, 188, 195, 196, 246, 288
Sitting still, 40, 41, 124, 136, 143
Situation, 31, 189, 235, 252
Ski-running, 145, 280
Skill, 82, 336
Slates, 131, 185, 244
Slaughter-houses, 318
Sleep, 126, 154, 156, 194, 204, 219, 234, 300
Solution, 89, 228
  of problems, 41, 202, 214
Sons, 282
Sorrows, 19, 31, 255, 289, 292, 303
Sources, 36, 39
Sparrow, 262
Speech defects, 325, 328
Sport, 96, 187, 261
Stammer, 220, 320

Standard, 61, 63, 67, 86, 92, 114, 139, 273, 276, 282
Statements, 15, 32, 56
Statistician, 20
Stealing, 287, 288
Sticking-plaster, 266
Stimulation, 58, 71
Stimulus, 63, 77, 306
Story, 126
Street, 130
Strength, 32, 40, 43, 76, 85, 95, 96, 110, 135, 139, 160, 207, 233, 249, 304
Stroking, 108
Struggle, 21, 45, 85, 106, 118, 170, 236, 276, 277
Stubbornness, 105
Students, 87, 166, 179, 181, 214, 220, 221
Stupidity, 158
Style, 48
Subjects, 50, 65, 171, 172, 215, 224, 242, 247
Subjugation, 63
Subordination, 73
Substitute, 127
Success or successes, 35, 45, 65, 68, 74, 82, 92, 94, 114, 116, 119, 162, 170, 203, 289
Sufferers, 112
Sufferings, 31, 36, 38, 40, 118, 193, 196, 221, 227, 287, 299
Suggestion or suggestions, 36, 59, 79, 84, 250, 255, 266
Suicide, 193, 227, 228
Sums, 124, 126
Sunday, 98, 99, 126, 214, 315
Superiority, 61, 79, 118, 211, 282, 284
Superstition, 32, 41, 44, 99, 114, 334
Supervision, 253
Supplication, 124
Supremacy, *see* Power
Suspicion, 43, 44, 49, 63, 140, 233, 254, 257, 267
Sweets, 108, 285
Switzerland, 20, 41, 47, 69, 84, 114, 144, 174, 199, 207, 212, 336
Sympathy, 17, 81, 112, 135, 222, 237, 275, 309
Symptoms, 110, 225
System, 28, 36, 37, 39, 42, 56, 67, 75, 92, 93, 101, 115, 144, 152, 160, 230, 316, 333

Table, 156, 177, 202, 227, 250, 252, 279
Tagore, Rabindranath, 213
Talent or talents, 33, 45, 47, 57, 74, 82, 84, 88, 90, 107, 147, 163
Taskmasters, 116
Teaching staff, 28, 30, 62, 68, 83, 90, 198, 216, 274, 289, 296, 298
Teachers, 15, 16, 17, 20, 21, 27, 29, 35, 37, 38, 39, 41, 42, 45, 49, 52, 55, 59, 61, 69, 72, 74, 75, 76, 77, 83, 84, 86, 89, 91, 92, 101, 103, 104, 105, 114, 117, 118, 119, 129, 130, 133, 134, 135, 136, 137, 139, 141, 143, 144, 145, 153, 158, 163, 167, 169, 171, 174, 180, 192, 197, 203, 205, 208, 209, 210, 211, 214, 216, 219, 222, 223, 224, 226, 228, 230, 234, 240, 248, 249, 250, 254, 256, 258, 259, 261, 263, 272, 277, 279, 289, 294, 296, 298, 302, 307, 308, 309, 323, 325, 336
  men, 125, 257, 292, 320
  nervous, 294
  old, 257
  pensions for, 85, 278
  salaries of, 83
  women, 124, 257, 274, 292
  young, 257
Tears, 125, 140, 155, 206, 214, 266, 267, 279, 289, 297, 303, 318
Teasing, 92, 184
Temper, 103, 109, 278, 279, 308
Temperament, 81
Temple, 40
Tendencies, 33, 46, 72, 79, 86, 88, 91, 109, 110, 136, 174, 232
  despotic, 101
  sado-masochistic, 305
Tension, 118, 249
Terror, 219, 234
Theories or theory, 33, 47, 48, 144
Thieves, 147
Thoughts, 47
Thrashing, 106, 108, 110, 111, 112, 113, 114, 115, 116, 117, 154, 160, 207, 248, 282, 300, 312, 316, 323, 326
Threatening, 53
Thrift, 60
Time, 27, 41, 48, 65, 67, 70, 97, 99, 133, 134, 136, 232, 271

INDEX

Time-tables, 47, 55, 58, 83, 91, 144, 209, 216, 271
Tiredness, 42
To-day, 92, 98, 208
To-morrow, 97, 98
Tooth, 324
Torments, 46, 112, 134, 195, 271, 279, 283, 302, 322
Torture, 31, 56, 111, 117, 158, 190, 191, 266
Town or towns, 134, 135, 273, 328
Tradition, 26, 27, 37, 45, 59, 151, 232
Tragedy, 60
Training, 29, 38, 86, 89, 99, 115, 133, 336, 337
Tram-conductor, 25
Tricks, 126
Trouble or troubles, 19, 32, 35, 40, 55, 73, 101, 190, 201, 221, 222, 233, 252, 271, 275, 292, 302, 317, 335
Truth, 51, 77, 144, 224, 260, 306, 334
Truthfulness, 61, 76
Tyranny, 58, 80, 118, 177, 198
Tyrant, 35, 103, 137, 178, 322, 324

Ugliness, 42, 61
Ugly, 59
Uncertainty, 35, 43, 179
Understanding, 40, 48, 49, 73, 76, 77, 105, 159, 177, 179, 185, 274, 275, 289, 334
  lack of, 178, 335
Unhappiness, 35, 255, 327
University, 150, 155, 264, 329

Values, 26, 30, 62, 75, 80, 81, 84, 179
Vanity, 35, 60, 80, 118, 170
Veneration, 25, 27, 127, 292, 320
Vice, 111
Victim, 111, 166, 195, 248, 310, 314, 325, 326, 329
Victory, 45, 155, 171
Vienna, 174
View or views, 18, 185, 251, 254
Virtue, 62, 82, 102, 334
Vitality, 32, 40
Vivacity, 270
Vocation, 30, 157, 160, 274
Voltaire, 157, 160, 274

Wasp, 54
Watch, 263
Weakness or weaknesses, 28, 43, 101, 218, 225, 232
Weapon, 45, 118
Weariness, 34, 42, 70, 335
Wife, 208, 209, 304
Will or wills, 32, 39, 45, 104
  -power, 34
Windmills, 56
Wisdom, 21, 28, 32, 81, 119, 204, 238
Wishes, 39, 88, 98, 102, 198, 232
Witness, 334
Women, 100, 133, 149, 280
Words, 48, 241, 281, 290, 294, 297, 299, 315, 326
Work, 26, 27, 30, 33, 34, 35, 37, 39, 46, 56, 67, 70, 71, 73, 84, 92, 95, 116, 139, 144, 153, 160, 163, 170, 175, 192, 196, 215, 235, 241, 249, 250, 273, 276, 277, 287, 293, 306, 372,
  hand or manual, 47, 56, 85, 280
  needle, 47
  practical, 47, 48, 147
  projects, 95
  theoretical, 47
Workshops, 46, 67, 68, 87, 161, 333, 337
Worry, 31, 50, 128, 135, 252, 260, 273
Wound or wounds, 15, 127, 314
Write, 256, 283
Writer's cramp, 201
Writing, 65, 68, 131, 188, 241, 265, 291, 299, 311, 328
  bad, 200, 326
  good, 161, 312
  left-handed, 265
Wrong, 58
Wrong-doing, 107, 108
Wrongs, 41, 106, 239

Years, 89, 114, 157, 179, 213, 220, 230, 271, 296, 300, 312, 314
Young folks or people, 28, 75, 84, 88, 91, 99, 136, 141, 144, 160, 171, 209, 227
Youth, 32, 43, 70, 100, 115, 127, 149, 174, 190, 193, 233, 234, 236, 335

Zeal, 71, 82, 134
Zeppelin, 277
Zoology, 145
Zurich, 131, 169, 174, 183, 191, 223, 224, 314, 315, 328, 329

GEORGE ALLEN & UNWIN LTD
LONDON: 40 MUSEUM STREET, W.C.1
CAPE TOWN: 73 ST. GEORGE'S STREET
SYDNEY, N.S.W.: WYNYARD SQUARE
AUCKLAND, N.Z.: 41 ALBERT STREET
TORONTO: 91 WELLINGTON STREET, WEST